THE BARN

Sally Coulthard is a bestselling author of books about natural history and rural life including *The Barn*, *A Short History of the World According to Sheep*, *The Book of the Barn Owl*, *The Hedgehog Handbook* and over twenty more titles. She lives on a Yorkshire smallholding which she shares with her husband, three girls and an assortment of unruly animals.

Also by Sally Coulthard

A Short History of the World According to Sheep

The Book of the Earthworm

The Hedgehog Handbook

The Little Book of Snow

The Bee Bible

The Little Book of Building Fires

The Book of the Barn Owl

Fowl Play: A History of the Chicken from Dinosaur to Dinner Plate

SALLY COULTHARD

THE BARN

The Lives, Landscape
and Lost Ways of
an Old Yorkshire Farm

An Apollo Book

First published in 2021 by Head of Zeus Ltd
This paperback edition first published in 2022 by Head of Zeus Ltd,
part of Bloomsbury Publishing Plc

1 3 5 7 9 10 8 6 4 2

A CIP catalogue record for this book is available from the British Library.

ISBN (PB): 9781800240865
ISBN (E): 9781800240872

Typesetting by Ed Pickford
Linocuts by Sarah Price

Printed and bound in Great Britain by
CPI Group (UK) Ltd, Croydon CRO 4YY

Head of Zeus Ltd
5–8 Hardwick Street
London EC1R 4RG
WWW.HEADOFZEUS.COM

For Mum and Dad

CONTENTS

4

Yan mud as good stop at yam 217

*The Cart Shed • Carts and Waggons • Rural Roads •
Turnpikes • Highwaymen • Rivers and Canals • The
Railways • Passengers • Rural Holidays • Walking and
Pedestrianism • The Great Depression • Market Gardening
and the Orchard*

5

Some h'ae luck, an' some stick i' t' muck 269

*Well-sinking • Water • Cholera and Typhoid • Mains
Water and the First World War • Privies • The Midden •
Food and Packaging • Rag-and-Bone Men • Rubbish • The
End of High Farming • The Great Land Sell-off*

'This is certainly a beautiful country! In all England, I do not believe that I could have fixed on a situation so completely removed from the stir of society.'

Wuthering Heights by Emily Brontë (1847)

'I suppose you are going back to Yorkshire, Mr. Stanhope? A very ugly county, Yorkshire!'

King George III to Walter Spencer Stanhope

PROLOGUE

'd propped a ladder against one of the walls inside the big stone building that dominates our farmyard. Its plastered limestone was grubby in the way that only agricultural spaces can get - a thin buttering of old seeds and bits of straw, mixed with black farmyard grime; all that sweat, shit and mud that had been kicked up over the years.

The Barn had been empty for decades. The previous owners of the farm had sold off most of their arable land in the 1980s and moved into more profitable pigs. The farm's days of cereal crops and cows were long gone. Now, with us as the new owners - a writer and a gardener - the pigs had also disappeared and all that was left was a run-down farmhouse, 12 acres of pasture, and one patched but perfectly serviceable limestone barn. The farm also came with its own metal Dutch barn, to store hay, and a large, dusty grain store. We'd bought a ghost ship; part wreck, part promise.

I'd started to brush down the internal walls, an almost pointless attempt at trying to make the Barn fit to rent out. A local sculptor had suggested he could use the threshing bay – the tall, central part of the Barn with its soaring ceiling – as a studio. Broom in one hand, and gripping the ladder with the other, I'd stepped up and stretched to the highest parts of the wall, to discover that, as the dust fell away, a pattern appeared.

It was a circle, the size of a dinner plate, scratched into the plaster, far above head height. Inside the circle, someone had scribed a daisy wheel – the kind of pattern schoolkids make with a compass and pencil, drawing arc after arc until the petals form. A beautiful, simple frippery. But then, after brushing slightly to the left of the circle, another appeared. Same pattern, same technique. And then another. And another. Until, smiling and thick with dust, I'd managed to uncover a frieze of six mysterious circles.

A quick phone call to an archaeologist friend revealed that these strange scratchings were 'witches' marks' – patterns etched into plaster to ward off bad spirits and bring good fortune. Apotropaic* marks, to give them their proper name, are absolutely everywhere if you know where to look: barns and other rural buildings, churches and chapels, but also cottages and large houses. This ancient form of graffiti

---

* From the Greek *apotropaios*, 'averting evil'.

– which is gouged not just into plaster, but stone and timber too – covers a wide span of rural history; many are medieval, but everyday folk carried on marking their buildings well into the eighteenth century. Far from being idle, careless doodles, they're both hopeful prayers and desperate pleas from our not-too-distant ancestors.

Those witches' marks got me thinking. Ritual scratchings like these are conversations, delivered directly from the past. It might be difficult to decipher their meaning but they speak nevertheless. It made me wonder about the people who had been around the Barn before us – generations of rural families who occupied a corner of the world where, for centuries, superstition, religion, nature, work and home life jostled side by side.

And while farming is still alive and well in this fertile corner of North Yorkshire, the Barn is a relic of a life long gone. The presence of the witches' marks made me ponder that perhaps other parts of the Barn, and the farm, could tell me something about what went before. Maybe they could give me clues about when and how the land was originally settled, show me how our ancestors rose to the challenge of growing food for a growing population, and hint at how they lived and thought. The Barn is also a repository of local crafts and skills that, if not already extinct, are fast disappearing. Its extensions and alterations are structural documents and display decades of change in agricultural life – from boom times to dereliction and back again – reflecting the broader social and economic character of rural life.

Over the past 250 or so years, since the Barn was built in its current form, this small patch of countryside – hidden and largely invisible to the rest of the world – would have experienced extraordinary changes. From the last of the Enclosures in the late eighteenth century to the Second World War, the fortunes of the Barn, the farm and the people who lived around it would have been blown, like a leaf in a gale, by the unstoppable forces of new agriculture and industry. Transport, education, food and farming, superstition, children's lives, war, the arrival of the railways, utilities, the role of the Church – changes in almost every area of society were played out, in miniature, here. This tiny, mellow slice of Yorkshire witnessed the dramas of history unfold, both large and small – from sweeping political change to local crises and domestic triumphs and tragedies.

Reaching even further back in time, the fact that the Barn is where it is suggests a landscape already primed for agricultural life. Some of the stones in the lowest part of the Barn wall come from another, older building or structure. Perhaps one of the large medieval ruins that lie close by, religious and administrative juggernauts that landed in this sleepy landscape nearly a thousand years ago. Or perhaps the stones were pilfered from one of the lost Roman byways or abandoned villas that farmers have unintentionally ploughed up over the years.

We came to the farm by accident. Or unconscious design. I still haven't made my mind up which it was. The landscape around the Barn has always, strangely, felt like home. As a child, my family would holiday in the small village of Gilling, on a sheep farm only two miles from here as the crow flies. Our own home was a couple of hours away, in the traffic-filled suburbs that sit between two industrial textile giants – Leeds and Bradford. Coming to the Gilling farm, for Easter holidays, felt exotic in its rural seclusion. I loved the unmistakable smells of lambing time and sheep manure, with its grassy sweetness. The deep pink sunsets settling on the stone-lintelled windows. My brother and I would spend hours searching for warm eggs and feral kittens hidden among the straw bales. And everywhere, unlike home, was just so peaceful. Not silent, though – the countryside is full of birdsong, bleating and farm machinery, which together produce a golden, alchemical hum.

University and then a career took me first to Oxford and then London. Cloistered life, studying archaeology and anthropology, was heaven but the capital took me by surprise, shredded my nerves, until I felt I could no longer cope and ran home in my late twenties, ill and with a deep sense of displacement. A year or so later, my parents retired and moved to the countryside, only a few miles from the Gilling farmhouse we'd stayed in two decades earlier. I went with them, fell in love with a gardener, and began the search for a home that could sustain both my need for solitude and my new husband's landscaping business. And so - after a chance conversation with an estate agent and some financial overpromising - we found our way here, to the farm.

The Barn nestles in the bottom of a shallow valley. An orotund Victorian once described it as 'a magnificent basin, ornamented by Nature's most lavish hand',[1] but I like to think of it more like a huge, flat roasting tray. The base of the tray is the valley floor - wide, open, and largely without buildings. The farm is tucked to one side, sheltered by the ridge that runs along the top of the valley, and so if you look out of the back of the Barn you see the hillside stretching steeply upwards. Gaze in the opposite direction and you see a flat plain of arable fields and pasture, dotted with the odd copse of trees. And then, a mile in the distance across the fields, a hamlet called Cawton. Thanks to the bouncy acoustics of the valley bottom, we can sometimes hear a distant dog barking as clearly as if it were in our farmyard.

It's part of a landscape known as the Howardian Hills, a patchwork of fields, ancient woodland and scattered limestone villages. Everything about the area is gentle and accommodating, it's just right, neither too hilly nor too flat, too remote nor too busy. It's a small area, squeezed between the craggily handsome uplands of the North York Moors and the lush, fertile vales to the south, east and west, and part of a much larger district – Ryedale, an ancient and vast administrative area named after the River Rye, which meanders through.

York's architectural embarrassment of riches is only a half hour south by car and yet, for the most part, we ignore city life. Almost everything we could need comes from our nearest market towns – Helmsley, a place once described, rather unkindly, as all fudge and honeyed stone, and Malton, its chubbier, no-nonsense big sister. On the whole, strangers have been kind about the area. Stonegrave, the nearest village to the Barn by the road along the top of the ridge, was once rather sweetly branded a 'tom-tit's nest, almost hidden from view' by Henry Merry Cross, a nineteenth-century local magistrate: 'The whole of this district is a veritable hunting ground to the antiquarian.'[2] One of the most notable discoveries of the day was Kirkdale Cave, about six miles north of the Barn. A large chasm was revealed by quarrymen in 1821 and sifted through by Reverend Dr William Buckland, a man torn between his theological beliefs and his passion for fossils. The cave contained remains of prehistoric mammals including elephants, rhinos, hyenas and the most northerly remains of a hippopotamus ever found. The bones convinced Buckland that the world was much older than the

Bible suggested and provided a faith-shaking explanation for geological events that had previously been attributed to Noah's Flood.

Herbert Read, one of Britain's most famous modern art historians and writers, also lived here. Viewed as one of a Yorkshire triumvirate that also included Henry Moore and Barbara Hepworth, Read was deeply progressive and yet his rural childhood, in the closing years of the nineteenth century, never left him. He was born and raised by a farming family, not far from the Barn, but after his father's death he was exiled from his beloved Ryedale and sent to an orphanage in West Yorkshire. The longing to come back to his rural Eden never left him, though, and so, as an adult, he returned to the area as a successful writer and bought Stonegrave rectory, a handsome late-seventeenth-century house that had also housed successive churchmen and owners of the Barn. There, he spent the last few decades of his life exploring his feelings about the local area, unpicking ideas of sense of place, roots and identity.

The landscape where the Barn sits is spectacularly old. People have lived here for millennia, drawn by the woodland, rich soil and natural springs. Farming has been central to its story – from the earliest times, people have manipulated nature to their own ends, altered the countryside and attempted to work within its rhythms. This is the story of that journey, or at least a short part of it, told through one building and its surroundings.

The book is divided into chapters that broadly relate to the different sections of the Barn and the farm, but the story brings in other parts of the immediate landscape – the farmhouse, the fields, the road leading to Stonegrave, and other nearby settlements. The book also ventures further afield, exploring places and events that would have seemed unimaginably exotic to the people who worked around the Barn but which had a direct impact on their lives.

Standing in front of the Barn, you see three distinct sections. The middle, oldest part, is the threshing bay – a space now open from floor to ceiling but which once had a wooden mezzanine floor. This was where wheat or oats were beaten to separate the grain from the stalks and the filled sacks hoisted up and stored. To the right of the threshing bay sits a later cart shed with a granary above. To the left of the threshing bay, the old stables with a first-floor hayloft. Attached to the rear of the Barn, at right angles, is a large cowshed; old photos also show there were originally other, smaller barns – for pigs and calves – linked together to create a courtyard or 'fold yard', as well as a smithy, a water well and a lime kiln. The farmhouse's midden was also tucked next to the Barn, a dumping ground for curious old bottles and broken blue-and-white teacups; their nineteenth-century detritus is now a source of endless pleasure for our children with their seaside buckets and spades.

Thanks to years of alterations, with little thought of aesthetics, the Barn wouldn't win any beauty prizes. It's remarkably ordinary. But it's a practical space. The stables are now a workshop full of gardening tools. The hayloft, granary and cart shed are occupied by artists and their studios, while the threshing bay – now the sculptor has moved on – protects a knackered old Land Rover in a thousand pieces. The original smithy is long gone but our farm still hosts a blacksmith; he's now in a different building, still hammering to the same beat, creating gates, railings and garden structures for neighbouring farms and further afield.

Bees, bats and birds have colonised the soft limestone walls and so we leave the Barn largely to its own devices. On my night-time dog walk, which takes me on a loop around the farmyard, I'm often dive-bombed by pipistrelle bats, or catch the occasional ghostly flash of a barn owl. Swallows come without fail every summer, after a heroic flight from southern Africa, raise a family for a few months in the rafters and then head back. But it's the human impact on the landscape that really fascinates me. Historic barns, and other farm buildings and remnants, help tell the long history of agriculture, trade and settlement in this quiet corner of the country but also provide a glimpse at wider trends in the world of our not-too-distant ancestors. The Barn is just one of thousands that pepper the countryside in various states of repair or ruin, and yet if we lose them, we lose generations of untold stories.

I

IS T'A STOPPIN'
ON, LAD?

IS T'A STOPPIN' ON, LAD?
Will you stay here long?

I often walk up the hill to collect the milk. The milkman leaves it at the top of our steep farm track and, if the weather is set fair, I have to beat the morning sunshine before the cream curdles and ruins breakfast. It's a breathless climb and, more often than not, I have a quick rest before grabbing the crate and setting off back down the slope. It's a view I never tire of. Farming paints a different picture in the valley almost every month: the rich plough-browns of spring slide into the wet, lush greens of summer. At the back end of the year, the colours change again, from the dirty yellow wheat stubble to the black and white geometry of winter.

From such a high vantage point, it's easy to mistake the valley for a diorama. Looking down onto such an expansive scene can briefly deceive the eye, an illusion broken only when a tractor trundles out from behind a hedge or a herd slowly get to their feet. It always strikes me that this small valley seems such a sensible place to have settled. Schoolchildren now learn that the valley was once the western fringe of Lake Pickering, a vast body of fresh water, during the last Ice Age. When the water finally drained away, it left behind a near perfect landscape – fertile lowlands tightly enclosed by surrounding hills. Patches of dense woodland, some of it ancient, now cover the basin and valley sides. Ash, oak and holly also mark out field boundaries, while alder and willow snake along its winding rivers and streams.

The weather is fairly benevolent too. Go 30 miles in any direction from here and it's different. Head upwards in winter, onto the North York Moors, and remote villages are often marooned for weeks with thick snow. Lancashire's Pennines – the backbone of England – capture much of the wet weather that drives over from the west, leaving the Howardian Hills and, indeed, much of North Yorkshire with less than half the rain of our western neighbours. The sheltered south-facing slopes of the Howardian Hills, including our steepest fields, also have a much gentler microclimate, more akin to southern England, than any Yorkshire person would care to admit.

The temperate fertility of the landscape was undoubtedly one of its most attractive features for its earliest pioneers. The shores of Lake Pickering, with its rich fauna, enticed small groups of families to set up seasonal camps as far back as 9000 BC,[*] and

---

[*] Star Carr is the most fascinating and important Mesolithic site in Britain. Five miles south of Scarborough, at the eastern end of what was Lake Pickering, the site is thought to have been a seasonal base camp for families

by the Bronze Age farmers had cleared wide sections of forest ready for crops. Not far from the Barn, we can trundle along the remains of a long Bronze Age dyke, a boundary that once marked the edge of an important territory and demonstrated the power and prestige of its builders. As much as these first farmers started to alter their surroundings, however, the ridges and contours of the natural landscape remained largely fixed. Reading and understanding the local environment, bowing to its confines and celebrating its generosity, was the only way agriculture could flourish.

✳

Only a few miles from the Barn there is a strange, otherworldly hole in the ground. During the winter months, thanks to a geological quirk, waves of hot air rise up from its dark mouth; during summer, it emits cool blasts that shake the grass and overhanging vegetation. To prehistoric people, this steaming, subterranean chasm must have seemed a place of unfathomable mystery.

The chasm is called Slip Gill. It is one of a handful of natural fissures in the local landscape known as the 'Windy Pits'. These narrow limestone caves form an extraordinary

hunting red deer, aurochs and wild boar. Highlights from excavations include headdresses made from deer skulls, thought to be used by shamans, harpoons for hunting and fishing, evidence of the oldest house in Britain, and the earliest carpentry in Europe.

network under the North Yorkshire countryside. To add to their sinister intrigue, over the years the remains of more than twenty of our ancient ancestors have been discovered at the bottom of these deep voids. In Slip Gill alone, four bodies – a man, woman and two teenage children – were uncovered, relics from Iron Age farming communities who dotted this landscape 2,000 years ago.

What is particularly striking about the Slip Gill 'family' is that they all met violent ends. Both adults had been immobilised, by having one leg deliberately broken, before being thrown into the hole. One of the children had a catastrophic blade wound to the jaw and the adult male had been scalped. Archaeologists believe the unfortunate victims of Slip Gill had been dragged to the entrance of the hole, ritually sacrificed, and then tossed into the 'underworld', in an act that would have held deep significance for the perpetrators. Stable isotope analysis of their bones also revealed that the dead were not strangers but local people, pulled from their own farming community. The earliest days of Yorkshire agricultural life were not always, it seems, gentle ones.

By studying the Windy Pits and other Iron Age sites, archaeologists have begun to reconstruct what life would have been like for the early farmers in this corner of north-east England. What emerges is a world of small communities, of family groups living in their own large, thatched roundhouses within a wider hamlet of four or five more families. Not all buildings would have been houses – some might have been used for storage, animal housing, or as workshops. These settlements are known as 'enclosed farmsteads' because they were usually surrounded by a large ditch and bank, a perimeter that would have prevented farm animals wandering off and wild ones from sneaking in.

Nearby hamlets would have traded, talked, feasted and perhaps even farmed together. People's days would have revolved around growing, harvesting and storing crops and tending to their animals, producing just enough food to live on and a little surplus, in good times, to trade for other commodities and luxuries. Cereals such as wheat, barley, rye and oats were already well established and consumed as bread, porridge and beer, while domesticated beasts – sheep, cattle and pigs – provided meat, hides, wool and manure. Iron Age farmers also had short-legged, powerful horses for pulling ploughs, chariots and carts. Take a rough Exmoor pony 2,000 years back in time and he'd fit right in. When harvests failed, however, crisis loomed, and this may explain the fate of the poor Windy Pits 'family' who were sacrificed and thrown into the darkness.

Across Iron Age Britain, sacrifice was an important part of rural life. The ritual destruction of a valuable object or living being was a way of offering thanks, or penance, for events that would have been central to daily concerns – a good crop, a successful lambing season, an illness, the weather and so on. Excavations from other Iron Age sites show multiple human sacrifices connected to the harvest. Seed was stored in underground pits, over winter, to ensure the survival of the tribe. Underground spaces were the realms of the gods; putting grain in the ground was an act of faith as much as a practical solution. And so, what better way to thank the gods for their protection than with the gift of a human life?

The Romans, when they came, brought with them large, elaborate villa complexes and a way of farming more labour-intensive than Iron Age villagers were used to. Agrarian society in this corner of Yorkshire was already organised, with established arable and pastoral farming, roundhouses and field systems, but the Romans added their own layer of administration, a fort at Malton, and a new pottery industry that supplied much of England with the latest must-have grey tableware. The landscape around the Barn had its own smattering of Roman villas – North Yorkshire powerhouses of farming and politics – including one just across the valley from the Barn in the now thriving village of Hovingham. From there, the wealthy owner and his family would have watched as an army of slave labour and tenant farmers called *coloni* toiled over crops and livestock to satisfy local demand and the military bases posted to the fringes of their conquered lands.

A Roman coin, dropped at the foot of the Barn, was discovered only two years ago by my middle daughter,

Isabella, who was ten years old at the time and digging a hole to plant a Christmas tree. The coin is minute – only just over a centimetre in diameter – but is packed with Roman self-congratulation. On the front of the coin is the head of Theodosius I, Emperor from AD 379 to 395, and on the reverse, the great leader in full military gear, astride a horse and raising his hand alongside the words GLORIA ROMANORVM – 'Glory of the Roman people'. Quite how the fields around the Barn and the Roman villa were connected, if at all, isn't clear, but coinage of a similar date was also found at both Hovingham and nearby East Ness in previous excavations. Local archaeologists believe that these Yorkshire villa farming estates were never more active than in the late fourth century[1] – how tempting it is to imagine a *colonus*, drawn from the local 'barbarian' community or an emancipated slave, working the land and paying for the privilege in produce or taxes.

The Roman presence didn't last. It's funny to think that only a few years after that small coin tumbled to the ground, the glory days were long gone. By AD 410 Rome had lost its grip on the peoples of Britain and abandoned North Yorkshire and the rest of the country to its fate. When the legions left, farmers slowly reverted to their old ways – living in simple, thatched farmsteads with everything under one roof.

The tiny settlement of Stonegrave became an important

spot in its own right, with a recorded history reaching back at least to the eighth century. In 757, Pope Paul I ordered Eadbert, King of Northumbria, to pull his finger out and 'restore the monasteries at Stonegrave, Coxwold and Jarrow'.[2] Quite what this building was, we don't know, but it was possibly an outlying post for what is now known as Whitby Abbey on the North Yorkshire coast. Remnants of the Anglo-Saxon building, including a glorious Celtic cross, and the grand title 'Stonegrave Minster' keep the heritage aflame. Outsiders sometimes arrive, expecting a cathedral, to be surprised by a sweet, self-effacing village church.

Relics of this occupation are also found in the DNA of the people who still live and work in the countryside around the Barn. Recent DNA analysis showed that the region's ancestral make-up is markedly different from the rest of Britain. Unlike most of the country, the majority of Yorkshire folk have their roots across the North Sea. Saxon, Teutonic and Norse Y-chromosomes appear in over half of Yorkshire's male population, compared to about a quarter across the rest of the country.[3] Place names also reveal Anglo-Saxon links – Hovingham, 'farmstead of Hofa's people', or Cawton, a 'cow farm'. Even Stonegrave, with its obvious-sounding label, isn't all it seems – the name has nothing to do with the church's graveyard. Recorded as 'Stanegrif' in the Domesday Book and 'Staningagrave' 300 years earlier, Anglo-Saxon settlements used the prefix 'stan' to denote some kind of stone-working,[4] while 'grave' meant to dig up, carve or mine. 'Engrave' and 'groove' come from the same root. As we'll see later in the book, local quarrying and limestone made the Barn what it was and helped it to grow and expand beyond its original modest start.

For the next millennium and beyond, from Anglo-Saxon rule to Viking occupation, Norman conquest to medieval feudalism, remarkably little changed in terms of the fundamental day-to-day activities of the average person working on the land. Farming with the seasons, planting a limited range of crops, looking after livestock, paying some kind of 'rent' to whoever owned the land in the form of crops or stock – the rhythmic routine of farm life remained the one constant. Indeed, North Yorkshire – and most of the country, for that matter – was still overwhelmingly rural at the end of the eighteenth century. Villages or cluster of hamlets were, by and large, self-sufficient communities, producing and eating their own food, making their own goods, mending their own things and, for the most part, marrying their own people. As their ancestors had done for centuries, many farmers still shared their homes with their livestock; remnants of this ancient way of life continued in remote areas of North Yorkshire even into the early twentieth century. Canon Atkinson, vicar of Danby (a local moorland parish) and keen antiquarian, described farmhouses where there was 'one room with a clay floor, for the occupation of the family, separated from an enclosed place formed by boarded partitions which formed a pig sty and calf pen under the same roof, by a narrow unlighted passage'.[5] Customs and celebrations too had their genesis in ancient, long-forgotten rituals.

The relationship between those who owned the country-side and those who worked the land also had its taproots in a system formed hundreds of years before. When William the Conqueror invaded England in 1066, and became its king, he set in stone the idea that all the land in the kingdom belonged, unequivocally, to one sovereign. Land ownership before that time was more fractured; since the end of the Roman era, Ryedale – like other parts of the country – had endured invasions by Angles, Saxons and Norse, creating not a unified nation under one ruler but a patchwork of smaller, independent kingdoms. Warriors and aristocratic families who were on the side of a victorious army would have their loyalty rewarded with acreage in the newly vanquished land. For the men, women and children already living and farming in an area, it's easy to imagine successive centuries of endless invasion, pillaging and plunder. But, for the most part, it seems life continued as it always had done, farming and paying your dues to a different master. New landowners wanted income from a buoyant rural economy, not waste land, and so allowing agricultural life to continue, largely uninterrupted, made sound economic sense.

At the time of the Norman Conquest, the land around the Barn was owned by Orm, Son of Gamal, an aristocratic landowner descended from Viking settlers. While many of his contemporaries had their land confiscated and handed over to Norman loyalists, Orm somehow managed to keep his estate. Three years later, while William was busy 'harrying the North', crushing the last of the uprisings against him and laying waste to vast sections of North Yorkshire countryside, by political sleight of hand Orm managed to keep his holdings intact. Many of the surrounding villages weren't so lucky – the eleventh-century monk Simeon of Durham wrote that it was 'shocking to see the houses, the streets, and highways, human carcases swarming with wirms, disolving in putridity and emitting a most horrid stench; nor were there any left alive to cover them with earth, all having perished by sword or famine, or stimulated by hunger had abandoned their native land'.[6]

With the country finally subdued, a system of land management settled into place that lasted until the seventeenth century. Under the feudal system, the king was the absolute owner of the land, but he parcelled it out to the nobles, knights and other tenants below him, who could then use the land to generate income. In return for this land, William's supporters had to give the king a portion of their time, loyalty or goods. Knights offered their military service, clerics offered ecclesiastical duties, and socmen – the most common type of landholders – offered 'socage', agricultural services such as ploughing or payment in livestock* or rent.

Much of the farmland surrounding the Barn was, for centuries, glebe land, which meant it was owned by the Church. Fields were allotted to villagers in return for payment of the tithe, this being one-tenth of their annual produce or earnings (the word 'tithe' derives from an Old English word *tēotha*, meaning 'tenth'). Looking at old maps of the farm, the ancient field names are revealing. The ecclesiastical connection is clear with names such as 'Parson's West Pasture' and 'Priest's Croft'. Other field names provide a fascinating glimpse into the occupations of villagers who tended to their individual strips – Chandlers (a candlemaker), Hunters West and Challoners. Names can pin a place to a time – 'challoner' is a word we don't use any more, but it was commonplace in early medieval England and described someone who made or sold blankets. Woollen bedcoverings were called 'chalons' or 'chalouns', after the French textile town Châlons-sur-Marne. Other names hint at what the land was being used for; a handful of the fields belonging to the Barn have the name

---

* 'Chattel' and 'cattle' are vestiges of this period and essentially the same word. Both words used to mean any kind of moveable property. Around the early fourteenth century, 'cattle' started to refer only to livestock, and then, from the late sixteenth century, to cows and bulls exclusively, while we still use 'chattels' to mean moveable, tangible assets.

'ruskey' – Ruskey First, Low Ruskey, Ruskey Fourth and so on. The word can also be spelled ruskie, rooskie and rusky, and refers to a straw basket that holds corn when you sow it, perhaps suggesting the land around the Barn has long been used for arable. It's interesting, however, that one document relating to the Barn, dating from 1685, uses the word 'Rosco' instead of Ruskey. This word has Norse origins and means a 'deer wood' or 'roebuck copse' – perhaps, instead, suggesting a hunting wood of some kind.

The medieval villagers who farmed the land around the Barn never owned it, but they did possess it in a way, a privilege that could be passed down through generations and came, as we shall see later, with a host of common rights. Most would grow a succession of crops in a particular order – usually wheat and rye in the first year, then oats, barley, peas or beans, and then leave the field fallow for a year to recover. While the field was fallow, animals were allowed to graze on the weeds and, in return, their poo added fertility back to the flagging soil. Stock owners were also allowed to let their animals roam across stretches of common pasture, wild meadow or poor, uncultivated ground. Rules created by the local manorial court or village committee would keep things in check – whether it was who did what where, how many livestock were allowed on a piece of land, or what time of the year different activities took place. Each village was unique in its approach and to a large extent autonomous, farming within the constraints of the local environment.

People had access to different places where they could grow or gather resources. Land could be available in the middle of the village, next to a dwelling, for growing fruit and vegetables, while animals might nibble the village green or a stubble field at the edge of the settlement. Families could also grow crops or keep stock on fields a few miles from the village, an arrangement that allowed everyone access to a slice of land, but also meant plenty of walking and carrying crops to and from the field. Where this was the case, isolated buildings often sprang up where there was distance between a villager's home and an important arable field or stretch of pasture. These simple field barns saved both time and labour – some were used to store hay for winter feed, others sheltered young or pregnant livestock. The villager could also cut and thresh his crop in the field barn and take the precious grain back home but leave the straw in the building. Any cows or sheep that were subsequently kept in the field barn could transform this straw into rich manure, which was then close to the field for spreading.

The strange, dark stones that make up the first few courses at the base of the Barn are, in all probability, a relic of a pre-eighteenth-century field barn. They're impossible to date – cottages and farm buildings in Ryedale often reveal material robbed from ancient Roman sites, dissolved priories or monastic granges. While most of the current Barn is a yoghurty, soft limestone, quarried from less than a mile away, the oldest founding stones are a less common, curiously hard grey-brown mudstone, now called Brandsby Roadstone. This stone, which looks a bit like slate, is made of thin, clearly defined layers and is easy to split into large slabs. Both the Romans and Saxons excavated this unusual stone for footings, road coverings and roof slates from a quarry six miles away from the Barn, but it also found its way into two fourteenth-century castles nearby – Gilling Castle and the now derelict Sheriff Hutton Castle. Quite why a hard-wearing mudstone makes up the first few feet of the Barn remains a delightful, if unsolved, mystery, but it suggests that whoever needed to build a small field barn would have had remnants of tracks or ruins to pilfer from.

During the middle of the eighteenth century, this ancient system began to change. Previously communal pasture and arable fields were amalgamated or 'enclosed'. The reasons for this we shall explore later, but the end result was that rather than lots of different people farming a large area of land, only one capable farmer, under the direction of a landowner, was needed. While the results of this land grab were devastating for the individuals who relied on their small, self-sufficient strips, the effect on farm design was profound. Enclosure had been going on in a piecemeal fashion since the fourteenth century, but its pace and scope exploded from the middle of the eighteenth century. Rearranging scattered holdings allowed tighter control of both crops and livestock. And, with enclosure as a weapon of management, the landlord could now create his ideal, efficient farmstead with an ideal, efficient tenant farmer, ready to do his bidding.[7]

The farmland around Stonegrave was divvied up between three local men of means: the Honourable Thomas Howard, Lord of the Manors of Nunnington, Stonegrave and West Ness; Sir Bellingham Graham, Baronet and High Sheriff, whose ancestor had been granted a baronetcy in 1662 for helping to restore the monarchy; and the rector of Stonegrave – Thomas Mosley – who was already collecting tithes from many of the fields around the village. Mosley was to be allotted two large parcels of land, the equivalent of one-sixth of the open fields and one-eighth of the common grasslands in the township of Stonegrave, including the fields and, no doubt, the field barn. In return for discontinuing the tithes, the rector was free to farm the land as he pleased.

And so began the next stage of the Barn's life. Almost as soon as the land was enclosed by Parliamentary Act in 1776, a new building sprang up on the old foundations. Still modest, but more ambitious in scale than the small field barn, this was a purpose-built threshing barn. A map commissioned at the time shows the new Barn, lonely in its isolation, but handily placed next to a 'stackyard', an area of open ground that stored wheat and barley, in haystacks, waiting to be processed.

Thomas Mosley, rector of Stonegrave, now he was free of tithed tenants, was turning his attention to more productive, commercial types of farming. A scientific revolution was sweeping across the nation – breakthroughs were being made in the fields of astronomy, exploration, plant sciences and chemistry. As the historian Richard Holmes has written: 'Nature [was] waiting to be discovered or seduced into revealing her secrets.'[8] This was the age of the public science lecture, the popular textbook, and the idea that scientific principles could be applied to almost any aspect of life, including agriculture. Many rectors were younger sons of landed gentry, Oxbridge-educated and treated as honorary gentlemen. The living at Stonegrave was also a generous one, with a substantial country house to boot, and the leisure time to engage in potentially profitable ventures. Such were the perceived benefits of the clerical lifestyle that the eighteenth-century astronomer William Herschel even attempted to persuade his own son into the role of clergyman, despite his own misgivings about the Church: 'A clergyman [...] has time for the attainment of the more elegant branches of literature, for poetry, for music, for drawing, for natural history, for short and pleasant excursions of travelling, for being acquainted with the spirit of the law of his country, for history, for political economy, for mathematics, for astronomy, for metaphysics, and for being an author upon any one subject in which [he is] qualified to excell.'[9]

In 1769, as botanist Joseph Banks and North Yorkshire's own Captain Cook were taking their first steps on a Tahitian beach, hoping to amass a new collection of plant and animal specimens, back in England self-taught farmer Arthur Young was busy scribbling his *Course of Experimental Agriculture*, which he published the following year. While not a particularly successful farmer in his own right, Young was an evangelist for the new field of 'scientific agriculture'. From new machinery to crop rotations, fertilisers to selective breeding, Young also urged the nation's landed gentry to ditch sentiment and become more 'commerce minded' about their holdings. Just a few years later, in 1802, when the scientist and Fellow of the Royal Society Humphry Davy gave one of his enthusiastic lectures on the potential of agricultural chemistry, he was clear that providing plenty for all was not the primary aim: 'the unequal division of property and of labour,' he concluded, 'the difference of rank and condition amongst mankind, are the sources of power in civilized life, and its moving causes, and even its very soul'.[10]

In the space of just a few years, the land around the Barn had gone from being made up of nearly thirty different strips or plots to just nineteen large, hedged fields. With enclosure allowing him to choose his own direction, Thomas

Mosley also followed 'modern farming' principles to the letter, neatly apportioning three fields each to turnips, oats, grass and wheat, one for barley, one for seeds, one for peas and so on. Building a new threshing barn was also part of this policy of improvement. Having specific buildings for a specific purpose, rather than one multifunctional field barn, was one of the rector's first steps toward specialisation. And a purpose-built threshing barn, positioned right next to his newly planted fields, made not only practical but also commercial sense. The threshing barn was big enough to allow not just one, but five or six men and women to thresh at the same time. It also had a wooden mezzanine level about ten feet off the floor, supported on thick timber beams. You can still see the holes in the limestone walls where the timbers slotted snugly in. The sheaves were beaten on the threshing floor, to separate the grain from the tough stalks. The straw, which was useful as animal bedding, could be stored either side of the threshing floor, while the grain, once bagged, was hoisted up to the mezzanine. The logic was impeccable – the mezzanine was just high enough not to get in the way of the threshers, beating the crops with their flails, but protected sacks of grains from rats and mice. Before this, many small-scale farmers simply kept their grain in their own homes, in relatively modest amounts; but if Thomas Mosley wanted to grow grain on any scale, he knew he'd need somewhere to store it.

This step towards modernity still had one foot in the past. While money had been invested in a smart new threshing barn, the push to build adjacent accommodation for a tenant farmer didn't come for another fifty years. Only in 1840 did the Barn finally get its own farmhouse and, even then, for the first fifteen years it was occupied by live-in farm labourers employed, no doubt, by the Church. The census from the time reveals a dislocated set of lodgers and, unusually, a mix of local men and a single woman: two male agricultural servants in their late teens and early twenties – Robert Douseling and George Fisher; two fifteen-year-old boys – William Bradley and Michael Reed; and a lone thirty-year-old woman – Maria Nightingale. It's an odd set-up – not only would it have been potentially scandalous to leave a single woman flanked by four relatively young strapping farmhands, but Maria is also described not as a housekeeper or domestic servant, as one might expect, but as a farm labourer. Such a situation would suggest that Maria was either a poor young widower, with no dependent children, or a casual worker desperate enough to shack up with male farmworkers. Either way, she'd have been an oddity in early Victorian life.

With the building of the farmhouse came a redoubling of efforts – the threshing barn was extended to create a cart shed and first-floor granary at one end, and stables with a hayloft at the other. In 1855, a tenant farmer and his young family finally moved in. John Hickes was a local man. Born and raised in Terrington, a village about four miles away, John was the younger of two poor farming brothers. Eight years before he came to Stonegrave, John, then thirty-seven years old, and his slightly older brother, Jonathon, were living and working together as bachelors and farm labourers. However, Jonathon held the tenancy to a modest 40 acres of land, and without fields of his own to farm, John would forever remain in his brother's shadow. And so, within the space of four years, John met and married a local girl, Jane, and fathered his first child, George. A daughter, Mary Jane, quickly followed, so by the time John was handed the keys to the Barn, the farmhouse and 200 acres, he was already head of a family of four. In the same year that he and his new family moved in, they had a second boy – also named John – and the following year welcomed another daughter, Susannah. By 1866, the couple had had two more healthy children – Sarah-Ann and Jonathon – and the farm, with their presence and energy, was beginning to thrive.

John and Jane Hickes and their six offspring had pulled off no mean feat. Within just a few years, John had moved up the agricultural ladder from landless labourer to tenant farmer. Not only that, but he had leapfrogged his older brother's acreage by a factor of five, secured a large farmhouse, and transformed himself from casual employee to full-time employer of consequence. Two hundred acres wasn't a large farm, but it wasn't a small one either and was significantly more than most labourers could ever have hoped for. Land meant status – John went from being a casual labourer to a man who managed land and other workers. Quite *how* he made the leap isn't clear, but he was undoubtedly capable and versatile; a good farm labourer needed to have a huge variety of seasonal skills, from building drystone walls to ploughing, laying hedges to threshing. Add into the mix a good dash of ambition and John had achieved the almost impossible task of rising up through the ranks.

Many of these tenant farmers found that, with hard work, there was a lot of money left over after paying the rent,[11] but for all their successes, the Hickeses never actually owned their farm or the Barn. The role of the tenant farmer could also be precarious – landowners enjoyed unrestricted control over what the land was used for and had the power to raise rents, change the farm's focus of activity or evict tenants. Farms were usually leased by the year, with few tenants' rights, and in many cases part of the tenancy agreement, until well into

the nineteenth century, included 'boon days'. These were days, given for free, to help the landowner with his own chores, whether it was reaping the corn or mending a road.

The landowner didn't hold all the cards, though. While short-term tenancies didn't encourage farmers to invest in their own land, they did allow them to up sticks and move if the farm proved unproductive or unprofitable. Moving farm was called 'flitting', from the Old Norse *flytja* (to relocate); farmers would sometimes flee under the cover of darkness, leaving their rent unpaid, which is where we get the phrase 'to do a moonlight flit'. A legitimate flit was a local event, which brought offers of muscle and transport from nearby friends and family. 'If you liked your neighbour it was a friendly thing to do,' recalled one North Yorkshire farmer, 'if you didn't like him you were glad to help him go. Either way you were sure to help.'[12]

The Hickes family stayed put, and decided to make a go of it. But it wasn't going to be easy; John would need plenty of farmhands to help to achieve his goal. The trick was knowing how to find them.

For hundreds of years, up until the middle of the nineteenth century, and well into the twentieth in many parts of Yorkshire, farmers looking for help, and villagers seeking farm work, would flood into the nearest market town to visit the annual hiring fairs. Also known as 'Mop Fairs' or 'Statties', the dates of these hiring fairs varied across the country but tended to coincide with one of the few quiet periods in the farming calendar.

In Ryedale, hiring fairs always took place in the week around 'Old Martinmas', 22 November.* The date would have been a significant one for the Hickeses; by that time, the summer crops were safely harvested and the winter seeds were in the ground, ready for next year. But, as a rural festival, it had a much older pedigree; for hundreds of years, Martinmas had signalled the end of the agrarian year and celebrated, with huge feasting, the annual cull of cattle and other livestock for the winter stores. Rituals associated with the autumn cull of animals have a long taproot: in the medieval form of Welsh, November is *Tachwet*, the month of slaughter, or *Y Mis Du*, the black month, while the Anglo-Saxons called November *Blotmonath*, the month of blood. Farmers would traditionally bring their livestock down from the moors or off the commons for an annual stocktake. Overwintered animals need winter feeding, or fodder, and any shortfall in supplies meant that excess stock had to be slaughtered and preserved for the lean,

---

* The date for the Yorkshire hiring fairs is a local oddity. Martinmas, or St Martin's Day, is celebrated in the rest of Britain on 11 November; the mismatch only makes sense when you know that, in the mid-eighteenth century, the country swapped from the Julian to the Gregorian calendar and eleven days effectively disappeared from the year. While most of the country accepted the new timings for saints' days and festivities, Yorkshire folk decided to stick to their guns and keep to the old date.

icy months ahead. Salted or smoked meat is still known as 'Martlemass beef'.

At the hiring fairs, men would dress up in their best clothes and head into the marketplace to meet with prospective employers. Depending on their skills, they might wear a token or badge of their trade - a tuft of wool for a shepherd, for example - while younger, less experienced lads might just tuck a plait of straw in their buttonhole, signalling a willingness to work. In general, the employment offered at hiring fairs split into two types - young unmarried farm servants, who would sign up for a year's work with lodging and food included - and farm labourers, usually older and more experienced workers who might live in a tied cottage or nearby village.

Farmers and farmhands would barter the terms of employment and, if an agreement was reached, the deal was sealed with a small amount of money called a fastening penny or God's penny, which could be spent on the fair's many other diversions - from fairground rides to fortune tellers - or down at the pub. Women looked for farm and farmhouse work too. No one quite knows where the name 'mop fair' comes from, but many a romantic country writer has pictured maids, hoping for work, carrying mops as part of the bucolic scene. Others have suggested that 'mop' was the name given to the workers' identifying flourishes, whether it was a horseman's whip or a twist of straw.

While employment was high on everyone's agenda, that didn't stop hiring fairs from being riotous fun – the wide-eyed recollections of one Yorkshire man, who visited the York hirings as a child in the early twentieth century, show just what a day out it must have been: 'What memories those fairs conjure up! It was a wide and fine street but could barely accommodate the massive fair, with its roundabouts, menagerie, shooting ranges, coconut shies, fortune-tellers, marionettes, living wonders of all kinds, moving-pictures, peep-shows, brandy-snap and gingerbread stalls and a dozen other attractions.'[13] For certain members of society, however, there was such a thing as too much fun and hiring fairs represented everything uncouth about rural life with 'the prevalence of pickpockets, the bad language [...] the labourers spent their Godspennies and more on wild beast shows, conjurors' booths and at the public houses which they frequented for want of anywhere else to go. Drunken orgies had consequences which may be guessed.'[14]

Clergy wrote with fevered anxiety about the scandalous mixing of men and women on hiring day, the free access to drink and wanton hedonism that seemed to be going on under their very noses. From the middle of the nineteenth century onwards, attempts were made to segregate the sexes at the hiring fairs, often by offering the female farmhands indoor accommodation and registration facilities. In bad weather the women welcomed, with typical pragmatism, the opportunity to step indoors out of the rain rather than stand out in the open with the boys; but come the good weather or the end of the hiring day and both sexes were once again reunited, much to the annoyance of one superintendent: 'the servant girls are as plentiful as the servant men at the Mop, and they throng the public houses, drinking, dancing and singing with drunken men and prostitutes, lying with the men in adjoining buildings and taking part in scenes of which no-one can form a correct opinion unless they have witnessed them.'[15]

In the larger market towns, hiring fairs attracted not just a few hundred farmworkers but vast, heaving crowds. In 1855, 10,000 men and 5,000 women, all seeking work and a good day out, packed the streets of the market town of Malton, just ten miles from the Barn and one of the closest local hirings. Some social commentators of the day were troubled by the cattle market connotations of the hiring fairs – conjuring up images of picky, sharp-tongued farmwives squeezing the arm muscles of strapping lads or lecherous foremen eyeing up the bonniest girls. Some farmers 'can compare the thews and sinews of a great many candidates', wrote journalist Thomas Kebbel, 'scanning them critically [...] and naturally regard them in no other light than that of animals'.[16] In return, farmhands also questioned the dignity of being 'given the once over' by prospective employers; across in Cumbria, one Penrith farmer remembers the last years of the hiring fairs in the 1930s: 'Workers resented having to stand in the street to be eyed and questioned, on display, rather like tups* at an agricultural show.'

Much of the criticism levelled at the hiring fairs may, however, have stemmed from worries about labourers and servants having any kind of leverage with their employees. The Yorkshire vicar Reverend John Eddowes made a career from complaining about the hiring fairs, occasions that, in his opinion, encouraged an insufferable disrespect for the natural order of things. 'As the hiring day draws near,' he despaired, 'the servants become more rudely independent, more disobedient and impertinent.'[17] At the hiring fairs, an interesting informal bargaining would take place between an employer such as John Hickes and any potential employees. Both had to come to a mutual arrangement, each seeking the best possible deal. Farmhands had the benefit of being able to visit more than one hiring fair over the course of a week or so, while farmers had plenty of potential workers to choose from. Many servants and labourers would hold off agreeing to a contract until they'd visited a few fairs; it was a risky strategy – agree to a placement too soon and you might miss a better offer, wait too long and all the good jobs might have gone. Farmers' reputations would also precede them – stories

---

* A 'tup' is an uncastrated male sheep.

of bullying treatment, long punishing working days, or even bad food served up by ill-tempered farmwives.

What was remarkable about the lives of live-in farm servants was that, although they were contracted for a year with bed and board included, they didn't get paid until their twelve months were up. While labourers would be paid daily, weekly or monthly, depending on the job, live-in farm servants had to wait an entire fifty-one weeks for their money. In the absence of regular wages, they could ask for 'subs' – small amounts of money that were taken off the final tally – but for the most part life operated on the basis of settling up at the year's end. The cobbler who had mended their shoes, the washerwoman who had cleaned their clothes, the tailor who had made the farm servant his or her one good set of clothes – all would be paid off at Martinmas. One of the few benefits of this system was that – if their wages were reasonable and they had not built up too many debts over the course of the year – young farm servants could start saving money towards perhaps leasing their bit of land, buying a few animals or starting married life with a lump sum.

John Hickes had started off his career as a farm labourer. Traditionally, farm labourers – who didn't have to 'live in' as part of their employment – would be paid more frequently[*] than farm servants, and often receive part of their wages in kind. Small amounts of food from the farm were often part of the deal – potatoes or a sack of flour – or perhaps the use of a small cottage. England's villages are awash with the remnants of these properties, now prettified into well-to-do dwellings and second homes, but for most of their existence, agricultural labourers' homes would have been bleak. The land surveyor John Tuke travelled past the Barn in the closing years of the eighteenth century, taking stock of farming life. He was horrified by what he found:

> The cottages of the labourers are generally small and low, consisting only of one room, and, very rarely, of two, both of which are level with the ground, and sometimes a step within it. This situation renders them damp, and frequently very unwholesome, and contributes, with the smallness of the apartments, to injure the health both of parents and children, for in such contracted hovels numerous families are often compelled to reside. In the North Riding the farmer is by no means well accommodated, but the labourer is much worse.[18]

---

[*] Titles such as daytale-men (those paid by the day) and month-men (often employed just for harvest) reveal the short-term nature of most rural labour.

One perk of the farmworker's life –
especially at harvest time – came in the
form of alcohol. A daily allowance of
farm-brewed beer or ale not only
greased the wheels of gruelling work
but also contained vital calories
that water alone didn't. The alcohol
content of the booze consumed
during the day was often weaker than
evening drink, but the results of home

brewing weren't always predictable. William
Marshall, a late-eighteenth-century agricultural writer and
Ryedale resident, wrote with concern that some harvest ale
was so strong it would 'stupify any man and make a sober
man drunk from morning to night'.[19] Even so, labourers
were allowed a gallon of ale a day by the farmers who
employed them.

The Truck Act of 1887 attempted to ban the drink allowance
for farmworkers, and some farmers even encouraged
their workers to swap it for a small increase in wages, but
the pleasure and ritual of the harvest ale and other drink
allowances proved seductive and the habit continued well
after the Act had forbidden it. In some cases, it was clearly
a deal-breaker; in the words of G. E. Mingay, a scholar of
agricultural life in Victorian England: 'Temperance reformers
might rail against the custom, but drink was a traditional

part of the wage, and it was difficult to get workers even to start a job without it.'[20]

Over in East Yorkshire, historian Stephen Caunce captured the oral recollections of men and women who had worked on farms in the early twentieth century, as the last of the old traditions slipped away: 'There was a lot of farms and each farm had five or six single lads, and we used to go to look at their horses, to see who had the fattest. And in harvest time we used to go and see who had the best stacks... Sometimes the farmer would come out and he would bring a bucket of beer – great big buckets, scoured clean – bring a dozen mugs and a basketful of beef sandwiches – stick 'em in the middle of the yard, and say "here you are lads!"'[21]

The fact that both farmers and potential employees could visit more than one hiring fair allowed both parties, year on year, to test the state of the market. Wages would fluctuate depending on conditions in the wider agricultural economy, the weather and its effect on the harvest, and availability of labour: some years farmhands could command higher wages, in others, farmers dictated the terms. It's interesting that in places such as North Yorkshire, where hiring fairs were well attended, formal trade unions struggled to take hold as they did elsewhere in Britain. Yorkshire farm wages often tended to be higher than in other counties – growing and confident northern industrial towns provided an expanding market for North Yorkshire's farming produce but also pushed up the wages of those agricultural workers who resisted the pull of the mills. James Caird, who took on the task of surveying British farms for *The Times* newspaper in the middle of the nineteenth century, noted that farmworkers in the north earned, on average, nearly 40 per cent more than their southern counterparts.[22] John Hickes would undoubtedly have had to compete with the lure of industry to secure help at the Barn.

The development of formal trade unions must have also been hampered by the nature of rural employment, especially in the north. Live-in farm servants were not expected by either party to stay on at the same farm for longer than two or three years – the arrival of the hiring fair in the annual calendar gave many the opportunity to kiss goodbye to a hated employer and try their luck elsewhere. As one Yorkshire hiring rhyme went:

Good Morning, Mister Martinmas
You've come to set me free
For I don't care for Master
And he don't care for me.[23]

One of the cheapest ways for John Hickes to get help was to employ children. Despite being a father of six young children himself, he would have had few qualms about employing other people's offspring; child labour was as much a part of the rural landscape as the crops and livestock – the poor relied on the wages of all the family. Being born into a poor farming family, John would have also no doubt worked from a young age himself – he'd experienced both the hardships and the necessity of young labour at first hand.

While we often think of industrial textile mills or coal mines as the crucibles of child labour, agriculture was one of the largest employers of both paid and unpaid children. An 1834 Rural Queries parliamentary report attempted to uncover what kind of work was being done on farms by small hands. What's fascinating and shocking is just how many different, and difficult, tasks children were expected to perform, depending on their age and experience. The very youngest were sent out in all weathers, alone, into the fields to scare away the birds or keep an eye over an unruly flock, while older children were responsible for pulling up root crops, harvesting grain, haymaking, herding cattle, catching vermin or driving ploughs.

The average age for a child labourer in farming was ten, but children as young as five were routinely corralled into working long, cold days, either in isolation or with unscrupulous employers. Writing about his childhood in

the middle of the eighteenth century, the journalist William Cobbett, author of *Rural Rides*, could 'not remember the time when I did not earn my living. My first occupation was driving the birds from the turnip-seeds, and the rooks from the peas. When I first trudged afield, with my wooden bottle and my satchel swung over my shoulder, I was hardly able to climb the gates and stiles; and, at the close of day, to reach home was a task of infinite difficulty.'[24] Another lad, Roger Langdon, began his working life at eight years old in the 1830s: 'For the princely sum of one shilling a week [...] I had to mind sheep and pull up turnips in all winds and weathers, starting at six o'clock in the morning [...] After this, until I was thirteen years of age, my life was not worth the living.'[25] Roger lived in with his farmer 'master' and suffered at the hands of the ploughman charged with his day-to-day care; drunken beatings were commonplace and, when Roger's parents tried to intervene, the violence got worse. But Roger's family could not 'keep him in idleness' and so he endured five more years of thrashings before he was set free.

While blows were raining down on young Roger Langdon, the government passed the 1833 Factory Act to improve conditions for children working in factories, which banned child workers under the age of nine. Farming, however, remained unregulated and an enthusiastic employer of children under ten until well into the second half of the nineteenth century. Local records show that the Barn had its own child labourers – two in the 1860s and another two in the 1880s – and, no doubt, plenty of unofficial young help during harvest. Nationally, the 1851 census showed that nearly 10 per cent of all farm labourers were under fifteen, although the true figure was probably nearly double that; children often slipped through the statistics – either because they were labouring on their family farms, or their work went unrecorded. In the same year, nearly one in six farm servants – who were contracted to work and live away from home under the farmer's roof – were under fifteen.

Many girls left home to go into farm service at twelve and while for poor families this had the benefit of there being one less mouth to feed, young girls were often at risk from sexual harassment and assault from both employers and fellow employees. As early as 1740, novels such as *Pamela; or, Virtue Rewarded* by Samuel Richardson shocked and titillated readers in equal measure with their tales of wealthy landowners making inappropriate advances towards their guileless, fresh-faced servants. For some children in service, the loneliness must have been intolerable. In 1875, scandal briefly visited the rector of Stonegrave, John Hickes's landlord, when one young servant found she could no longer cope: 'A young girl, a native of Cantley, near Doncaster, living as a domestic servant with the Rev. A. W. Wetherall [...] obtained possession of some poison from her master's medicine cabinet, and took it, with a fatal result. She left a document behind her, stating she was "tempted by the devil".'[26] One can only imagine what that temptation might have been, living and skivvying over 60 miles from home under the care of an unmarried, middle-aged man.

The Barn, and the farmhouse, also had its fair share of young female domestic servants. It's almost unimaginable to modern Western sensibilities that a child might be responsible for cooking, cleaning and looking after a stranger's entire family, and yet the Hickeses employed domestic after domestic with dogged consistency. By 1881, a local girl of just fourteen – Annie Johnson – was the farmhouse's only live-in servant and was responsible for sourcing and preparing all the meals, washing clothes, feeding the chickens, working in the dairy, cleaning the house, making the fires, changing beds, and a multitude of other spirit-sapping chores. Annie herself was the youngest of six children born within the space of nine years to a farming family in Wombleton, a village only a few miles from the Barn. But Annie's father was no John Hickes, and with just 13 acres to make a living from, a wife, six children and an elderly mother to care for, he would have welcomed the opportunity for his youngest daughter to make her own way.

At this time, four of the farmer's own children were still living at home. Now aged between sixteen and twenty-five, the Hickeses' offspring were all much older, and better educated, than Annie, but would have felt no awkwardness about employing her services. Attitudes to childhood were just one of the many contradictions of the Victorian era – on the one hand, sermons, poetry and literature of the period were often cloyingly sentimental about children's purity and simplicity, while society at large relied on armies of underage servitude. While *Alice in Wonderland*'s Lewis Carroll was writing, with chilling unctuousness, to the mother of two young girls he liked to photograph nude – 'Their innocent unconsciousness is very beautiful, and gives one a feeling of reverence, as at the presence of something sacred'[27] – over at the Barn, Annie was enduring a sixteen-hour shift catering to the needs of two adults, four grown-up children, a large farmhouse and an array of farm animals.

Female domestic servants like Annie, on isolated rural farms, lived a precarious existence. In the absence of any protection, in every sense of the word, many young women in service found themselves pregnant. An illegitimate child brought not only social disapproval, but instant dismissal. Many young domestics found they had no choice but to conceal the birth of a baby and dispose of the body; the locations are heart-breaking – privies, dung heaps, ditches – but reflect the desperation of women anxious to avoid detection and prosecution.

Annie's predecessor at the Barn, Ann Barker, a twenty-two-year-old domestic servant, would have undoubtedly got wind of one such incident in 1871, less than a mile away, at a neighbouring farmhouse. The *Yorkshire Herald* ran the story:

'On Monday, an inquest was held at the house of Mr. Jackson, East Newton, by A. Wood, Esq., deputy coroner, on the body of a female child. Mr. G. Jackson stated that thinking the cistern would be full by the heavy rain he lifted the cover, when he saw something floating at the top, and on taking it out he found it to be the body of a child. Mrs. Jackson charged a girl named Elizabeth Barr with the offence. She denied it at first, but afterwards confessed she had the child three weeks ago, during the night, and that she put it in the cistern. Mrs. Jackson did not notice any change in the girl. She had only been to her service a week previous to the occurrence, and never complained that she was ill. Dr. Haynes, of Helmsley, made an examination of the body, said that the child was of premature birth, and that it had never breathed [...] The girl was committed to York for trial, on Wednesday.'[28]

In the end, Elizabeth was charged with the new crime, created just ten years earlier, of 'Concealing the Birth of a Child' and sentenced to three months' imprisonment. Locals must have considered her to have had a lucky escape; under the new law, any woman found deliberately concealing the body of a baby that died in or shortly after childbirth could look forward to up to two years in prison. And if the jury – which until the 1920s would have been all male – decided the baby had been deliberately killed, Elizabeth could have faced the noose.

The discovery of an illegitimate child also had consequences for the father. The 1576 Poor Law had aimed to lift the parish burden and make putative fathers duty-bound to acknowledge and maintain any illegitimate offspring. Under the 1733 Bastardy Act, the rules were tightened so that a man could face prison until he agreed to marry the mother of his child or repay any relief costs the parish incurred. Proving an unwilling man's paternity would have been challenging for a young mother but, at the very least, there was a legal acknowledgement of a male parent's financial duty to his illegitimate child. For many an unrestrained gadabout in a position of trust, this obligation must have been irksome. One such individual was Captain John Bolton of Bulmer, a village between Malton and the Barn. The story is fascinatingly grim, not just for its gruesome details, but because the girl involved was both a pregnant rural servant and a foundling herself, no doubt the product of an unhappy liaison just eighteen years before.

Bolton had been in the militia. After marrying and settling down, and fathering six children, he applied to the Foundling Hospital in Ackworth, West Yorkshire, for domestic help. A twelve-year-old girl – Elizabeth Rainbow – was duly dispatched to a small estate in rural North Yorkshire, not dissimilar to the Barn's. Six years later, the Foundling Hospital received a strange letter from Bolton's neighbour, which informed them that Elizabeth had gone missing and that they were concerned for her safety as there had been rumours that Bolton might have got her pregnant. The hospital swiftly contacted the local Justice of the Peace and a warrant was issued for Bolton's arrest. Bolton, infuriated, dashed to the local courthouse and demanded a warrant for his neighbour's arrest in return, charging them with defamation.

While in the courthouse, Bolton learned that a constable had been dispatched to the house. In a panic, he galloped home, only to discover the constable uncovering the body of Elizabeth Rainbow in his cellar. At the trial, it emerged that Bolton, on finding out that Elizabeth was pregnant, had forced her to take abortifacients. When those didn't work, he waited until his wife and children were out of the house and strangled Elizabeth to avoid the disgrace and financial responsibility of fathering a bastard, then dug up the cellar and dumped her body in the soil. Bolton was taken to York prison, where he was sentenced to hang. Elizabeth had been five months pregnant.[29] The murder, which took place in the 1770s, clearly struck a chord with local men and women and became the subject of a popular folk song. Thirteen snappily bleak verses tell the tale, sung to the much older tune of 'Death and the Lady', and would have been warbled by the Barn's harvesters and horse men alike throughout the nineteenth century. 'I should have been her guardian and her friend,' runs one particularly apt line – a warning and a reminder of the vulnerability of young women and girls in farm service.

Children and teenagers were also recruited by gangmasters, subcontractors who provided farmers with a pool of cheap labour for seasonal tasks such as harvesting or haymaking. Conditions were tough – twelve- and fourteen-hour shifts were not uncommon – exacerbated by long, often double-figure, walks to and from home. One woman, writing about her experiences as a child working for a Lincolnshire gangmaster in the 1850s, recalled leaving school at eight years of age to work fourteen-hour days in a gang of fifty other children; her misery continued for the next four years until she found factory work, which, despite its brutality, compared to farm life 'felt like Heaven'.[30]

Child labour was cheap. Most earned barely a third of the male adult farming wage. Under-tens took home not even a quarter of the amount their fellow adult workers did. Children could also be picked up and dropped casually – employed for a few hours at a time, for a few pence a day – but few objected to the practice. The view of one rural vicar, writing in the 1840s, echoed the feelings of the time: 'We have had a few instances', he noted with alarm, 'of boys kept at the school until they were seventeen, and it was found that they could not at that age, and after habits acquired in attending school so long, turn to that kind of labour. They continue to loiter about the village and become idle.'[31]

Sometimes escape seemed the only option. Job Smith was a young boy employed as a live-in farm servant at a farm in Stonegrave. Just after Christmas Day in 1874, Job ran away but was found two weeks later and ordered to return to work. He stuck it out for two more days and then absconded again, complaining that 'he had been required to do too much work; that was why he left'.[32] The farmer disagreed and took the boy to court, claiming lost earnings and legal costs, insisting that 'he had set the lad to do no more than anyone else would give him'. The court ruled in the farmer's favour, ordered the boy to return and to pay nearly £2 14s in compensation and costs, a sum that would have taken Job – who was paid nine shillings a week – six weeks to pay off.

As a semi-illiterate farm servant, Job would have few other options than to return to the farm that employed him. Just a few years earlier, the 1870 Elementary Education Act had made some provision for the education of primary-aged children. The Act established boards to oversee the creation of school places for all children between the age of five and thirteen. However, it didn't make education free and whether a child received any kind of schooling depended on a number of different factors, not least whether their parents could afford to forgo their offspring's wage or pay the school fees.

Children who lived more than two miles from a school were also exempt from mandatory attendance, a clause that would have applied to a large number of rural children.

The suffragette Hannah Mitchell remembered being denied an education – even after the 1870 Act – so that she could help her father around the farm. Her three brothers and older sister were allowed to attend school, while Hannah stayed behind, an injustice that informed her later passion for women's rights: 'in early spring [...] even lovely flowers failed to console me for a bitter disappointment. Standing among them weeping, I told my uncle that my sister was to start school the following week. I had expected to go with her but my mother said she needed one of us at home.'[33]

The decision not to make elementary schooling free came from competing pressures. Politically, the idea of state-funded schooling wasn't popular among certain sections of society – many feared that an educated workforce would be a dangerous one or, at the very least, pointless. Only a few years earlier, Sir Charles Adderley,[34] Vice-President of the Committee of Council on Education, had made his thoughts clear on the subject: 'any attempt to keep the children of the labouring classes under intellectual culture after the very earliest stage at which they could earn their living, would be as arbitrary and improper as it would be to keep the boys at Eton and Harrow at spade labour.' Other voices of dissent objected to the economic threat posed by removing valuable child labour from the mills and farms of the country.

Stonegrave's residents were, in some ways, luckier than many others. Since the early 1670s there had been a small charity school in the neighbouring village of Nunnington, which took in a handful of children from both villages and was paid for by donations and legacies. Nearby Hovingham had a similar arrangement; in the early eighteenth century, a kindly benefactor had left enough money to pay for the schooling of four children, boosted a few decades later by another donation that took the number of young scholars to sixteen. There was, however, no formal setting for the education of the village children until Lady Worsley – who lived at Hovingham Hall – built a school. On 3 October 1864, forty-two local children sat down to their very first lessons at Hovingham Church of England School. Over a hundred and fifty years later, the school is still central to village life and welcomes the same number of young children, including our three girls.

The 1870 Education Act was a milestone, but children routinely slipped through the net. Even when the 1891 Elementary Education Act made elementary school free, the economic reality for many rural families was that they needed their children's earnings more than their literacy. Richard Scurr, an agricultural labourer whose father, John, had worked in the Barn's fields before Hickes took over, was fined a day's pay in 1896 for not sending one of his seven children to school regularly. Richard had, ironically, been one of the few children, along with his older sister Ruth, to receive schooling – at least for a few years of his young life. A brief education in a rural schoolroom wasn't enough, though, to reverse the fortunes of the Scurr family and many others like it. By his teens, Richard was a farm servant for a local farmer and, once married, returned to Stonegrave to be a farm labourer. Ruth became a maidservant for a large house.

Rather than send their children to the local school, the Hickeses hired a governess, the sure-fire status symbol of the aspiring Victorian middle class. The role was a curious one. A member of the educated middle class herself, a governess was usually a young woman whose family had fallen on hard times. The death of a father or a poor financial decision could leave a middle-class family in dire straits. Working in a shop or on a factory floor was seen as demeaning for a genteel young woman – one of the only 'respectable' jobs was to work in the bosom of another well-to-do family. In 1851, around 25,000 women earned their living by working as governesses. Pay was typically poor, although board and lodging were provided. The novelist Charlotte Brontë spent her early twenties as a governess to a wealthy Yorkshire family, the Sidgwicks, a situation she found both isolating and socially ambiguous. Charlotte was charged with the care of two young children. Writing to her sister Emily, Charlotte said she found the loneliness and indifference of her employer hard to bear. Of the mother, Mrs Sidgwick, Charlotte wrote that she 'does not know my character & she does not wish to know it. I have never had five minutes of conversation with her since I came— except when she was scolding me.' And, at one mealtime, when one of the Sidgwick children tenderly took Charlotte's hand, saying, 'I love 'ou, Miss Brontë,' Mrs Sidgwick quickly chastised her son: 'Love the *governess*, my dear!'[35] Charlotte left the Sidgwicks under a cloud in July 1839 but only a few months later conceded that she needed to find another position. 'I *hate* and *abhor* the very thought of governess-ship,' she raged, but knew she had little choice.

The Hickeses' governess was a twenty-year-old woman called Minnie Hale. Minnie, like Charlotte Brontë, was also far from her home in Hartlepool, County Durham. Minnie's father had been born to a well-to-do family but, as the second son, wouldn't inherit and worked as a customs clerk. The year Minnie arrived at the Barn, her father, mother and younger siblings were already living in India. Whether Minnie stayed behind in Yorkshire by choice or financial necessity isn't known but she worked under the Hickeses' roof in the knowledge that everyone who was close to her was on the other side of the world. Any complaints she had about life as a governess would have had to wait for months, until their return. Life as the Hickeses' governess also took Minnie away from society and the chance to make a judicious match. Soon after her father returned from India, Minnie's mother died, leaving Minnie no choice but to care for her father and her younger siblings. Her spell as a governess at the Barn, followed by the domestic responsibilities imposed on her as the eldest daughter, ensured Minnie would never marry and have children of her own.

The only child Minnie didn't teach was the Hickeses' eldest son, George. For a child of a once-impoverished labourer, fifteen-year-old George was already enjoying an opportunity his father could only have dreamed of – full-time education as a boarder at St Michael's School in Malton.

Girls were employed less frequently in heavy farm work than boys, but it wasn't unknown. Moral crusaders felt that farm labouring was turning young girls into 'coarse women', but few had the luxury of choice. Those girls who did stay at home often had to childmind their own sisters and brothers so their mother could work instead – girls no older than seven or eight would regularly be left in sole charge of their younger siblings and babies, or frail older relatives. As girls grew into women, many would continue to toil as part of a rural husband and wife 'team'; but as the wives of labourers, their contribution is often invisible in the records. Tuke, in his late eighteenth-century survey of the land around the Barn, is one of the few observers to notice how critical women were to the rural economy:

> 'nor ought it to be forgotten, that to the females a very large share of it is to be ascribed: their industry is not exceeded by that of the women of any country; equalled by few: the dairy is entirely theirs; and no trifling labour attends it: they perform at least half the harvest work; they labour at that season with the men, and many of them as well; they weed the corn; they make the hay; they mould the fields; and perform a multitude of the lesser occupations of husbandry.'[36]

Those girls who did work in the homes of others, either as domestic servants, farm servants or governesses, were often local, but this was not always the case; employers sometimes knew little about the true character of their staff before they welcomed them into their homes. While petty theft and child cruelty were common complaints against female staff, the story of one particular woman – Mary Bateman – served as a stark warning for rural families, like the Hickeses, looking to employ help.

Mary had been born into a modest farming family at Asenby, about 20 miles from the Barn, in 1768. By all accounts she was an intensely bright child, but wayward. Her father finally sent her into service with a local family in nearby

Thirsk when she was thirteen – not a particularly young age for a rural domestic servant – but almost from the moment she arrived, Mary began a career of spectacular thievery, con artistry and, eventually, murder. What started with pilfering from her employer soon developed into a catalogue of bizarre and, at times, astonishingly cruel hoaxes and poisonings. One of her better-known deceptions involved 'The Prophet Hen', a chicken she claimed laid magical eggs bearing the poorly spelled inscription 'Crist is Coming'. Credulous admirers would line up and pay to see the doomsday hen in action, not realising that Mary had etched the words on the eggs with acid and kept reinserting them up the poor hen's oviduct.

In another deception, Mary persuaded a widow to sell all her worldly possessions and leave the money and the care of the widow's four young children to her. True to form, Mary pocketed the cash, sent the infants straight to the workhouse and disappeared into the ether. After a catalogue of thefts, frauds and poisonings, Mary's undoing came when she killed a woman whom she claimed she was ridding of 'evil spirits'. Rather than cure her, Mary had been slowly poisoning the woman over weeks, with contaminated puddings, but the husband became suspicious and the whole sorry affair soon came to light. On 20 March 1809, Mary was hanged for the crime but, by this point, she had become something of a celebrity. Sensing there was some money to be made, the local infirmary charged visitors three pennies a head to see her corpse, which they subsequently flayed, tanned and sold as macabre souvenirs.[37]

Farmers' wives would have been particularly interested in Mary's story, not least because they were usually the ones responsible for hiring female help. While male servants often slept in accommodation away from the family – in the Barn's case, they slept in a small loft space above the scullery or in the hayloft – female employees bunkered down in the main house. Child domestic servants, like Annie Johnson, may not have had a bedroom at all, and slept in the kitchen or shared a room with the other female servants, just yards from the rest of the household. Female farm servants and domestics, like their male counterparts, were not expected to stay at one farmhouse for more than a few years, hopping from one place of employment to the next. It's hard to imagine what kind of uneasy truce existed between family and female servant, sharing such intimate, close quarters and relying so heavily on each other for the day-to-day survival of the farm.

L. P. Hartley famously wrote: 'The past is a foreign country.' As a successful tenant farmer, Hickes and his family enjoyed a relatively comfortable existence, but an unescapable fact of rural life even as late as the early twentieth century was how close most agricultural workers and their families lived to financial ruin and penury. The poverty and squalor of newly emerging industrial cities – such as Bradford or Leeds – is well documented and yet life in the countryside was, in some ways, even tougher. Images of ruddy-cheeked farming families, healthy from the endless supply of fresh food and home-grown produce, don't tally with the reality of life for many labourers and farm servants in the eighteenth and nineteenth centuries. In many cases, the amount of money coming into the rural home just wasn't enough to cover food or any other basic necessities.

The average family size, across Britain, in the mid-nineteenth century was two adults and four children. And yet the wages varied hugely across industries. While rural labouring families earned a weekly household income of 11s 6d (about £35 in today's money), mining families earned two and a half times as much (29s a week), while manufacturing families took home even more at 33s a week.[38] No wonder, then, that many a desperate country dweller abandoned the fields of their childhood home and made a beeline for the mill towns.

Unlike successful tenant farmers such as John and his family, the money that most rural families made simply didn't stretch as far as the wages of their urban counterparts. Three-quarters of an agricultural labourer's household income was spent on food and, of that amount, more than 70 per cent was spent solely on bread; the rest bought a tiny quantity of meat and a thin smattering of extras like cheese, milk, butter, tea, sugar, salt and yeast.* Far from being a nation of smallholders, only one in five rural families could afford to keep a pig and just one in three had access to a garden or an allotment where they could grow their own food.[39] Even fewer kept a cow. In his round-up of North Yorkshire, Tuke despaired that 'labourers in the country are often worse supplied with milk, than the same class of people in the town'.[40] There will be more to say about milk later. For the majority of the Barn's life, up until the Second World War, the experience of the people employed on the farm would have been dominated by poverty and, at times, hunger. As the historian Ruth Goodman has written about rural life in Victorian Britain: 'Large numbers of people woke up famished and spent their working days – and much of their working lives – in a state of semi-permanent wanting of food.'[41] How bitterly ironic that men, women and children who spent their days sowing, growing and harvesting food, and tending to animals, had so little for themselves.

The reasons for this are myriad and complex, but two issues shine through. As we have already seen, the medieval open-field system of farming gave villagers common rights to graze their animals and grow a selection of crops on small strips of land owned ultimately by the Crown. But the era

* To give you a modern comparison, the British people now only spend around 20–25 per cent of their total household income on food consumption. Poorer countries, such as Tanzania and Bangladesh, typically spend around 50–60 per cent of their income on food. (Source: UN's Food and Agriculture Organization Report 2018)

that followed the English Civil War saw an increase in the power of private landlords, who wanted to parcel off large fields for their exclusive use. Such enclosures had originally been used for sheep farming – wool made many a fortune in medieval England – but from the mid-eighteenth century onwards they were increasingly devoted to the large-scale raising of crops and livestock to feed newly emerging urban populations. England was rapidly growing – in the 200 years between 1500 and 1700 the population more than doubled from around 2 million people to 5 million, while the price of grain increased sixfold; arable farming was starting to make some real money. By the eighteenth century, demand for meat and dairy products from London and other growing urban markets was also encouraging landowners to enclose fields for cattle rearing.

One of the benefits of the old open-field system was that – at least in those cases where it functioned well – farming was a collective activity, and most people would have enough to subsist on. Farming practices were overseen by the local manorial court and foreman, who would ensure that the community was kept in line. Everyone farmed, so no one saw themselves as a 'farmer', and most families kept themselves afloat with a mixture of agriculture and other work, such as weaving wool, making baskets, local mining, collecting fuel and so on. Even the local clergymen farmed in between sermons.

By 1815, however, most of England's farmland – including the Barn's – was enclosed. Under the new system, villagers became waged agricultural workers who were obliged to take on a string of casual jobs that left them with no social protection and rendered them vulnerable to fluctuations in the wider economy. The pre-enclosure subsistence farmer was poor but tended to spread his liabilities across a number of income sources or items for barter, such as grain, timber, textile work, meat, eggs and so on. As a waged labourer, you were entirely at the whim of the market. During the nineteenth century, any period where there was a surplus of workers caused wages to plummet, while the introduction of labour-saving machinery, such as threshing machines in the 1830s, drastically reduced the man-hours required. As one, unusually sympathetic, enclosure report from the turn of the eighteenth century noted, 'The poor and persons with little capital (such as butchers, common shepherds, etc.) derive benefit from open fields and commons, by being enabled to keep horses, cows, and sheep [...] It will be difficult to prove that in any case the poor have been benefited (by enclosure). No instances of benefit on this score have been stated to me. On the contrary, an increase of poor has been the general complaint.'[42]

If enclosure had dealt the decisive blow, changes in women's work ensured that rural families stayed down and out. Domestic hand spinning and other forms of textile work had been a ubiquitous and welcome source of income for rural women since the Middle Ages, allowing wives to work and look after children at the same time. The wife's wage, however small, was often the difference between survival and destitution for rural families. By the time the new threshing section of the Barn was finished in the 1780s, the county had begun its transition to machine spinning and factory production, leaving domestic textile workers with the difficult choice of finding other forms of rural income (if indeed there were any to be had) or trying their luck in the 'big smoke'. Even at the time, there were worries about the wisdom of heading for the mill towns, not least because factory work was so unpleasant.

Small-scale manufacturing had a long history in Ryedale – alum, iron for forging and sailcloth, for example, had been produced there for centuries. What worried commentators such as Tuke was the scale of burgeoning industries such as cotton weaving and their effect on both the health and morals of the farming community: 'agriculture and manufacture have never been found to flourish in the same country,' he said disapprovingly. 'Where people are collected together in large numbers, their morals are likely to be depraved, their health injured, and [...] their strength weakened.'[43]

For some, the promise of a better life was just too tempting to ignore. Between the late eighteenth and early twentieth centuries, millions of people attempted to escape rural poverty. Many got no further than the nearest town, while others left friends and relatives behind to head for sites of heavy industry and big cities such as Leeds, Liverpool and Manchester. Between 1841 and 1911, Britain's rural villages lost more than 4 million of their residents through internal migration.[44] Another 10 million Britons took the almost unthinkable leap of faith and headed for the far side of the world. The Barn watched its own workers leave the local village in a steady flow – in 1831, the village of Stonegrave had a population of 189. By 1881 it had dwindled to 140, and by 1900 to only 127.[45]

Newspapers ran weekly advertisements enticing rural dwellers and their families to sail away to a new life. Ports such as Whitby, Hull and Liverpool offered passage to Australia, New Zealand, America and Canada for just a few pounds. And it wasn't just labourers and servants who were packing their bags. As part of the improvements made to land, farm buildings were often built or expanded. Landowners could see the potential to increase the profitability of their holdings and were asking tenant farmers for higher rents in return. While some tenant farmers could meet these costs, plenty couldn't. Among those who pushed for enclosure, it was an article of faith that it always brought improvement. And yet, at least in the short term, for many people the reverse was true. When farm tenants were asked – by shipping companies – to give their reasons for leaving, the subject of rents came up time and time again.

The second half of the eighteenth century had seen a dramatic rise in farm rents, often as much as 50 per cent.[46] Many farmers from across North Yorkshire left for Nova Scotia, citing such motives as 'on account of the grate [sic] advance of rents' or 'Provisions, Rents and every necessary of life, being so very high'.[47] Of the seventy adult passengers on just one ship, the *Two Friends*, which sailed from Hull to Halifax, Nova Scotia in the 1770s, at least half were tenant farmers or farm labourers pushed out by high rents or chasing a better livelihood.[48] Yorkshire had the largest acreage enclosed of any county in England and, it seems, plenty of farmworkers willing to start a new life abroad.

Michael Francklin, lieutenant governor of Nova Scotia, concentrated his energies on recruiting disgruntled agricultural workers from Stonegrave, Hovingham and other nearby settlements. He placed emigration agents in a number of key villages to pinpoint potential settlers from among local farming communities. Remarkably, over a thousand local residents upped and left, including two families, the Fawcetts and the Coateses. The Fawcett brothers – William, John and Robert – were industrious Methodists but had grown tired of trying to make a living against the backdrop of rising rents. They set sail, with their young children, in 1774. Thomas Coates, his wife and their young daughter had left two years earlier. For both families, the move proved to be a gamble worth taking. When Thomas Coates died in 1813, he had nearly a thousand acres of farmland and a large property to his name, while the Fawcett brothers became wealthy and prominent figures in Canadian farming and business life. News of their success would have no doubt trickled slowly home.

The loss of skilled farm tenants did not unduly worry those who rented out their holdings - the inconvenience of finding a new tenant farmer was more than outweighed by the increased profitability of agricultural lettings. Tenancies in Stonegrave and a handful of surrounding villages, for example, made record profits in the 1830s and 1840s, just at the time the Reverend Thomas Mosley was looking for a farmer to rent the Barn's new farmhouse. Sir Bellingham Graham - one of the three large landowners who split Stonegrave's land between them, along with the rector and Thomas Howard - had had a particularly fruitful year in 1834, making 20 per cent more than the previous year's receipts.[49]

The fact that agricultural workers were attempting to improve their lot by emigrating was, for some, a national disgrace. In the 1870s, George Jennings Davies, landowner and clergyman, wrote witheringly that the rural labourer had learned to 'hate England, and is only anxious to shake off the dust of his feet at the door of all the squires and parsons, and to set out for Australia or some other distant place [...]

where he imagines he has nothing to do but to eat colonial beef steaks, and dwell in a house with a spare bedroom for each of his children, forgetting that an industrious man can live in England and that a lazy one cannot live out of it.'[50] Other, more circumspect, commentators worried for the future of the country, when so many of its essential workers had dropped tools and headed abroad. Henry Rider Haggard – Victorian agricultural reformer and successful adventure novelist – warned that the countryside was in tatters: 'The labourers "back to the land". That is the cry of the press and the fancy of the people. Well, I do not think they will ever come back; certainly no legislation will ever bring them. Some of the rising generation may be induced to stay, but it will be by training them to the use of machinery and paying them higher wages.'[51]

Colonies were desperate for agricultural labour and skilled farming knowledge, and, for the British government, emigration offered a unique opportunity to unburden themselves of an ever-increasing number of poverty-stricken, jobless rural workers. From 1834 the Poor Law Commission would sanction the emigration of any of its poor that a parish was prepared to fund. By the end of the nineteenth century, nearly 40,000 paupers from England and Wales had been sent overseas by their parishes. Few politicians expressed any concern, with the notable exception of the reform-minded MP Charles Buller, who, in 1843, claimed

74

that Britain was 'shovelling out paupers to where they may die without shocking their betters with the sight or sound of their last agony'.[52]

Undeterred by Buller's views, the pauper emigration scheme would pick up pace in the 1850s. Further legislative changes allowed workhouses to send abroad any 'poor orphan or deserted child under the age of sixteen years'[53] under its care. A number of other independent organisations and charities also sent their orphans to the colonies, with children often ending up as indentured servants on farms. Between 1869 and the late 1930s, more than 100,000 'orphans' were sent by Barnardo's and other philanthropic organisations to Canada alone, while a further 130,000 were shipped off to both Canada and Australia from the 1920s to the 1970s. In reality, only about one in ten of the children sent were actually parentless. Many were rural children who had been put by destitute parents into the workhouse system or charitable institutions, hoping they could reclaim their sons and daughters when their situation improved. Sometimes parents would go back to collect their offspring only to find they had been sent abroad, or they would receive an 'after sailing' notification telling them their child had already left. Once on foreign shores, few of Britain's young farmhands ever saw their childhood fields again.

2

WE'VE GOTTEN WER MELL, HURRAH HURRAH!

WE'VE GOTTEN WER MELL, HURRAH HURAAH!

We've cut the last sheaf!

A stiff wind often whistles through the valley. For most of the year, it comes from the west and races around the Barn. Almost as soon as we arrived on the farm, we started planting trees to act as a windbreak. We asked for trees instead of wedding presents and guests took to the idea with relish. Now, over a decade later, we have a young mixed woodland, full of chestnut, cherry, oak and rowan trees, many of which have grown on a lean, as if pulling away from the prevailing weather.

In early summer, however, a balmy breeze often blows in the opposite direction, bringing with it a clear, cloudless sky. These are the days when we make hay. Like a coordinated ballet, for a week or two tractors come and go, cutting, turning, then raking the grass into windrows. Once the grass is first mown it's left in the swath, to start drying out. Over the next few days, the hay needs occasionally aerating or wuffling, a laborious job for a man with a pitchfork but now done in minutes with a tractor tedder and its rotating spikes. The best bit is when the baler finally arrives and gobbles up the neat rows, spinning the hay into huge round cylinders. When a bale is ready, like a hen laying a huge egg, the baler lifts its behind and drops a still-rotating, bouncing bale onto the field. Darting in between, a smaller tractor skewers the bales on its forks and makes a beeline for the open barn doors.

I find haymaking exhilarating, not least because it could so easily rain for the week and potentially ruin the crop. It's also hugely satisfying to see the Dutch barn, dark and sweet-smelling, stacked high with hay. The bales will feed horses and sheep over winter and it's vital to make the hay good and dry, just as generations have done before us, so it doesn't go mouldy or, even worse, start a fire. Wet hay bales are notorious for self-combusting, a costly and surprisingly common mistake. At the end of haymaking, I'm also thankful that this is our only crop. For the successive farmers who've grown grain in this region, haymaking is just the beginning of an anxious summer. The real test comes a few weeks later, with the harvest.

For all the hardship of rural life, North Yorkshire country folk knew how to celebrate. And of all the festivals of the year, the most significant was the harvest supper. The scholar Eugene Aram, a local man, wrote in the eighteenth century: 'They are commonly insisted upon by the reapers as customary things, and a part of their due for the toils of their harvest, and complied with by their masters, perhaps more through regard of interest than inclination. For, should they refuse them the pleasures of this much expected time, this festal night, the youth especially, of both sexes, would decline serving him for the future, and employ their labors for others who would promise them the rustic joys of the harvest supper, mirth and music, dance and song.'[1]

At the Barn, the communal meal to celebrate bringing in the harvest was known locally as the 'mell supper'.* This festivity', gushed the clergyman and antiquarian John Brand, 'is undoubtedly of the most remote antiquity. That men in all nations where agriculture flourished should have expressed their joy on this occasion by some outward ceremonies has its foundation in the nature of things. Sowing is hope; reaping fruition of the expected good. To the husbandman, whom the fear of wet, blights &c., has harassed with great anxiety, the completion of his wishes could not fail of imparting an enviable feeling of delight.'[2]

---

* The word 'mell' is a singularly ancient one; the word may come from the Old French *mesler* or *meller*, which means 'to mix or mingle', while two more likely options delve even further back in time – the word '*mel*' used to mean 'a feast or a fixed time for eating', while '*mele*' meant to crush or grind flour. Both these words have their roots in the late Neolithic cultures who brought farming to Britain's shores around seven thousand years ago. We still use the word 'meal' to mean both a time to eat and ground grain.

Harvest was the zenith of the rural year, a reckoning of all the hard work over the past twelve months and the busiest time on any arable farm. Horse-drawn reapers, which helped speed up the harvest, had been introduced across the county from the middle of the nineteenth century but, to all intents and purposes, the event was as it always had been and relied on a vast body of helpers to bring home the grain. Writing about the lives of North Yorkshire farmers in the 1970s, rural historians Marie Hartley and Joan Ingilby observed: 'Within living memory corn was harvested by a team of workers in a manner little changed since the Middle Ages [...] A great force of people – women, children, men of all sorts of occupations – set forth into the fields.'[3]

Timing was everything. The corn couldn't be too ripe or the seeds would fall off during gathering. And the weather had to be clear and warm for days in a row. Before the invention of weather forecasts in the 1860s by Admiral Robert FitzRoy,* farmers had to rely on a capricious cocktail of gut instinct, nature observation and superstition to decide when to begin the harvest. While most weather lore didn't hold up

---

* Admiral Robert FitzRoy is considered to be the founding father of the Met Office. A brilliant seaman and meticulous collector of data, FitzRoy was able to make accurate predictions about the weather for sailors and fishing fleets. He transmitted his forecasts by telegraph and *The Times* began publishing his daily reports in 1861. His remarkably accurate weather charts not only saved countless lives at sea but also allowed farming communities more control over their sowing, growing and harvesting schedules.

to scrutiny, a few sayings did have some use, including 'Red sky at night, shepherd's delight. Red sky in the morning, shepherds take warning'; a rosy sky at sunset meant that high pressure would most likely bring good weather. The weather on St Swithin's Day (15 July) was also closely monitored by farmers, who followed the proverb: 'St Swithin's day, if thou dost rain, For forty days it will remain; St Swithin's day, if thou be fair, For forty days 'twill rain no more.' While there is no record of it ever raining consistently for forty days and forty nights in North Yorkshire, there is some truth in the rhyme's predictions. The location of the jet stream in early July largely dictates how the summer weather will progress. If, on St Swithin's Day, the jet stream is southerly, an unsettled summer is likely to follow. If it's northerly, July and August will probably be dry and clear. Rural workers also kept an eye out for natural clues that suggested sunny days might be around the corner. *Swallow's Almanac* of 1633 noted confidently: 'Signs of hot weather. Many bats flying abroad sooner than ordinary. A white mist arising out of moors or waters, either before Sun rising or after Sun setting. Birds flying high in the air. Crows or ravens gaping against the Sun. Store of flies playing in the Sun shining towards night.'[4]

Harvest time, with its sultry, warm weather, was also prone to thunder and lightning storms. Dramatic weather had long attracted superstitions, especially from those people who farmed under its dark skies. The day of the storm, for example, was thought to foretell the future; writing in 1556, the scientist Leonard Digges noted that 'Sondayes Thundre, shoulde brynge the death of learned men, Judges & others: Mondayes Thundre, the death of women: Tuesdayes Thundre, plentie of grayne: Wednesdayes Thundre, the death of Harlottes, & other bloodshed: Thurdayes Thunrdre, plentie of Shepe, and Corne: Frydayes Thundre, the slaughter of a great Man, and other horrible murders: Saturdayes Thundre, a generall pestilent plage and greate deathe.'[5] In certain parts of the country it was thought that lightning could help the corn to ripen, while some villages attempted to scare the thunder away by ringing the church bells.[6]

Working out in the fields in a storm was not without its risks, as one rural couple found out to their cost. In the summer of 1718, the poet Alexander Pope was staying at Stanton Harcourt in the Oxfordshire Cotswolds. While he was there, he heard the shocking news that on 31 July two young lovers – John Hewit and Sarah Drew – were struck down by lightning, just days before they were to wed, while harvesting a field of barley. Pope was so moved by their plight, he penned an epitaph for the local church:

'Near this place lie the bodies Of JOHN HEWIT and SARAH DREW An industrious young man And virtuous young maiden of this parish CONTRACTED IN MARRIAGE; Who being with many others at Harvest work, Were both in

one instant killed by lightning on the last day of July, 1718.
Think not by rigorous judgment seiz'd; A pair so faithful
could expire; Victims so pure, Heaven saw well pleas'd.'

Pope couldn't resist writing a naughtier second poem for
his own amusement: 'Here lye two poor lovers, who had the
mishap, Tho very chaste people to die of a Clap.'[7]

When the optimum moment for harvest arrived, and the
weather was set fair, no one was left idle. All hands were
outdoors. Thomas Hardy perfectly captured the mood in his
bucolic novel *Far from the Madding Crowd* (1874): 'all the men
were a-field under a monochromatic Lammas sky, amid the
trembling air and short shadows of noon. Indoors nothing
was to be heard save the droning of blue-bottle flies; out-of-
doors the whetting of scythes and the hiss of tressy oat-ears
rubbing together as their perpendicular stalks of amber-
yellow fell heavily to each swath. Every drop of moisture
not in the men's bottles and flagons in the form of cider was
raining as perspiration from their foreheads and cheeks.'[8]
Local men, women and children were all drafted in, often
supplemented with gang labour or itinerant workers who
travelled up and down the country helping with the harvest
and sleeping rough, taking shelter in a hayloft or under a
thick hedge.

In the 1980s, historian Charles Kightly recorded a dying breed of country voices – men and women who had experienced the last days before the mechanisation of farming changed the landscape forever. 'Within living memory,' he concluded, '[harvest] could call for over a month of unremitting dawn-to-dusk labour from every man on the farm, and frequently the women, children, Irish and other temporary hands as well.'[9] Despite the large numbers of people involved, harvest time was rarely chaos; everyone knew their roles. As a general rule, both men and women used the sickle – a short-handled tool for cutting wheat – while men 'mowed' the barley and oats using larger, more cumbersome scythes. Economy of movement was everything; 'When I was a lad in the 1890s,' remembered one North Yorkshireman, 'women used to shear. Two good strokes right round and they had a shaff [sheaf] which they held under their arms.'[10]

Anyone mowing with a scythe was followed by a team of helpers – usually women and children – tying the corn into sheaves with bands skilfully twisted from stalks (a process called 'scramping') and stacking them into small piles called 'stooks'. In a day, a skilled worker, with a nimble team of binders and stookers, could harvest one or two acres of wheat, and perhaps as many as three or more of oats and barley. It was hot, thirsty work but the choreographed, unrelenting nature of the harvest prevented anyone taking a rest until the task was complete.

Food and refreshment were an accepted part of the farmer's responsibility to his harvest workers; meals taken in the field, with names such as 'beaver' or 'bever', had been a tradition for hundreds of years and continued well into the nineteenth century. The *Modern Husbandman*, a survey of the agricultural year by the Hertfordshire farmer William Ellis, published in 1750, noted: 'During harvest-time [...] all the men working in the fields have beaver, which is equivalent to luncheon. It is taken at 10·30 a.m. but only lasts twenty minutes. During harvest and hay time an extra meal, called fours, is taken in the fields at 5 p.m.'[11] The antiquity of this harvest food tradition was hidden in its name – *beaver* comes from the Old French* word *beivre*, 'to drink'. Around the Barn, though, the workers didn't take beaver but '*bait*', a word still used across the region to mean a packed lunch. Bait comes from the ancient Norse '*beit*', meaning food.

When almost all the corn was down, the cutting of the last sheaf was hugely symbolic. For thousands of years, it was thought that the spirit of the corn lived among the crop. Harvesting the grain effectively made this fertility sprite 'homeless' and so it was important to make the last sheaf into a 'dolly' or other woven decoration to capture the corn spirit and give her somewhere to reside until the following year.

---

* The language spoken in the northern half of France from the eighth to the fourteenth century.

The corn dolly* (or other regional shapes such as rings, tufts and, in the case of North Yorkshire, spirals) would be kept safe and dry in the farmhouse until after Christmas, when she would be ploughed back into the soil on Plough Monday and returned to her rightful place.†

Customs surrounding the 'corn spirit' are found across Europe and many share similarities in the cutting of the last stalks. No one wanted to be responsible for slicing off the final sheaf – and therefore killing the corn spirit – and so everyone had to throw their sickles at the last standing stalks of corn and luck would take its course. The last sheaf was known by different names in different regions, including the mare, the hare, the gander or the old woman, and whoever was responsible for the final blow was treated to a small reward – the first drink at the meal, a

* When mechanisation eventually replaced the hand harvest, it was found that shorter crops were easier to machine-cut. Machines not only removed the workforce, for whom the tradition had been a part of harvest life for millennia, but they also made long-stemmed varieties of corn, which best suited the corn dolly craft, all but redundant.

† Plough Monday or 'Fond Plufe' celebrated the resumption of work after the Christmas celebrations. Farm lads would drag a plough through the village, collecting money with menaces, not dissimilar to trick-or-treating. Blackened faces, cross-dressing, dancing and vandalism were all part of this ancient misrule custom, which celebrated the fact that the shortest day was over and spring was just round the corner.

coin or a wish. The cutting of the last sheaf was also often accompanied by a special teatime treat, brought into the field and shared among the crowd. Hot cakes, apple pies and plenty of ale or tea would replenish the workers, a meal that became known as 'kern supper'.* The sheaves in their piles or 'stooks' would be left to dry out and finish ripening for two weeks or 'while the church bells rang twice'.[12] Once the stooks had dried, they were loaded onto a cart and brought back to the farmyard either to be stored in a barn or, more often – owing to lack of space – made into large stacks ready for threshing later in the year.

After the corn had been harvested and carted off the fields, women and children were allowed back onto the land to 'glean'. Gleaning was a right of the poor, under customary law,† to gather any leftover crops or scattered grain from a field that had just been harvested. With enough time and nimble fingers, gleaners could collect plenty of residual grain – 'as much wheat and barley as would make them flour for the

---

* There are contrasting opinions as to why it was called 'kern supper'. While some believe kern to be the same word as 'corn', others link it to 'churn' because it was customary to produce a churn filled to the brim with cream to be circulated among the workers.

† Customary laws are those based on long-standing customs or historic patterns of behaviour that have come to be accepted as a rule or legal requirement. They're often unwritten and passed down over generations.

winter and meal for a pig',[13] representing perhaps as much as a sixth of a labouring family's annual income.[14] The right to glean was a lifeline for those who otherwise struggled – often widows, children and single women – and had been exercised for thousands of years. 'When you reap the harvest of your land, do not reap to the very edges of your field or gather the gleanings of your harvest', instructed the Bible. 'Do not go over your vineyard a second time or pick up the grapes that have fallen. Leave them for the poor and the foreigner.' (Leviticus 19:9–10).

In 1788, a landmark legal case shook this system to its core. Mary Houghton, who was gleaning from the fields of a wealthy Suffolk landowner, James Steel, was taken to court and sued for trespass. Steel won. The court had decided that, despite centuries of precedence, gleaning was a privilege not a legal right, and that granting the right to glean would 'raise the insolence of the poor'. Mary Houghton was made to pay the crippling sum of £35 5s for the plaintiff's damages (about a year's wage for a skilled tradesman), alongside her own legal costs, rendering her and her children debt-ridden for the rest of their lives.[15]

The decision to remove the right to glean was part of a wider trend. During the eighteenth and early nineteenth centuries, the rural labourer had to contend not only with enclosure but also a marked reduction in their traditional customary rights, which had been in existence for hundreds of years. As part of the medieval open-field system, villagers had certain 'use rights' – such as estovers[*] (the right to take wood from the forest), pannage (allowing pigs to graze on acorns and beechmast) and turbary (the right to cut peat). Under this system, after the harvest had been safely gathered in from the fields, anyone who worked and lived in the manor was also allowed to put their animals out to graze the leftovers. In addition to these cultivated fields, there was also waste land, which wasn't good enough for crops but was available to livestock for grazing. Taken as a whole, these various common rights made a significant contribution to the livelihoods of villagers before enclosure.

Customary law and enclosure, with its wholesale transformation of property rights, didn't mix well.[†] As E. P. Thompson, celebrated historian of the English labouring classes, noted, during the 'eighteenth century one legal decision after another

---

[*] The language associated with these ancient rights is fascinating and paints a picture of the daily activities and concerns of rural labourers. Estover rights, for example, included four different elements – *House-bote* (timber for house repairs and building), *Fire-bote* (fuel for the fire), *Plough-bote* (timber for repairing farm implements) and *Hay-bote* (wood for repairing fences). 'Bote' as a word has its origins in the early Germanic speakers of Iron Age Europe and means benefit, profit or atonement. 'Man-bote' was an amount paid to a lord as compensation for killing one of his men, or to the family of a murdered man.

[†] A considerable amount of land with common rights still remains in Britain – much of it lowland heath and moorland – but it owes its existence not to any act of benevolence or local charity, but to the fact that landowners did not see it as productive enough to be enclosed in the first place.

signalled that the lawyers had become converted to the notions of absolute property ownership and that [...] the law abhorred the messy complexities of use law'.[16] In hindsight, the *Steel* v. *Houghton* case wasn't about whether gleaning was a financial imposition on a landowner. The Houghtons were a shoemaking family and one of the few in the local area to own their own home with a small patch of land. The family were also, unusually, highly literate and had openly expressed their opposition to local plans for enclosure. After the court case, which awarded punitive damages to Steel, the Houghtons were forced to sell their house and land, leaving the path clear for a local landowner to snap up a bargain and complete the enclosure process. Within a year, Mary's husband was dead and, after her small savings dried up, she remained in receipt of weekly poor relief until her death in 1806. 'The last vestiges of the Houghtons' independence had disappeared.'[17]

Despite the *Houghton* v. *Steel* ruling, the poor continued to glean. Few had any other option. Many tenant farmers allowed surplus grain to be gathered as they simply didn't have the time, inclination or resources to collect the gleanings by hand for themselves. Gleaning was also part of an informal social contract within the community, an acknowledgement of a moral duty to the poor that went beyond any change in the legal framework; the activity was even famously depicted by the nineteenth-century French artist Jean-François Millet in a painting of three peasant women bending to pick up wheat after the harvest. The painter's sympathetic depiction of grinding poverty aroused the anger of landowners and conservative critics, but many others read it as a radical plea to remember the importance of charity to the countryside's most vulnerable workers. Even in the early twentieth century, gleaning continued in many parts of the country. In his memoir *Peasant's Heritage*, Ralph Whitlock – who was born six months before the outbreak of the First World War – remembered a Wiltshire childhood where farming and rural life were a never-ending struggle: 'No farmers in our district ever dreamt of turning away the gleaners from his fields. There was, however, an unwritten law that gleaners might not enter a field until every sheaf was taken to the rick.'[18]

The rules surrounding gleaning were clear: farmers would leave a 'guard sheaf' or 'gleaning policeman' – just a single stook of sheaves in the field. Its removal signalled to the gleaners that the field was finally ready for picking over. The hours for gleaning were also regulated. In many areas, the beginning and end of the gleaning day was signalled with the ringing of the church bell. Far from being an unwanted restriction, local gleaners welcomed the marshalling of such precious resources. Most of the gleaners were women, with husbands and children to wake, feed and get ready for the day. The gleaning bell prevented 'ardent souls from getting up at two in the morning and starting gleaning before the mothers of the household could get a look in'.[19]

Bill Partridge, as a child in Suffolk, also remembered gleaning in the early years of the twentieth century: 'We used to goo [sic] gleaning the corn after harvest – the mother and all the children'd goo gleaning [...] As soon as the field was clear, as soon as they'd carted the shocks [stooks] out o'field, the women could goo in there and glean it: but some o' these farmers used to hoss-rake it afore they'd let 'em goo in, and they'd not git so much then.'[20] The 'hoss rake' was the horse rake. During the nineteenth century, some progress had been made introducing horse-drawn rakes to help scrape up the harvest, and while many of the early models struggled with the high ridges and deep furrows of the ancient arable landscape,[21] by the end of the century they had improved to the extent where they not only significantly reduced the labour needed to collect in a harvest but also left little corn behind for the gleaners to collect. Simultaneously, many farmers also introduced horse-drawn reaper-binders, which could cut and tie up the corn automatically. These machines cut the corn closer to the ground than the hand implements they replaced, allowing the horse rake to pick up even more of the last few ears of corn ordinarily left behind for the gleaners.

Fewer rewards meant fewer gleaners and yet it wasn't until the introduction of combine harvesters just after the Second World War that gleaning completely disappeared from British fields. During the inter-war years, as we'll see later, when much of Britain was under a cloud of economic depression and political upheaval, farming was suffering its own roller-coaster ride. During the First World War, farming had boomed – the government had put in place a state-regulated and subsidised system that not only boosted the pay of agricultural workers but also increased the profits and productivity of the land for farmers. When these new protections were removed in 1921, farmworkers' wages fell by as much as 40 per cent. Gleaning once again became a lifeline. As one former gleaner remembers from this time, it was often a race to pick up the slim pickings: 'The news spread about that so-and-so's field was ready for gleaning, the farmer's ready. There'd be such a rush and you'd go and glean it.'[22]

The harvest was such an important financial reckoning that if it went wrong, the effects would have been devastating for a farmer. Poor weather aside, there were other risks to the crop, not least the potential for fire. Tinder-dry material and a run of rainless days were the perfect ingredients for a blaze. In early September 1855, the same year the Hickeses moved into the farmhouse, disaster struck in Stonegrave:

'On Tuesday last, about half-past four, p.m., as Mr. Thomas Featenby and his men were busy leading corn into the stackyard, they suddenly discovered that one of the large wheat stacks, recently erected, was on fire. Every effort was immediately made by Mr. F. and his men, and a number of neighbours who were quickly on the spot, but although a plentiful supply of water was at hand, we are sorry to state that all efforts proved ineffectual to stay the progress of the raging element, which in spite of all opposition very quickly enveloped the whole stackyard, compromising six long and two round wheat stacks, the produce of thirty acres of land, a good crop, all in excellent condition; also several oat stacks, the produce of about nine acres of land.'

Despite being insured, Featenby soon discovered that the compensation he was due didn't come close to matching his losses. It turned out that the fire had started as a result of the labourers' 'very careless and highly reprehensible' habit of smoking in the stackyard, and the insurers quibbled to the last. The spectacular blaze, which 'was seen many miles distant, and continued burning nearly all night',[23] was an event of immense local significance. Labourers and farm servants, and their families, would have known that a disaster of such magnitude for the tenant farmer would, ultimately, have consequences for the following farming year and their chances for local employment.[*]

* Poor old Featenby's bad luck didn't stop there. Only a year or so later the hapless farmer found himself headline news again, when another of his young employees managed to run himself over with a waggon and three horses. The boy, who was in charge of delivering produce to Malton, lost control of the beasts down the main street. The horses' hooves and

Once the excitement and high stakes of harvest time had died down, it was back to work. The next job was threshing. 'Thrash' and 'thresh' are essentially the same word and give away the nature of the work. The job of a thresher was to hit the dry corn to separate the grain from the straw. The skill was in the beating – hit the corn too hard and you damaged the straw, a valuable crop in itself for bedding and feed, but hit it too lightly and the grains remained fast.

When the Barn was just a threshing barn, between the 1780s and the early 1850s, the job would have been done by hand. Or, more accurately, by flail – a stick made from willow or ash with a shorter stick, called a swipple, hanging loosely from the end. This jointed beating stick was held lightly in the hands and gently twisted as it was brought down onto piles of corn laid on the floor. The swipple landed flat, knocking off the grains without breaking the straw. Depending on the size of the farm, workers might thresh alone, in pairs or in groups. Communal threshing or threshing in pairs needed precise coordination – taking alternate swipes at the corn in a rhythmic, tick-tock beat. Miss a step and you'd more than likely take a blow to the head.

the wheels of the waggon 'passed over his face and legs', causing serious injury, and the horses galloped on to the crossroads before crashing headlong into the front of Mr Snow's draper's shop. The boy and the horses survived, just.

The Barn, with its modest arable acres, would have been able to thresh all its grain indoors, inside the threshing bay; but for a large harvest, grain was often threshed out in the open. Writing in the late eighteenth century, the Yorkshire-born agricultural writer William Marshall was thrilled to witness a public threshing, scribbling that the 'thrashing [sic] affords the contemplative mind a pleasing sight; and would afford the pencil a picturesque subject'.[24] He marvelled at the large-scale organisation of the event – 'the whole country, for many miles around, are collected. The days of thrashing are considered as public days, for all who choose to enter, ample provision of meat and drink being made for this purpose. A wake or a fair is not a scene of greater jollity.' Vast sheets, made from hessian, were laid on the ground, with the crop placed in a large circle, thinly spread. A group of threshers then moved around the circle, working in pairs, beating the crop to a strict rhythm. As the seeds fell off, women and children with rakes moved in to push the grain to the corners of the sheet, where it was collected and bagged.

But even as Marshall watched, he was all too aware that the days of public threshing were numbered. Threshing required hundreds of man-hours – as much as a quarter of all agricultural input in terms of labour was taken up with the task during the winter months – but by the late eighteenth century, the time of Marshall's musings, horse-powered threshing machines were already starting to make an appearance. Nunnington, one of the villages close to the Barn, was unusual in its very early adoption of mechanised threshing in the 1790s. There, agricultural experimenter and gentleman farmer Edward Cleaver bought a threshing machine for the princely sum of £100, the equivalent of two years' skilled labour. Local landowners, including Thomas Mosley, rector of Stonegrave, with his enthusiasm for 'improvement', must have flocked to see Cleaver's machine in operation. It was hard to deny the efficiency of the new machines, which, at a stroke, swept away hours of rural drudgery. Writing only a few years later, Marshall enthused: 'This may be considered as the most valuable discovery, in machines of agriculture, which has been made for centuries past. Not merely as lessening human labour, but as relieving farm workmen from their most unhealthy employment.'[25] Arthur Young, author and proselytiser of the new agriculture, agreed; the threshing machine is 'by far the most capital mechanized invention in husbandry that has appeared this century'.[26]

The hefty cost of purchasing one of the new threshing machines initially deterred small farmers but, by the early nineteenth century, their presence was numerous enough to be a cause of concern for rural labourers. Threshing was traditionally a winter job, a source of casual employment for lean times of the year. Harvest time still needed all hands on deck, but without the security of winter work, many rural labourers faced starvation over the colder months. The rural labour market was also swamped by men demobbed after the Napoleonic Wars ended in 1815. By 1830, rural workers in the heavily arable counties of the south and east had reached the end of their tether; protestors, who soon became known as the 'Swing Rioters',* smashed threshing machines, set fire to stacks and demanded an end to job losses. The reaction to the Swing Riots was swift and punitive. Local government was put in charge of trials and, of the 2,000 or so farmworkers involved, over 600 were imprisoned, more than 700 transported, and 271 sentenced to death. The Swing Riots were one of the first national demonstrations of agricultural workers' grievances, but they changed little in terms of conditions and prospects. Average wages for farm labourers carried on falling, in real terms, between the late eighteenth century and 1850.[27]

Many an agricultural treatise of the day lamented the demise of hand threshing as a quaint rural practice but spoke little of the effects on the labourers left behind. As the eighteenth century came to a close, William Marshall had seen which way the wind was blowing: 'It were almost a pity that a scene, at once so picturesque and so truly rustic, should

---

* The shadowy figure of Captain Swing was believed to have signed and sent threatening letters to local jury men, farmers, landowners and other important figures before carrying out various incendiary acts. He was, in fact, fictitious, a character created by the protestors as a smokescreen so that the genuine ringleaders wouldn't be detected.

sink into oblivion, as in all probability it will in a short course of years.'[28] By the middle of the nineteenth century, the flail had all but failed: 'the even, steady, and poetical sound of the thrasher's flail is rarely heard resounding the boarded barn; and that useful and simple instrument – amongst the oldest in husbandry [...] is likely at some future time to be placed in museums amongst flint arrows of the Britons, the querns of the Saxons, and other remains of antiquity.'[29]

You can't miss a threshing barn when you see one. Most have a large, wide doorway; such a grand opening not only allowed carts full of grain to trundle in and out but also gave the threshers plenty of light to work by. They often – as is the case at the Barn – also have a smaller door on the wall opposite the large entrance. Both small and large doors would be opened when it was time to winnow the corn, the task of separating the husks or chaff from the grain. For that, it was useful to have the cross-draught that was created by opening the 'through doors' (or 'thruff' doors, as they're known in North Yorkshire). The labourer could then hold a shallow basket full of grain, toss the contents in the air, and let the wind take the light chaff away in the breeze while the heavier corn fell to the floor. Few people notice but threshing barns are often orientated to make the most of the wind. The Barn is no different – labourers would have known that, during most of the year, a stiff breeze zipped west to east along the valley bottom. Building the Barn perpendicular to the wind – along a north–south axis – funnelled the air through the thruff door and out through the large doorway opposite.

Hand winnowing was a centuries-old skill but also one of the first farming chores to be mechanised. The winnowing machine first made an appearance in Scotland around the 1730s. Writing about agriculture in the north, later that century, one improver noted: 'The winnowing machine is in universal use here; we believe very little if any corn is dressed by any other means: They were first made by a farmer of mechanical genius called Rogers who lived at Cavers near Hawick, and whose grandson, now a carpenter there, still makes them.'[30] Rogers, it turns out, had spotted and copied a broken machine, thrown out of a granary near Leith, which had been brought over from Holland twenty years earlier. The design – essentially a handle that wound a rotating fan – had itself been 'borrowed' from an ancient Chinese machine called a *fengshanche*, which had been in use for at least two thousand years. Once the simplicity of the design was understood over here, winnowing machines were often made locally and cheaply, putting them well within the reach of most farms.

Hand winnowing was labour-intensive. For a relatively small outlay, the landowner or tenant farmer could buy a hand-cranked winnowing machine and drastically reduce costs. One man, operating alone with a machine, could now do the work of five adults with winnowing baskets, saving time and money in the process. Writing at the end of the eighteenth century, Tuke noted that almost all North Yorkshire farmers had switched to winnowing machines in the past few years – the 'thruff doors' on the Barn had only been in place since its construction in the 1780s but within a few years were already obsolete. During the nineteenth century, threshing and winnowing machines were combined into one larger machine, although small farms often still used separate threshers and winnowers up until the Second World War. These threshing-winnowing machines were, at first, powered by horses, but by the 1850s it was the turn of steam power to reign supreme – farms would often hire portable steam engines to process the grain, or neighbouring farms might club together to share the costs of purchasing their own machine.

The effect of horsepower, followed by steam, on productivity was profound. Between 1800 and 1900, the amount of labour needed to harvest a crop plummeted. To produce an acre of wheat at the beginning of the nineteenth century took around sixty man-hours; by the turn of the twentieth, it was only fifteen, just a quarter of the time and manpower needed a hundred years earlier. From the mid-nineteenth century onwards, mechanisation picked up its skirt and ran even faster, drastically reducing the need for manpower still further. In 1850, one in five men worked in farming. By 1900, it was only one in ten.

The introduction of both winnowing and threshing machines also did away with the need for a large, dry space to fling around a flail or winnow grain. The Barn's expansion in the 1850s, with a hayloft and stables to the left and cart shed and granary to the right, coincided with the arrival of a mechanical threshing machine and removed the need for a dedicated threshing barn. Threshing barns were big buildings to fill but farmers soon found other uses for the space. Some became places to process and keep animal fodder, such as oats and turnips; others found a new role as cow houses, milking parlours or storage bays. The Barn was no different. In the 1850s, out went the need for a large airy space to fling a flail and store grain at head height. The mezzanine floor was unsentimentally pulled out and the threshing space turned into a store for animal feed and the access point for both the first-floor granary and the hayloft. The thruff door, which had allowed a gentle breeze to float through the threshing barn, was unceremoniously blocked up and never used again.

While some commentators of the day worried about the effects of mechanisation on rural labourers, for many people the sweeping changes that were affecting agriculture were simply part of a larger, and inevitable, march towards industrialisation and increased productivity. Writing in the

People's Journal in 1847, one journalist echoed the profit-oriented zeitgeist of Victorian capitalism:

'A painful question is often asked – What is to become of the poor farmer? I reply, what has become of the poor hand-loom weaver – of the four-horse coach proprietor – of the road-side inn keeper – of the Gravesend sailing boats – of the hackney coaches! Even the poor old watchmen, who called the hours all night and cleaned boots and shoes half the day, have given way to the able, active and efficient new police. These are the days of movement and progression – and agriculture cannot withstand the common fate. The poor farmer and poor tenant who are in the wrong position will necessarily make way for more useful members of society.'[31]

Just a few decades later, in the 1870s, the English nature writer Richard Jefferies mused that 'The changes which have been crowded into the last half-century have been so numerous and so important that it would almost seem reasonable to suppose the limit had been reached [...] But so far from this being the case, all the facts of the hour point irresistibly to the conclusion that the era of development had just commenced.'[32] Alongside the mechanisation of labour-intensive jobs such as winnowing and threshing, agricultural science was starting to change the relationship between the farmer and his soil. The land would be expected to work harder than ever before.

✳

For thousands of years, farmers have attempted to supercharge the fertility of their soil. Time-honoured methods included ploughing in crop stubble, leaving fields fallow, or adding animal dung. During the eighteenth century, however, a handful of experimental improvers began to tinker about with crushed bones. One trailblazer was Anthony St Leger who, in the 1760s, made the important discovery that 'bones were an excellent manure'.[33] St Leger was a successful soldier and MP, and would become famous for founding the St Leger Stakes horse race. Less well known was that he was passionate about agriculture and the growing science of agronomy. In 1762, he moved to an estate in South Yorkshire, where he started to conduct informal experiments on the effect of bones on soil health.

St Leger soon discovered that the smaller the bone fragment the better but, at the time, the only way to crush bones was by hand and hammer. News of the trials spread quickly, though, and within just a few years a new trade – mechanical bone grinding – was established. Only a few miles away from St Leger's estate, entrepreneurs in Sheffield began to lead the way in milling bones. The city had a long-standing and thriving cutlery industry, which produced bone-handled knives, forks and spoons. Their manufacture created mountains of bone waste, which the cutlers had to pay to bury. With St Leger's discovery, a troublesome waste product quickly became a valuable raw material and a boon to local farmers.

By the early nineteenth century, scattering ground bonemeal was not only common practice but followed with such fervour that the demand for bones soon outstripped supply. Writing in *The Spectator* in 1841, one journalist described the appetite for powdered carcasses. Yorkshire, it seems, was at the heart of production:

'I do not know if bones are valued as a manure in any part of the Continent of Europe but it is certain that of late years they have attracted in a very particular degree the attention of the English farmer. Bones are collected in the streets of London and other great towns [...] In the Thames, above London Bridge, may almost always be seen a few sloops and cutters, chiefly from Hull, which are occupied in this trade. They take the bones on board generally in a more or less putrid state and stow them in bulk in the hold: here they soon begin to ferment, giving out an odour by which the bone-ships are detected at a considerable distance; and when the cargo is discharged at Hull, it is frequently reeking and smoking hot from decomposition. This probably softens the textures of the bones and renders them more easy to be crushed in the mill.'[34]

While grinding mills crushed many of the bones, where labour was especially cheap or – even better – free, manual bone breaking continued. The workhouse proved an ideal factory for this grim, repetitive task. The Andover Scandal of 1845-6 highlighted just how appalling many of the conditions were for inmates who were supposed to be under the care of Poor Law guardians.* In the case of the Andover workhouse, men, women and children had been so hungry that they had resorted to eating the scraps and marrow from the rotting bones they were employed to crush. Those who were supposed to be keeping an eye on the workhouse were also, it turned out, enjoying the benefits of cheap fertiliser. According to a subsequent House of Commons report: 'The bone-dust was disposed of by a kind of mock auction; the greater part was bought by the guardians.'[35] The story caused a stir – first-hand accounts shocked readers of *The Times* newspaper, which covered the story extensively – but few questioned the wider economic picture behind the tragedy.

* Each workhouse was run by a Board of Guardians elected by local ratepayers who occupied property worth at least £25 a year. Magistrates were also entitled to Board membership. One of the jobs of the Board of Guardians was to establish a Visiting Committee who would visit the workhouse every week to check it was being run correctly and listen to inmates' concerns.

It's interesting to think about just exactly who was involved in the Andover Scandal. As we've already learned, the early nineteenth century was characterised by economic circumstances that hit the rural labourer particularly hard – increased mechanisation of farming, a rising population, a huge labour force demobbed following the end of the Napoleonic Wars. Add a series of poor harvests between 1828 and 1830 and the result was that many rural workers found themselves bereft. The New Poor Law of 1834 was designed specifically to do two things – to discourage the provision of poor relief to anyone who refused to go into a workhouse and to make workhouse conditions so unpleasant they would be viewed as the absolute last resort for those in need. It's telling that a large number of inmates from the Andover workhouse during the nineteenth century are described as 'agricultural labourers' and 'farm servants' in the census, and the Board of Guardians are predominantly gentleman farmers. As the *Hampshire Advertiser* reported in August 1845: 'It appears that at Andover, as in other Unions, the duties of guardians are considered as heavy drawbacks on their time, most of them being farmers, and from the extent of the Union, the majority living at great distances from the house.'

Britain couldn't produce enough bones to keep up with demand from farming and so the lion's share was imported, much of it through the port of Hull in East Yorkshire. In 1821, the value of all the bones imported into England stood at around £16,000 (about £1 million in today's money). By 1837 it had rocketed to over £250,000 (over £15 million). The carcasses came from far and wide – one ledger from Hull in the year 1827 records vast volumes of bones coming from the Netherlands, Denmark, Sweden and Norway, Germany, Russia and Prussia. Alongside these northern European exporters, bones also flooded in from places such as Buenos Aires, North America, Egypt and the Mediterranean. And, while many of the bones came from slaughterhouses, butchers and leather factories, some of the ships' contents came from even grimmer sources. In the United States, many of the skeletons came from the systematic slaughter of the great buffalo herds of the western prairies. At the beginning of the 1800s, America had around 30 million buffalo. Thanks to government efforts to remove buffalo herds as a way of starving Native Americans into submission – as one US Army officer boasted, 'Every buffalo dead is an Indian gone'[36] – fewer than a hundred beasts remained in the wild by 1880.

Carcasses were also rumoured to have come from grave-yards. Again, the Andover Scandal reared its head. According to a parliamentary report: 'For the last three or four years there had been a new church building in Andover on the site of an old one, and the burial-ground had been much interfered with. When the foundation of the new church was dug, quantities of bones were thrown up, and among these there was a quantity of human bones. They were bought by a farmer in the neighbourhood to manure his meadow land. A portion of these bones was most properly buried; but another portion was sold to the collector of bones in Andover, and by him sold to the workhouse. It was well known that they were human bones.'[37]

Remains were also shipped overseas from Egyptian archaeological sites[*] and, perhaps most controversially, battlefields. The idea of collecting body parts and putting them to practical use wasn't a new one; in the early nineteenth century, for instance, the teeth of fallen soldiers were collected from battle sites and used to make dentures.[†] Nor were dead men's teeth the only macabre keepsakes picked up by battlefield tourists. After Napoleon's defeat at Waterloo, 'British travellers rushed to the battlefield where

---

[*] On one occasion, an entire nine-ton consignment of embalmed cats was shipped from Egypt to Liverpool. The cats, which had been discovered in the late 1880s by an Egyptian farmer, had been mummified for posterity by their owners, a common practice in antiquity. The cats were duly unwrapped, stripped of their fur, and their dry bones packaged up for shipment to England, where bone merchants Messrs Leventon and Co. quickly snapped them up for fertiliser. (*Bristol Mercury and Daily Post*, 11 February 1890)

[†] Traditionally, false teeth were made from ivory or bone, but these tended to deteriorate quickly in the mouth and were expensive. Real human teeth were cheaper and longer-lasting but trickier to source. Poor people sometimes offered to have healthy teeth pulled and sold on, but other sources of human dentures included teeth scavenged from battlefields, gallows' victims or those dug up from corpses by tradesmen who called themselves 'resurrectionists'. 'Waterloo teeth' were still appearing for sale in dental catalogues as late as the 1860s. (Source: British Dental Museum https://bda.org/museum)

the great general had been routed'.[38] Skulls, bones, buttons, horse hooves and even body parts were eagerly collected. The Irish poet Eaton Stannard Barrett, writing in 1816, remarked on a friend who had 'brought home a real Waterloo thumb, nail and all, which he preserves in a bottle of gin'.[39]

Whether the bones of dead soldiers were actually scooped up deliberately and sold for fertiliser remains a moot point. While the practice wasn't officially condoned, journalists had their suspicions it was going on. One, writing in 1823, claimed sensationally:

'It is estimated that more than a million bushels of human and inhuman bones were imported last year from the continent of Europe to the port of Hull. The neighbourhoods of Leipsic, Austerlitz, Waterloo, and all the places where, during the late bloody war, the principal battles were fought, have been swept alike of the bones of the hero and of the horse which he rode. Thus collected from every quarter, they have been shipped to the port of Hull and thence forwarded to the Yorkshire bone-grinders, who have erected steam engines and powerful machinery, for the purpose of reducing them to a granulary state [...] It is now ascertained beyond a doubt, by actual experiments upon an extensive scale, that a dead soldier is a most valuable article of commerce; and, for aught known to the contrary, the good farmers of

Yorkshire are, in a great measure, indebted to the bones of their children for their daily bread.'[40]

America quickly followed suit. The *Pittsburgh Dispatch*, in 1889, even suggested those who had died should be grateful their remains were being put to good use:

The importation of human bones from Africa into this country suggests new hope for the Heathen. The bones of Africans and Arabs which have been lying in the sand of the Sahara for goodness knows how long, are to be manufactured in various ways for our benefit. And in this, as I have said, there is hope for the heathen, for we know that while:

A Yankee missionary can,
With his melodious tones,
Convert the living African.
Who worships sticks and stones;
And now a shrewd American
Will eke convert his bones![41]

Bones, whether animal or human, were not the only methods of enriching the soil. The seventeenth-century garden writer Leonard Meager, in *The Mystery of Husbandry* (1697), spent a good deal of time deciding which, out of all the fragrant options, was his favourite poo. Few had thought to ask the question 'What Dung doth most enrich the Earth?', but Meager carefully weighed up his options:

'The most Expert of the Ancient Husbandmen, appoint three sorts of Dungs: the first of Poultry, the next of Men, the third of Cattel. Of the first sort, the best is had out of Dove-Houses; the next is of Pulline, and other Fowl, except Geese and Ducks, which is hurtful [...] The next to this, is Man's Ordure, if it be mixt with other Rubbish of the House: for of itself it is too hot, and burns the Ground. Man's Urine, being kept six Months, and poured upon the Roots of Apple-trees, and Vines, causeth them to be very fruitful, and giveth a pleasant Taste to the Fruit. In the third place, is the Dung of Cattel.'[42]

Meager was unusual in his appreciation of 'man's ordure'. While most of the world had, for thousands of years,* embraced the use of human excrement or 'night soil' as fertiliser, British farmers were queasy about it. But they needed to do something. The pace of industrialisation and population growth in the late eighteenth and early nineteenth

* Ancient Rome, for example, had poo collection down to a fine art – scavengers collected human excrement from the city trenches that served as sewers and sold it on to farmers. Urine was also collected to sell on to fabric dyers and fullers.

centuries was starting to worry agronomists – soil degradation was happening before their very eyes. British farmers were demanding more 'bread and meat'[43] from the land, to satisfy the needs of an ever-expanding urban population, without fully understanding that the soil had its limits.

At the same time, towns and cities were beginning to overflow with unprecedented volumes of sewage. A number of agricultural writers started to ponder the wasted potential of 'humanure'. Forward-thinking farmers, like John Hickes, would have taken great interest in what the *Rural Cyclopedia* – an A to Z of all things farming – had to say about 'night-soil'. It is 'one of the most powerful and important manures', stated the author, but sadly 'has not, in any form, been employed by the farmers of England to the same extent as the Continent, although it is certainly by far the most powerful of the organic manures'.[44]

The Europeans had been successfully splattering their fields with human faeces for some time: in Flanders, farmers mixed it with water and sprayed it on by the gallon, while the French, with their usual flair for refinement, had found a way to dry human excrement and rebrand it as *'poudrette'*. But even though experiments had repeatedly shown that human waste could beat 'the best stable manure',[45] the British remained coy. Part of the resistance came from the fact that farmers already had some effective fertilisers at their disposal, including bone and, later, guano – 'the white gold of seabirds'. Peruvian guano had been used by indigenous communities as a natural fertiliser since the third century BC, but it wasn't until the early nineteenth century that it attracted the interest of western agriculturists, desperate for ways to boost crop yields. The turning point came in 1838, when two Franco-Spanish merchants sent guano samples to William Myers, a successful Liverpool businessman. Myers experimented with the bird droppings and was so impressed with the results that he not only put in a large order for more but decided to invest in the nascent business.

It wasn't a trade for the faint-hearted. When the first guano ships arrived on British shores, 'the stench was so miserable', wrote the English historian Frederick Pike, 'that the entire urban population has fled to the nearby hills'.[46] Despite the appalling smell, between the 1840s and 1880 guano became one of Britain's most sought-after commodities. In the space of just four decades, traders scraped nearly 12 million tons of avian excrement off Peru's islands and shipped them over to Britain, France and the United States. The trade was both filthy and exploitative, employing enslaved Polynesians and Chinese in brutal and degrading conditions. It's thought that between 1849 and 1875, as many as 90,000 indentured workers were brought to the guano islands – almost all of whom died either en route or after they arrived off the western coast of South America. The American traveller George W. Peck noted in 1854 that the islands seemed to him to be 'a kind of human abattoir, a slaughter-house of men; and I feel a relief in being away from them, as one feels who has escaped out of some gloomy dream'.[47]

The fact that the British were busily importing bird shit while failing to address their own public effluent crisis infuriated one journalist, who noted bitterly in 1851: 'we import guano and drink a solution of our own faeces'.[48] The problem, however, was one of expense. British farmers like John Hickes didn't tend to use human excrement because of the increasingly steep cost of shifting it from city centres to rural farmland. Even though the logistics for moving large quantities of night soil around the country finally dropped into place with the arrival of the railways after the 1850s, the idea never really took off on a national scale. In the end, science beat sanitation to become the prime mover behind Britain's fertiliser industry; in 1918 the German chemist Fritz Haber[*] received the Nobel Prize for inventing the Haber-Bosch process, which created ammonia fertiliser cheaply from nitrogen and hydrogen gases. Haber had, in effect, magically worked out how to pull fertiliser from air and put it in the ground. His work enabled the mass production of agricultural fertilisers and led to an unprecedented increase

---

[*] Fritz Haber, as well as working out how to feed the world, discovered how to exterminate it. Alongside his fertiliser work, Haber played a major role in the development of chemical warfare. With the outbreak of the First World War, Haber, an ardent German nationalist, threw himself into the development of poison gas.

in growth of crops. The days of bone, guano and humanure were over.

✳

Another way for farmers to improve their land was lime. Farmers have been using lime on their fields since at least the sixteenth century. It's made by heating up limestone rocks to a high temperature, which produces a powdery, highly caustic alkaline substance called quicklime. It's incredibly useful stuff: mix it with water and sand and you get mortar; thin it down and you can use it as a disinfecting whitewash for barns and dairies; you can plaster with it, render walls and paint with it. Farmers also used lime as an antiseptic and preventive medicine for cattle; in Yorkshire it was common practice to burn a 'need-fire', a bonfire with lime added on top to create a 'cleansing smoke'.[49] Cattle would be driven through the fumes as a preventative for 'murrain', an umbrella term for a host of diseases that afflicted livestock, some of which were little understood at the time.

On farmers' fields, lime worked a kind of alchemy. Not only did it reduce the acidity* of the soil, which affected a crop's ability to thrive, but it also broke up clods of earth

---

* Soil acidity is the farmer's perpetual challenge. Most cultivated crops prefer a slightly acidic pH but soil that gets too acidic stops plants taking up nutrients. It's essentially a man-made problem – growing crops such as wheat actually makes the soil more acidic, as does spreading manure and other fertilisers. Lime – which is alkaline – helps to restore the balance.

into a lighter, fluffier texture. Different soils naturally have different pH levels – the beauty of lime was that it could transform 'waste land' into crop land, especially areas that were boggy or had recently been woodland. Growing arable crops, however good your land, also leaches the soil, making it more acidic over time; plants can't take up nutrients as easily in very acidic soil and so a farmer needed to keep 'sweetening' the earth with lime. The problem is that lime's magical effects are short-lived. And so, every few years, it would be time to call in the lime burners.

To make lime, the Hickeses needed a kiln. Until the late nineteenth century, Britain had hundreds of thousands of lime kilns dotted across the landscape – they're unmistakable chimney-like structures, several metres high and wide, with an opening at the top and a curved draw hole or 'eye' at the bottom, where you lit the fire. Even as late as the 1950s, making and using lime supported a vast network of rural people – every part of the process needed labour, whether it was quarrying the stone, carting the rocks to a lime kiln, or lime burning itself. Limestone is also extremely heavy and so, although some farmers had to cart limestone long distances, many built their kilns as close to the quarry as possible.

The lime kiln for the Barn was literally a stone's throw away from a supply. The landscape around the farm is awash with small quarries and evidence of disused kilns. Herbert Read called the landscape 'pocked' and, as we already know, quarrying for limestone even gave the village of Stonegrave its name. The Barn's limestone came from a mere 300 metres away, at the top of the ridge – a quarry that had been worked since the beginning of the nineteenth century to supply local farmers and landowners. The close availability of such a useful material would have been a boon for the Hickeses, who could use the stone not only for burning but also as building material for expanding the Barn, limewashing its walls and mortaring its joints.

Lime burning was a specialist but dangerous skill, something that rural labourers could do to earn extra money on the side, especially over the quieter winter months. The Hickeses' kiln was built into the hillside, midway between the Barn and the quarry. Constructing the kiln on a slope made it easier for the lime burner to tip fist-sized lumps of stone into the top of the kiln without needing a ladder. The kiln was filled with alternating layers, like a trifle, of limestone and fuel, and then lit from underneath.

Once the process was started, that was the point of no return. For the next three or four days the lime burner had to stay by the kiln, watching over the process with a beady eye. Reports of men sleeping next to their kilns are not

uncommon, but it was a risky strategy – large limestone rocks often exploded in the intense heat and the carbon monoxide fumes from lime burning were deadly. Accidents happened with depressing regularity, especially when labourers snuggled near the kiln for warmth. One local report, from 1860, is typical of the time: 'the body of John Berry, labourer, aged 36 years, who was found dead at the Brancliff lime kilns [...] Wm. Richardson, one of the labourers at the lime kilns, went to stir the fire about one o'clock on Saturday, and found the deceased lying dead and quite stiff, in the "eye" of the kiln. The deceased [...] has led a drunken vagabond life for some time, sleeping out of doors the whole of last winter, and frequently at the lime kilns. There appeared to be no doubt that he had been suffocated by the gases emitted from the lime kilns.'[50]

Once the lime burning had finished, it was time to spread it onto the fields. Hickes and his men would shovel the lime, now in crumbly, corrosive lumps, straight from the eye of the kiln into a waiting cart. It was a dusty, unpleasant job that stung the eyes, burned the throat and left your nose running with blood; no wonder Victorian writers used the expression 'as thirsty as a lime burner'. Once the cart was full, the farmer led the horses into the field and walked up and down in a straight line, flinging lime onto the soil, and waited for the next rainfall to wash it in. Not only was lime useful for the fields but a 'burning' would also provide the farm with mortar and limewash. The lime that still holds the Barn's building stones together, plastered its walls and whitewashed the interior was no doubt burned by local lads, in its very own kiln.

The process of burning limestone transformed an inert substance into a reactive, almost magical ingredient that could transform the fortunes of a farm. It's perhaps no wonder, then, that such a potent but hazardous process would attract folk beliefs well into the nineteenth century and beyond. Over in the Yorkshire Dales, where locals have been burning and spreading lime for centuries to improve the marginal uplands, lime burners would offer thanks to their kilns by leaving small gifts inside. Even in the mid-twentieth century, lime kilns still attracted curious rural rituals. An encyclopedia of superstitions, published in the 1940s and documenting the dying embers of country folklore, described a strange restorative: 'A cure much practised, even to-day, is to carry the child to a lime kiln [...] and let it breathe the smoke or the gas fumes—or, as it was put, the "harmonious air".' The book also describes a love oracle: 'Steal alone at night to the nearest lime-kiln, and throw in a ball of blue yarn, winding off in a fresh clew [ball] as you come near the edge. Grasp hold of the thread lying in the kiln. You must then ask who holds the other end, and the name of your future life partner will be uttered.'[51]

Build your lime kiln in the wrong place, though, and you could expect disaster – as the antiquarian Thomas Crofton Croker observed in his 1824 *Researches in the South of Ireland*: 'An industrious peasant, who purchased a farm in the neighbourhood of Mallow, from a near relative of mine, commenced his improvements by building [...] a lime kiln.' Soon after, the 'fairies' – who didn't approve of where he'd built it – caused him to lose 'his sow with nine boniiveens (suckling pigs), his horse fell into a quarry and was killed, and three of his sheep died'. Although the kiln had cost the peasant five guineas, 'he declared he would never burn another stone in it, but take it down, without delay, and build one away from the fort, saying, he was wrong in putting that kiln in the way of the "good people," who were thus obliged to go out of their usual track.'[52]

Lime burning, like many other farm processes, was ripe for modernisation. As the nineteenth century progressed, the development of a national rail network began to give farmers access to cheap powdered lime created on an industrial scale. This removed, at a stroke, the need for both the lime burners and the kiln itself. Remnants of these once ubiquitous structures now scatter the countryside, but few people recognise their former purpose. The Barn kept its kiln longer than most; the proximity of the quarry at the top of the hill kept Hickes's costs low even with the lure of ready-made powder. But by the middle of the twentieth century, it was increasingly difficult to find local workers willing to do such dirty, dangerous work. Few attempts had been made to improve safety in the farming environment during the nineteenth century. The Threshing Machines Act of 1878 was the first to address the issue of protecting farmers from accidents, and the 1880 Employers' Liability Act made it possible for a worker to hold his employer responsible for injuries resulting from a foreman's – or another employee's – carelessness. But it wasn't until the 1950s and the passing of three key pieces of legislation – the Agriculture (Poisonous Substances) Act, the Mines and Quarries Act and the Agriculture (Safety, Health and Welfare Provisions) Act – that homespun lime burning became more of a liability than a money-saver. By the 1960s, the Barn's kiln had been dismantled and the stone reused elsewhere, leaving nothing but a shallow dip in the hillside to show for its century of service.

✳

With the soil sweetened, the farmer could sow his crops for the coming year. Before the threshing part of the Barn was built in the 1780s, the surrounding fields would have been planted with four dominant crops – wheat, rye, barley and oats – plus field beans and forage peas. All four grain crops were used for bread-making but barley was also essential for brewing and animal feed, and oats for oatmeal and horse feed. Wheat and rye were often grown in the same field – the resulting mixed crop was called maslin and was also used for bread-making. Beans and peas were largely destined not for the table, but for use as animal feed. Planting legumes also helped fix nitrogen back into the soil,[*] which the previous arable harvest had depleted. The fallow year allowed the soil to recover and the weeds, which inevitably grew, could be grazed over the warmer months. But animals had to be slaughtered before winter as there wasn't enough greenery to sustain them.

From the late eighteenth century onwards, farmers also began to introduce new crops across the county, including oilseed rape[†] and turnips, and different ways of rotating the crops they grew. For hundreds of years, farmers who grew cereal crops had to leave a third of their land fallow at any one time. There was logic in this – arable farming depleted the soil and so, to restore the goodness to the land, the farmer needed to leave the soil to recover. If you weren't growing crops, however, you weren't making money. Early

---

[*] The science of nitrogen was in its infancy in the 1770s, the element only having been discovered in 1772. But farmers and agricultural writers had long known that legumes did something beneficial to the soil.

[†] The Romans probably introduced rape seed to England and it was occasionally grown until the Middle Ages, when it was used as a 'break crop' and dug back into the soil as an improver. Oilseed rape really took off during the Industrial Revolution, when its oil was used as an essential lubricant for machinery, while the residue from the oil-extraction process was useful as an animal feed.

experiments in the Low Countries in the fourteenth century had shown that there was a way of breaking the cycle; by growing turnips on the land when it was fallow, you could not only improve the soil and return it to fertility (turnips also fix nitrogen in the soil) but the root vegetables could feed large numbers of sheep and cattle in the cold, dormant months, meaning they didn't have to be culled over winter. And, as a bonus, the manure from all the turnip-munching livestock added extra goodness to the land.

An influential Whig politician, Viscount Charles Townshend (1674–1738), had seen this system in action during a visit to the Low Countries and decided to experiment with it on his Norfolk estate. The viscount famously became known as 'Turnip Townshend', but not just because he was an 'early adopter' of the root crop in England. It was Townshend's endless proselytising for the practice that really earned him his nickname – he talked of little else, apparently: 'he was particularly fond of that kind of rural improvement which arises from Turnips,' observed one exasperated listener, the poet Alexander Pope. 'It was the favourite subject of his conversation.' The Low Countries system was long-winded since it involved the rotation of crops up to seven times in one cycle. But impatient British farmers soon whittled it down to four: winter wheat harvested in summer; turnips harvested the following spring; barley harvested the next summer; followed by a final round of clover and grass. When

Thomas Mosley, the rector of Stonegrave, got his hands on the enclosed land around the Barn, one of the first things he got his labourers to do was plant a few fields of turnips. Not only could he now concentrate on grain crops – which he could process in his new threshing barn – but he could also provide fodder for animals over winter. Thanks to a simple root vegetable, farming productivity doubled. Such was the admiration for the turnip among the agricultural community that particularly impressive examples were showcased in Victorian news reports. The rector of Stonegrave would have felt a twinge of envy at the monster turnip grown on fields belonging to his fellow landowner Sir Bellingham Graham: 'A remarkably large turnip', gushed the *Yorkshire Herald* in 1835, 'was lately produced in a field [...] at Stonegrave. Divested of the root and greater part of the top, which was small, it weighed thirteen pounds; and it measured 2 feet 6 inches by 2 feet 4 inches in circumference.'[53]

Another farming innovation was the widespread adoption of the potato. Although the tuber had first arrived on British shores sometime at the end of the sixteenth century, Britons didn't warm to it as a staple food. John Tuke, writing in 1800, noted that in North Yorkshire: 'Potatoes first became an object of field husbandry in this district, not more than forty years since; before which time they were little known beyond the garden of the gentleman; within that period, they have got universal possession, from the table of the rich, to the daily board of the cottage.'[54]

Northern Europe was, and had always been, a grain continent and the arrival of the new root vegetable was initially greeted with suspicion; many feared it was poisonous or only fit for animal consumption. The French parliament even went so far as to criminalise the potato between 1748 and 1772, believing the tubers caused leprosy; the potato ban was only lifted thanks to the efforts of a potato-loving Frenchman, Antoine-Augustin Parmentier, who served in the Seven Years War (1756–63) as an army pharmacist. Captured by Britain's Prussian allies, he was fed a prison diet of potatoes and survived the experience of incarceration; after his release, Parmentier vowed to ensure that their nutritious qualities were made widely available in his homeland. He quickly set about demonstrating different ways to cook potatoes, hosted potato-themed dinner parties, and successfully persuaded the French government to lift the embargo. Even King Louis XVI was an enthusiast – 'One day France will thank you for having found the bread for the poor!' he announced, after reading Parmentier's *Treatise on the Culture and Use of Potatoes* in 1789.*

---

* Parmentier's name lives on in the classic French dish *pommes Parmentier*, small cubes of potato cooked with garlic and herbs.

In Britain, however, many were uneasy about the potato's links to Catholicism. Spain had been instrumental in introducing the potato to Europe from South America. When Spanish conquistadors conquered Peru in the sixteenth century, they were searching for gold but would take home a different treasure – the tuber. During the 1560s, potatoes were grown on Spain's Canary Islands and by the 1570s they were being cultivated on the mainland and sent by the Spanish court as exotic gifts to key Catholic figures across Europe. Two centuries later, in 1765, the slogan 'No Potatoes, No Popery!' was used by a parliamentary candidate in Lewes in East Sussex on England's south coast.

In the end, pragmatism won the day; farmers could see that potatoes not only yielded more calories per acre than grain but also offered some kind of insurance policy against poor grain harvests. Across much of northern Europe, people had – like Antoine-Augustin Parmentier – discovered the virtues of the potato tuber in time of war. During military campaigns, soldiers on the move would empty granaries for their own use, often leaving local farmers bereft or, worse, destroying crops as a deliberate act of sabotage. Potatoes, grown and stored underground, out of sight, offered peasants a fighting chance. Perhaps even more convincing was the potato's ability to counteract some of the worst effects of harvest failure. Famine was a feature of farming life: between 1523 and 1623, for example, England suffered seventeen catastrophic national crop failures. France, between 1500 and 1800, had around forty.[55] Severe, life-threatening food shortages regularly occurred more than once a decade – countries could not, it seems, consistently feed themselves, especially with their growing urban populations.

Part of the problem may have been down to what has been dubbed the 'Little Ice Age', a period of climate cooling between the mid-fourteenth century and the early nineteenth. While the overall temperature drop over this 500-year period was probably only around one degree, parts of Europe and North America experienced sporadic and dramatic dips, especially over winter. The effect was often disastrous – canals and rivers froze, Alpine villages were gobbled up by advancing glaciers and, most significantly, farmers had to contend with hugely unpredictable harvests. The Little Ice Age also had some interesting cultural side effects, not least the spectacle of ice fairs. Between the seventeenth and early nineteenth centuries it wasn't uncommon for the River Thames to freeze over, often for weeks in a row. The first River Thames Frost Fair was held in 1608 – a jamboree of ice-skating, stalls, drinking feasts and bowling. Although the last fair was held in 1814, two years later came an even deeper freeze. Dubbed the 'Year Without Summer', 1816 is thought to have inspired Mary Shelley to write *Frankenstein*, much of which is set in arctic conditions. It also inspired the invention of the bicycle. In 1816, German farmers experienced a terrible oat harvest, and with nothing to feed their horses over winter, farmers were forced to shoot their steeds rather than watch them starve. Inventor Karl Drais von Sauerbronn, spurred on by these tragic events, created a horseless mode of transport. His pedal-less *laufmaschine* – propelled by the rider's feet pushing against the ground – became the forerunner of the modern bicycle.

By the time the threshing barn was operational, at the end of the eighteenth century, Britain had experienced two decades of poor grain harvests. John Younger, a Borders shoemaker, wrote extensively about his experiences of growing up with the spectre of hunger during those lean years; a succession of nationwide bad harvests forced him to 'chew beech, brier and thorn buds' and left him dreaming of boiled potatoes:

'...to be generally pinched of all matters in the consistence of human food for the space of two or three years—to be bleached skeleton-thin by a kind of protracted famine, wasting by daily degrees the blood from the young heart— was a sad concern, producing a feeling none can thoroughly comprehend from mere description, and few I wish may ever understand from sad experience, to go hungry to bed on a winter night, an unfortunate sister lying within hearing, with a leaching infant (a loved one) draining her hungry heart to the bottom of its deepest sigh.'[56]

The 'witches' marks' etched high up in the lime plaster on the Barn would have been carved at this time; what seem like superstitious scribblings to modern eyes would have been a heartfelt, hopeful gesture from a rural labourer. These markings are the setting in stone, literally, of people's anxieties and aspirations, both spoken and secret. They're made with an instrument that produces a fixed diameter – a stonemason's dividers or, more likely, a set of sheep shears. The hexafoil* daisy-petal shape is important – the circular design was thought to offer protection on the principle that evil spirits would be trapped or entranced by the shape's never-ending line.

With grain harvests at the forefront of many country-dwellers' minds in the late eighteenth and early nineteenth centuries, these old, careful scribblings were perhaps a prayer for a good harvest or a talisman to keep the grain safe and dry. Such beliefs and practices were so embedded in the rural psyche that they even travelled with farming men and women who emigrated. Witches' marks turn up on nineteenth-century buildings wherever British colonists landed, across Australia and Tasmania and up and down the east coast of North America. Pennsylvania has plenty of them, painted and scribed both on the inside and the exterior

---

* A hexafoil is a geometric pattern created by overlapping six circular arcs to form a flower with six petals.

of barns. The building type most covered in these symbols is – tellingly – the granary.[57]

✳

Towards the end of the eighteenth century, the British government launched a campaign to promote potato-growing as a way of ameliorating the effects of harvest failure. In 1795 the Board of Agriculture released a pamphlet – 'Hints Respecting the Use and Culture of Potatoes' – which encouraged farmers not only to plant potatoes as a productive crop but also to allow their labourers to 'plant for themselves, in such angles and corners as might otherwise be neglected'. The pamphlet also suggested that clergy might 'in their several parishes, to have the goodness to communicate the above to their neighbours: and at the same time, to encourage, as much as they can, the farmers and cottagers to plant potatoes this spring, in order that the kingdom may experience no scarcity, if the next harvest should prove either very late, or not sufficiently productive in bread corn.'[58]

With the weight of Parliament behind this new food source, and the spectre of starvation never far away, the potato went from novelty vegetable to household staple over the space of just one generation. Ireland, in particular, took to the potato with gusto. By the 1840s, almost half the population depended on the calorie-rich potato for sustenance. Landownership in Ireland at that time was largely concentrated in the hands of

English and Anglo-Irish Protestant families, many of whom were absentee landlords. Tenant farmers were often relegated to small parcels of land, which, even in boon years, barely provided enough food to live on. The introduction of potatoes – and one variety in particular, the Lumper (so called because of its productivity) – had been a lifeline, a way of negating the extremes of poor harvests. The tuber had seemed a sensible bet – the Irish poor could grow enough to feed their families from a small plot, leaving landlords large areas of their estates to grow grain for export back to England.

When potato blight spread into Ireland from northern Europe, its effects were catastrophic and epochal. The damage caused by the airborne fungus *Phytophthora infestans* had first been spotted on America's eastern seaboard in 1843 and the disease quickly crossed the Atlantic in a shipment of seed potatoes heading for Belgium. A damp spring in 1845 helped the mould spores sweep across Europe and settle on Ireland's west coast in the early autumn, ready to wreak havoc. Successive blasts of disease ruined potato harvests in Ireland not just for one year, but five years in a row. While around 100,000 people are thought to have died in other European countries as a result of blight, in Ireland it caused a devastating level of mortality. Conservative estimates put the death toll at around a million people between 1846 and 1851 (out of a population of around 8.5 million), with a further 2 million fleeing abroad.

But it was political ideology, rather than the potato fungus, that dealt the deadliest blow. Britain simply chose not to do enough to mitigate the effects of the famine even though, for much of the period, there were other food sources available. The political middle classes of Britain at this time fervently opposed any kind of interference in the form of sustained relief, believing that all the Irish poor needed to do was learn to be more self-reliant and judicious with their resources. Laissez-faire was the name of the game – the markets and society would check themselves. Not only was this 'right' economically, but morally and spiritually – if divine intervention was behind the famine, so members of the government argued, then to intervene was to go against God's will. Sir Charles Trevelyan, English civil servant and administer of Irish poor relief at the time, summed up the lethal philosophy: the famine was, in his eyes, 'a direct stroke of an all-wise and all-merciful Providence' and 'the judgement of God sent the calamity to teach the Irish a lesson'.[59]

While the government position was clear, not everyone dismissed the potato famine as divine retribution. The Quakers were one of the few religious communities to offer their support, including a Yorkshireman called James Hack Tuke, who travelled to Ireland to witness for himself the effects of the blight. In a series of letters written from County Mayo, he saw 'Human wretchedness' and 'living skeletons' and launched a scathing attack on landowners, naming and shaming those who had instigated a series of heartless evictions. The British Relief Association, formed in 1847, also threw its weight into the cause. The association, which was worried not only about the Irish blight but also the failure of potatoes in poor regions of Scotland, was largely the idea of the British Jewish banker Lionel de Rothschild. Money and power talked – within just a few days of being established, the British Relief Association had received a £2,000 donation from Queen Victoria and, more importantly, a letter to be read out in Anglican churches asking for prayers and donations. While the government dragged its heels, the British Relief Association's mission worked its hardest to squeeze money out of rich and poor parishioners alike. Even the poorest of Stonegrave residents put their hands in their threadbare pockets. On 13 March 1847, just a few months after the charity was formed, Stonegrave church held a 'collection for the Irish and Scotch' after a sermon by Reverend Edward Hawke. His words must have been rousing – Stonegrave's congregation of under two hundred people, mostly poor agricultural workers and their families, raised an astonishing £21 11s 9d, the equivalent of two years' wages for a labourer.

Enterprising farmers would try any crop if there was a market for it – hemp for rope-making, hops for beer, plants for dyeing – but Yorkshire had two specialities that few other counties dared to try. One of these was the fuller's teazle, a spiky plant grown for one express purpose – to raise the nap on woollen cloth. Fuller's teazles are covered in tiny, hooked bristles and were used to 'tease' or fluff up the surface of the cloth, which could then be cropped with shears to create a smooth surface.

For centuries, this job was done by hand, using teazles set into a small wooden frame rather like a large dog brush, but during the Industrial Revolution the process was mechanised and teazle-covered revolving cylinders called 'gig mills' made light work of the job. But a full gig used thousands of teazles at a time, all of which needed constantly replacing. The demand for teazles became insatiable. Unlike the wild teazle, fuller's teazles are fiendishly tricky to grow in Britain, not least because they are a heat-loving Mediterranean plant,[60] but demand from the voracious woollen mills in West Yorkshire gave a few farmers enough confidence to try out the crop.

Luckily, pockets of Yorkshire were blessed with the right soil and good drainage – 'a thin sweet surface and marly bottom'[61] – and so a small but significant trade in teazles provided a welcome source of income for both farmers and smallholders. The teazles were sold primarily to one place – Leeds. Once they were harvested in late summer, dried and boxed up, the teazles were loaded onto carts or waggons and driven into the city; the journey there and back, by road, was only profitable if it could be achieved in one day, limiting teazle-growing to those areas within one day's ride to middlemen in Leeds or directly to the woollen mills. The county soon found it couldn't provide enough fuller's teazles to meet Leeds's endless demands – many more had to be brought up from the West Country, which also traditionally grew teazles, and later, from growers abroad. In the heyday of the 1850s, waggons piled high with teazles travelled so regularly from North Yorkshire to Leeds that 'the horses knew by themselves which pubs to stop at on the way'.[62]

Perhaps the most surprising crop, though, was North Yorkshire's brief dabble with tobacco. Almost as soon as the plant first arrived from the New World in the middle of the sixteenth century, the habit of smoking its dried leaves became very popular. Despite King James I's demonising of tobacco in his *Counterblaste to Tobacco* of 1604 – 'A custome lothsome to the eye, hatefull to the Nose, harmefull to the braine, dangerous to the Lungs' – levels of consumption remained high, and tobacco imports soon attracted such heavy taxes that many British smokers decided to grow their own.

In the century following its introduction, tobacco-growing proliferated across forty counties and was one of Britain's biggest exports to Holland and Belgium. It soon became clear that the domestic market was threatening to interfere with the highly profitable business of importing tobacco from British-owned slave plantations in the southern states of America. In 1652 the government passed a law banning any planting of tobacco on English soil, strengthened eight years later by a second Act. The message to potential tobacco growers was loud and clear:

'Whereas divers great quantities of Tobacco have been of late years, and now are Planted in divers parts of this Nation, tending to the decay of Husbandry and Tillage, the prejudice and hindrance of the English Plantations abroad, and of the Trading, Commerce, Navigation, and Shipping of this Nation; For prevention thereof, Be it Enacted or Ordained by this present Parliament, and by the Authority of the same, That no person or persons whatsoever, do or shall at any time from and after the first day of May, One thousand six hundred fifty and two, plant, set, grow, make or cure any Tobacco, either in seed, plant or otherwise, in any Ground, Field, place or places within this Nation.'[63]

The Speaker of the House of Commons also stated publicly, and falsely, that tobacco didn't grow well in British soil, hoping to deter any mavericks who thought they might dodge the law and give it a try. But try it they did in North Yorkshire in the late eighteenth century. When farm labourers started to build the threshing section of the Barn in the early 1780s, just a few miles away the fields would have been filled with the smell of burning tobacco. Only a few years earlier, a retired plantation worker from Virginia had decided to give a group of local Ryedale farmers a lesson on how to grow and cure tobacco 'for the pipe'. The crops were a resounding success, but by 1782 had come to the attention of the authorities, who promptly publicly burned the entire lot, threw the farmers in prison and fined them the extraordinary sum of £30,000 (nearly £3 million in today's money).[64]

The lesson was learned. Throughout the nineteenth century, tobacco remained the most important source of import revenue for the treasury – the government was never going to allow British farmers to grow a crop that was bringing in enough duty to defray almost the entire cost of running the British navy. One journalist, writing in 1886, noted that excise duties on tobacco raised around £10 million a year, about £500 million in today's money. The cost of the navy for the same year was around £11 million: 'smokers must be regarded as an important class of taxpayers,' he sympathised, but tobacco is primarily 'the luxury of the poor and, that being so, it is rather hard that it should be taxed more heavily than any other article of consumption known to Englishmen'.[65] Dissent fell on deaf ears, however, and British farmers remained prohibited from growing tobacco until 1910. By that time, farmers had lost interest, invested elsewhere or simply couldn't face competing with large-scale foreign growers. The moment had passed.

3

EE COULDN'T STOP A PIG IN A GINNEL

EE COULDN'T STOP A PIG IN A GINNEL
He couldn't stop a pig in an alley (a reference to bowed legs caused by rickets)

Agricultural Societies and 'Improvement' • *The Farmhouse* • *Oxen* • *The Cattle Shelter and Fold Yard* • *Cows* • *Dairy* • *Pigs and Pigsties* • *Horses* • *Animal Welfare* • *Waggoners* • *Tractors and 4x4s* • *Vermin* • *Rats and the Granary* • *Chicken* • *Sheep*

The old stables in the Barn are now a workshop filled with oily tools and paint pots. At the back of this space, built high into the wall, is the old tack rack. This much-altered room retains few clues as to its past life, but the humble wooden peg rail, with its five dowels for harnesses and saddles, is a reminder of the great draught horses who once rested here. Everything about the space – from the three-foot-thick limestone walls to the vast timber beams – is reassuringly thick-set. Even the handmade iron nails, which were thwacked into the walls to hang extra tack, are vast and square-headed; dangling on one of these nails is a perfectly preserved leather bridle. Horses haven't worked on the farm for nearly a century and yet it just hangs there, patiently, as if waiting for the waggoner to come back and gently slide it over the horse's ears.

From the stable door of the Barn, you can look across the yard to the back of the farmhouse. The two buildings couldn't be more unalike. The Barn was built in solid local limestone but is decidedly ad hoc – each new construction stage solved a pressing practical problem. The farmhouse, by comparison, represents an idea. It's a page from an architect's pattern book, a statement of late-Georgian-style fashion with its high ceilings and sash windows. I often feel the farmhouse and the Barn have an uncomfortable relationship; they can seem like two very separate places. While the farmhouse has a shaky confidence, with its smart proportions and genteel symmetry, it's the Barn that truly dominates, a building completely at ease with itself and its surroundings.

In 1837, the Yorkshire Agricultural Society was formed. Its aim was clear: to promote the very latest in farm mechanisation and prize-winning livestock. The committee planned to hold a great event every year, where farmers could show off their best beasts and remarkable innovations, to be judged by the great and good of northern landowning society.

In the first year of competition, among the now familiar farmyard categories such as 'Best Large Breed Sow' or 'Best Pen of Five Ewes', was another, smaller prize. Ranked on the list between 'Horses' and 'Implements' was the category 'Servants'. Five pounds would go 'To the Labourer in Husbandry who has brought up and placed out to service the greatest number of children without receiving Parochial Relief'. First prize went to 'A. Kiddy, Labourer to R. Dennsion Esq. aged 82, – brought up 14 children', thrashing the nearest competition, a Mr John Tweedy and his eleven gainfully employed offspring.[1] Every living thing on the farm, it seemed, was ripe for advancement by apostles of the agricultural revolution.

Despite this rather dubious judging category, the spirit of the Yorkshire Agricultural Society was defiantly upbeat and progressive. It was one of many societies to emerge over the next few decades, along with numerous farming publications, shows and agricultural how-to books, including, in 1844, Henry Stephens's landmark *Book of the Farm* – an exhaustive read that offered guidance on all things farm-related to an eager audience. 'Agricultural improvement' was the topic of discussion on many a gentleman's lips – how to apply new methods of production, breeding and efficiency to the nation's farmland. Just as industrialists were working out how to squeeze every ounce of productivity out of both machines and men, so too landowners and successful tenant farmers saw an opportunity for radical change. All eyes turned towards specialisation, land drainage, new seeds and varieties, pest control, and bigger, fatter, fast-maturing stock to feed the ever-growing urban population.

For all the fevered excitement among the well-to-do, who had the means to pump capital investment into new farm buildings, machinery and animal husbandry, for many small farms the changes were slight and piecemeal. Even during the nineteenth century, most tenant farmers grew only enough food to feed their families and sell a small amount of surplus. Short-term annual tenancies also left little scope for increasing output or investing in long-term programmes. As Tuke noted in the late eighteenth century, with not a little disapproval of North Yorkshire farmers: 'it is a matter of regret, that a great want of attention among the generality of farmers, in improving their stocks, should still prevail; which can only proceed from a narrow and ill-judged parsimony as spirited improvers are scattered over most parts of the Riding'.[2] Similar feelings were echoed across the land by agricultural mavericks frustrated at cash-strapped farmers' reluctance to throw out the old ways: 'It is, indeed, deeply to be lamented', sighed one irritated expert,

'that such distinguished examples have not been more generally followed. Notwithstanding the acknowledged stride which agriculture has made in this country within the last half century, yet no science has been slower in its progress towards perfection; and even admitting numberless existing instances of intelligence and spirited management among farmers of the higher class, it is still an undeniable fact, that the great mass are men of a very opposite description. Brought up without sufficient education to enable them to comprehend the first principles of their art, acquiring it mechanically, as a mere trade, and either too dull or too indolent to seek information from books, they reject every proposed improvement as the visionary schemes of mere theorists, and even neglect them after their value has been proved by experience.'[3]

The Barn, however, was targeted for improvement and during the 1850s tripled in size. Reverend Hawke, who had so passionately implored the villagers of Stonegrave just a few years earlier to donate to the Irish famine, continued his predecessor's drive towards 'modern farming' and tacked a cart shed and granary onto the right of the threshing barn and a stables and hayloft to the left. The only thing that was missing at that stage was a tenant farmer to run the new holding. And, as we already know, John Hickes and his family would arrive in 1855.

A decade and a half before, in 1840, the previous incumbent – Reverend Edward Bland – had commissioned a farmhouse to be built just a few strides from the Barn. Unlike most of the other farmhouses in the immediate area, it was to be constructed from handmade red brick and grey slate, not the gentle, pale limestone and clay tiles that so define the vernacular in this part of the world. This was a new way of doing things. As part of the spirit of improvement, alongside new farming methods there was also a move towards 'model farmhouses' that were architecturally polite and neat, with a sensible, predictable layout and clear division of function. Nationally, plans were drawn up for housebuilders and architects to follow so they could create the ideal farmhouse regardless of where in the country they found themselves.

And so, in a deliberate attempt to distance the Barn's new farmhouse from local tradition, Welsh slate was shipped around the coast, at great expense, and bricks sourced from a city brickmaker, most likely in York or Scarborough. Bricks also signalled wealth. They'd been used in the region since medieval times, when they were initially imported from the Low Countries. By the middle of the fourteenth century, York was firing its own bricks, but they were still expensive, an architectural luxury synonymous with high status. Building in brick, even as late as 1840, in a county rich with natural limestone, sent a clear message that North Yorkshire farming was no longer the preserve of the poor. Agriculture was becoming a sound investment worthy of a model farmhouse, model barn and model tenant.

Reverend Bland would have overseen the building work but, as with many Victorian ventures, exploitation wasn't far under the surface. Many of the farmhouse's new building materials came from industrial sites that boasted some of the worst working conditions of the era. Brickmaking was particularly unpleasant; one writer for *The Builder*, a trade magazine not noted for its sentimentality, jotted down his thoughts just after the farmhouse was constructed: 'Frequently have our hearts bled to see the degrading labour to which the brickfield has subjected our species, and most revolting of all to see women put to the drudgery of horses and engines; little children too, who in a country like this should be at school, disguised past recognition in the mixed sweat and plasterings of clay and mud which encumbered their attenuated frames.'[4] Welsh slate was produced in working conditions of similar wretchedness. One of the largest slate quarries of the time, Penrhyn quarry in north-west Wales, was owned by Richard Pennant, MP and, from 1783, 1st Baron Penrhyn. Pennant also owned multiple sugar plantations in Jamaica and over a thousand slaves. The wealth Pennant generated from sugar and slavery was pumped into his slate quarry, turning it from a regional enterprise into a world exporter and the biggest quarry of its age. Pennant was, unsurprisingly, a staunch anti-abolitionist, defending slavery to the last, but also an employer of child labour back on home turf.

When the farmhouse was finished, it looked more like a town villa than a rural dwelling. This was deliberate, making the statement that farming was now an upright, forward-thinking occupation for upright, forward-thinking men. These 'double-pile' houses pop up across the country – all with similar layouts – and look very much like a child's symmetrical drawing of a house. The basic floor plan is four rooms, the two principal living rooms at the front, often south-facing for health benefits, and two at the rear – usually a kitchen and a dairy. Of all the rooms, the position of the dairy was critical – it had to be on the coldest side of the house, usually the north-east corner, to keep milk, home-made butter and cheese fresh.

Rather fittingly, these square double-pile houses were often originally built for clergy or minor gentry, as a statement of fashion and up-to-date architectural appreciation. By the early nineteenth century, when men of substance were turning their attention to farming, these buildings also found their way onto improved farms. One of the key differences was a central hallway. This meant that – unlike older, 'out-of-date' farmhouses – there was no need to pass through one room to get to another and staff could go about their business without disturbing the family. The farmhouse was also, significantly, built with its front door and principal windows facing away from the Barn – a key difference from earlier farm layouts, where human housing and animal shelter jostled amicably side by side. The farmhouse was not only deliberately separated from the noise and bustle of the Barn but orientated so its inhabitants wouldn't have to trouble their eyes with a messy vista of farm life.

Upstairs in the farmhouse, there are three large bedrooms for the family, and a small room for female staff. The builder of the farmhouse also tacked a modest cottage onto the gable end of the building, with a scullery and range downstairs and sleeping space with ladder access above. This was accommodation for male farm servants who otherwise would have had to make do with an unheated attic space in the main farmhouse or hayloft to sleep in.* The scullery would have also been used as a warming or rest room for the farmworkers, and was known locally as the 'slum' or 't'kip'.[5] Others called it a 'paddy loft', no doubt named after the Irish migrant labourers who passed through during harvest. Next to the cottage, another afterthought was added just after the Hickeses arrived – a small single-storey washhouse. Although the range in the cottage scullery could heat small amounts of hot water in its kettle, large volumes of water needed heating on a specially built 'copper', a huge metal bowl built over a brick oven. Annie or any of the other domestics who passed through the Hickeses' farmhouse would have had to heat endless rounds of hot

---

* The whole notion that people might enjoy a bed to themselves is a relatively new one. Parents might share with children, female servants with the mistress of the house, male live-in servants with each other, or children with staff. Some seasonal servants wouldn't have even expected a bed at all and would have made do with a sleeping space in a dry barn, attic space or workshop floor. The seventeenth-century Yorkshire farmer Henry Best instructed his foreman to 'sette then up boardes for bedsteads and to lay in strawe ready against that time; they usually made three beds ready for them in the folks chamber an if ther be anymore, they make the rest in the Barne, killne, or some other convenient howse for that purpose'. (Source: Flather, A., 'Gender, Space and Place: The Experience of Servants in Rural Households 1550–1750', University of Essex)

water, not only for cleaning the house and family baths, but for washing bedding every Monday. Every fluid ounce of steaming, boiling hot water had to be scooped out, ladle by ladle, and carried in buckets into the home.

$$\maltese$$

Extending the Barn in the 1850s, and the construction of stables, would have allowed horses to be kept on the farm for the first time. For anyone familiar with the North Yorkshire landscape, the choice to have horses rather than oxen would have been seen as the epitome of 'modern farming'. For centuries, local farmers had relied on oxen, both as draught animals and, to a lesser extent, a source of meat. While we traditionally think of horses as the pulling power behind agriculture, until the middle of the nineteenth century oxen constituted at least half of the national draught herd and, in many parts of the country, an even greater percentage.

Oxen are castrated male cattle[*] and were valuable working beasts on the land. Oxen offered sheer muscle power, which was especially useful on steep slopes and muddy tracks; they excel at the 'dead pull', heaving great weights from a standing start, and were perfect for heavy ploughing and hauling great loads of stone and timber. Sledges were a common sight

---

[*] Female cattle could, and were, sometimes trained as draught animals but were more valuable as milkers and calvers.

in North Yorkshire up until the early twentieth century, especially on farms with uneven ground or poor trackways. Far from being an archaic form of transport, the sledge had many advantages over the wheeled wagon, and not just on snow. Wheels tended to need smooth flat surfaces, a rare occurrence in a hilly agricultural landscape with poor roads, and sledges also had a low centre of gravity, making them less likely to tip over when fully loaded with limestone or fuel such as peat or turf.

When it came to oxen, bigger was better – as one eminent breeder in the 1840s joked, 'we had no criterion but size, nothing would please but elephants or giants'.[6] They were also cheaper to keep than horses; oxen could graze, unsupervised, on rough pastureland or unenclosed commons, while horses needed bringing home every evening, and more nutritious grazing and fodder. Oxen would start work at two years old, pull until they were six or seven, and were then sold off at the local market for fattening up to produce 'the huge marbled roasting joints favoured by catering establishments, large wealthy households, and by epicures'.[7]

Yet by the late nineteenth century, these massive beasts had all but disappeared. The pace and nature of change in agriculture left the draught ox redundant. Pre-enclosure, oxen had access to swathes of free grassland, especially on uncultivated ground, but new improvements in land reclamation and drainage meant that farmers could turn waste land into profitable arable fields, leaving few places for the large herbivores to graze. The demand for cheap beef also rocketed, especially from rapidly expanding urban areas. Up until the mid-nineteenth century, most working people didn't eat much meat; around 1800, for example, only 15 per cent of the average weekly food budget went on meat, usually a small scrap of bacon reserved for the male breadwinner.[8] Meat was, for most, a rare treat.

As the Industrial Revolution picked up pace, however, not only did wealthier families begin to expect meat as an everyday dinner-table staple, but even less well-off families who worked in factories and heavy industry could afford to buy meat since they earned higher wages than their rural cousins. By the 1840s, for example, working-class families in industry spent four times as much money on meat – albeit of low quality – as agricultural families.[9] Oxen matured too slowly to feed this demand; farmers now wanted cattle that would gain weight rapidly – in just two years rather than the traditional six or seven – and have a high proportion of meat to bone and fat. Developments in farm machinery, such as lighter ploughs – which horses could pull more quickly than oxen – gave equids the edge over the steady, plodding bovines.

Transport improvements spelled further disaster for oxen. For centuries, Britain's roads were little more than dirt tracks, along which both oxen and, less often, horses would heave heavy loads to market or the nearest waterway. As we'll see later, with the advent of industrialisation and the opening up of urban markets to rural produce, it became imperative to build more robust, compacted stone roads. Oxen, unlike horses, have cloven hooves, which makes walking on stony, hard roads uncomfortable. Ryedale tracks, according to Tuke, were no friend to the poor ox, a place where 'no roads are harder or more stoney'. 'There,' he continued with not a little tenderness, 'his feet let him down.'[10] The only way to make an ox roadworthy was to shoe it, but this was a notoriously difficult business. Not only does each hoof need two small shoes – one for each 'toe' – but an ox's hoof is thinner and more difficult to hammer nails into than a horse's. And that was if you could get the ox to stand still for long enough – any farrier brave enough to attempt it usually had to tip the vast animal over onto its side and carry out the procedure while the beast flailed around on the floor.* This was a task to be attempted only by the most skilled of farriers: 'The feet of the oxen being drawn together with strong ropes, they are

---

* Farmers did try to create tight pens or 'crushes' to hold oxen. As oxen don't like standing on three feet, each hoof had to be lashed, one at a time, to the pen while the farrier attached the shoes. Complicated sling contraptions were also built, which suspended the ox off the floor in a sturdy frame so the farrier could get access to all four feet. Needless to say, the ox rarely enjoyed it.

always cast or thrown down, which is sometimes attended to with accidents, the beast being irrevocably lamed, strained or otherwise injured.'[11] And so, while oxen had reigned supreme in a world of beaten earth roads and unenclosed lands, the nineteenth century left it languishing in the mud. But the ox didn't disappear altogether. Periods when horses were scarce, such as the failure of oat harvests (which farmers fed to horses) or wartime requisitions for the army, often saw a resurgence of draught oxen. Moorland regions – with their steep hills – and areas with heavy clay soil carried on using oxen into the early twentieth century. One of the very last farms in the country still to use oxen for the harvest and haulage lay just six miles from the Barn, in Helmsley. In 1963, a journalist in the *Whitby Gazette* reported: 'Old time butchers used to tell me that there was no beef equal in flavour or texture to that of bullocks used for ploughing and draught work until they were four or five, and then fattened off... one never or rarely sees oxen yoked in North Yorkshire [...] the Last in the North were on Lord Feversham's Duncombe Park Estate [...] and the man who shod them is still alive.'[12]

Before the mid-eighteenth century, most farmers operated on the basis that the only way to improve an animal was to feed it more. Using that logic, the fattest animals were sent to market for slaughter, while the smaller, weaker ones would stay on the farm to be bred from and, hopefully, fattened up.

As the principles of science began to work their way into the agricultural world, however, improvers turned their attention to livestock. Robert Bakewell (1725–95) began experimenting with cows and sheep on the tenanted family farm at Dishley in the Midlands. He concentrated his efforts on inbreeding – a process of rigid selection, mating and culling for certain characteristics. Hitherto, across the country, livestock of both sexes were often allowed to graze together freely, breeding at random and producing a pick-and-mix assortment of offspring, but Bakewell decided to keep his males and females apart – only allowing mating between specific animals to produce the largest, meatiest beasts. He also perfected the art of 'in-and-in' breeding, the slightly queasy and repeated mating of close relatives including father to daughter, mother to son, and brother to sister, exaggerating any traits he wanted to keep.

Two disciples of Bakewell, Robert and Charles Colling, went on to improve the Shorthorn breed of cattle, directing their efforts towards creating the ultimate beef beast. The story of their most famous creation – the Durham Ox – perfectly demonstrates the passion and excesses of nineteenth-century livestock breeding.[13] Pictures of the Durham Ox are thought to be the most commonly reproduced images of any livestock animal in British history and, while many a country pub is named after it, few know the tale of the eponymous hero. The Colling Brothers were ambitious farmers in County Durham, and Charles had been a student of Bakewell's. Cattle indigenous to the region were typically Longhorns, big animals but lean – more suited to draught than steak. Charles and Robert, however, had their eye on a new breed of Shorthorn cattle imported from the Netherlands. After some enthusiastic and prolonged attempts at inbreeding, the Durham Ox was born – an animal of such immense weight and size that it became an overnight sensation.

At the age of five, the animal was sold for £140 to a Mr Bulmer, who travelled around the country exhibiting the beast in a specially made horse-drawn carriage. After just five weeks, Mr Bulmer, sensing a quick profit, sold his ox and carriage to Mr John Day for double what he had originally paid. Almost instantly, Day received offers from other eager buyers – including one for the extraordinary sum of £2,000, the equivalent of around thirty-six years' wages for a skilled labourer. But Day was no fool, and played the long game, hauling the poor animal from city to city, from market town to market town, for six years, raking in takings from the thousands who flocked to see it; one day's work in London earned Day the sum of £100, about £5,000 in today's money.

With a girth of over three metres and tipping the scales at nearly two tons, the Durham Ox was a mighty beast indeed. But his corpulence proved to be his downfall when, in February 1807, after having travelled more than 3,000 miles around the country, the poor animal slipped while being led from his carriage and dislocated a hip. After a few weeks, with the ox showing no sign of recovery, Day called in the slaughtermen. Ever the showman, he erected a tent around the animal and charged spectators a fee to witness its last moments; he also sold pieces of the Durham Ox's skin as souvenirs.

The Durham Ox had proved a point – that selective inbreeding created animals that could satisfy the appetite of an exploding British population. Between 1700 and 1800 the population had doubled, from 5 to 10 million. A hundred years later, in 1900, the population had ballooned to nearly 40 million. Vast edible animals – it was hoped – would feed Britain's hungry workers, while beef fat or tallow, of which these grossly overweight bovids were a plentiful source, would grease the wheels of industry and provide candlelight by which to do it.[*]

The era of selective breeding turned farm animals into celebrities – paintings of plump beasts were commissioned, prints sold, and merchandise such as china plates and pottery models churned out in huge quantities. The Durham Ox's

---

[*] Tallow, which is rendered animal fat, proved to be an incredibly useful by-product of the meat industry. It was used widely in soap-making, frying, printing, tanning, candle-making and, importantly, lubricating the steam-driven engines, including locomotives and steamships.

fame even reached Australia, where Victorian prospectors homesick for their native country named a tiny hamlet after it. Not everyone was comfortable with Bakewell's legacy, however. Some commentators worried that inbreeding was meddling with 'God's plan'; one contemporary agricultural writer, Richard Parkinson, noted they were 'setting themselves in opposition to their Creator by endeavouring to destroy his works'.[14]

What did become clear was that Bakewell had forever changed how the value of certain livestock would be measured. As one improver of the day enthused, 'the value [of the animal] lies in the barrel, not in the legs'. Livestock became interesting only as a carcass. 'The live animal is conceptualised as already dead. It exists to be manipulated at will, as long as the required human value is created.'[15]

For most of farming history, barns for housing cattle weren't very common; cattle were expected to ride out the worst of the winter weather outside in the fields or, if the farmer couldn't afford to keep them, they were slaughtered. Cows that remained outside in cold weather used up a lot of energy keeping warm, and, as a result, lost condition or slowed down their milk production. By the middle of the nineteenth century, many farmers had begun to realise that cattle fattened more quickly or produced gallons more milk if they were kept cosy and dry, especially over the winter months. Keeping them under one roof, in a sheltered building, also allowed a farmer to measure and control how much food his cattle ate. A further advantage was that he could easily utilise all the manure his cows produced, mucking it straight out from stalls onto a dung heap ready for spreading.

The Barn got its own large cattle shed in the 1870s, tacked on at right angles. While the threshing bay was orientated north to south, to catch the valley breezes, the cow shelter was now built east to west. There's good logic in this – the open-fronted cattle shelter, facing south, would catch the sunshine, and let in plenty of light to keep the herd happy. Smaller animal barns – pigsties and calf stalls – were also added parallel to the threshing barn, creating a courtyard or 'fold yard', where manure was deliberately allowed to accumulate, and cattle could wander in and out of their shelters at will. The word 'fold' is an ancient one and has survived only thanks to farming. In Anglo-Saxon, *folde* originally meant earth or ground, but the word soon took on the narrower meaning of livestock enclosure; many medieval villages also had 'pinfolds', small walled pens where stray livestock would be impounded until their owners came to collect them for a fee. A 'pinder' was the person in charge of the pinfold. The fold can denote the space, but it can also refer to the animals: a fold is a flock of sheep or a herd of cattle and, of course, a community or group who share common values.

On a modest but reasonably profitable farm like the one belonging to the Barn, the Hickeses would have kept a herd both for meat and for dairy. Female calves would bolster numbers for the herd, while male calves could be sent for slaughter or fattened for later. By 1891, the Barn had enough cows to warrant the employment of a live-in 'cowboy' – John Cable, a sixteen-year-old hired to herd and tend to the cattle. While few rural labourers could afford to buy their own cows, it wasn't unusual for craftsmen and other buoyant tradesmen to own one or two beasts. 'Cow-keeping' was a sideline, but land was tricky to come by, and so cow owners often resorted to the last few scraps of pasture left behind after enclosure. Writing about the cow-keepers near the Barn, one rural historian commented: 'Some of these, who had no land, rented cow gates on the verges of the lanes set out in the enclosure awards. Here old men and old women acted as cow-tenters and looked after them. For instance at Pickering, twenty-five cows grazed on one side of the beck and twenty on the other, whilst at Helmsley about ninety cows belonging to some fifty cowkeepers used to be pastured in a large field called Beckdale. The practice ceased about the end of the First World War.'[16]

With cow ownership came the danger of falling victim to the unlikely crime of cow theft. It seems difficult to imagine how one might spirit away nearly a tonne of nervous energy, but for the farmers around the Barn cattle stealing seems to have taken place with surprising regularity. The plan was always the same and comically protracted: the thief would walk casually into a farmer's field, lead away two or three cows, and then herd them slowly all the way to the local market town, where they'd be sold to another – unsuspecting – farmer. In the case of the farmland around the Barn, it would have taken a thief at least six hours to coax the beasts along a busy main route to Malton, in full view of local onlookers. Newspaper reports of the day show that the hapless criminals were almost always apprehended, but these small-scale rustlers appear not to have been deterred by the risks attached to making off with other men's cattle in plain sight. Robert Webster's tale is just one of many: on 10 October 1848, Webster managed to lead two cows away from a farmer's field in Stonegrave and get them all the way to Malton, where he tried to sell them in the local pub. After agreeing a price of £19 (over £1,000 in today's money), the prospective buyer got jittery and questioned Webster about where he had got the cows from. Webster panicked and fled, but the story didn't end there. A few months later, our light-fingered friend was apprehended boarding a ship in Hull, bound for New Orleans – he was clearly hoping for a new life abroad. Webster left the country but not in the way he hoped; he was charged, found guilty and transported for ten years, a not unusually harsh sentence for the crime of cattle stealing.

The Hickeses would have enjoyed their own fresh dairy produce, but in their day cow's milk was a drink laced with danger. Traditionally, milk had been viewed as a 'risky' foodstuff, partly because it spoiled so quickly, partly because it didn't travel well, and partly because – although ideas about contamination weren't well understood – milk often harboured deadly bacteria or was adulterated by unscrupulous sellers.

For all their proximity to the cows that produced it, few rural labouring families could afford to buy milk on a daily basis and would enjoy their small slice of dairy in the form of a tiny sliver of cheese or butter. The old Yorkshire phrase 'Ee couldn't stop a pig in a ginnel'* provides a clue to the absence of significant amounts of dairy produce – and its associated vitamin content – from the nineteenth-century rural diet. Rickets, which gives children characteristic 'bandy legs', was a disease born out of poverty and poor nutrition. The condition is caused by a lack of Vitamin D, which we get from one of two sources – sunlight and food such as eggs and dairy. Many children in Victorian Britain suffered the twofold affliction of poor nutrition and lack of exposure to the sun, as a result of home- or factory-based indoor work or smog-enveloped city life. Rural youngsters

---

* The word 'ginnel' is a lovely, obscure relic; early versions of the Cornish, Irish and Scottish Gaelic languages all have similar words – *gannel*, *grinnel* and *grinneal* respectively – all of which mean a narrow alleyway.

probably had more access to sunlight than their urban cousins but, ironically, enjoyed less meat and dairy.

Farmers or cow-keepers with their own herds faced the choice of whether to eat their own dairy produce or sell it on. Farmers could take their butter, by horse, to Malton, which since the early eighteenth century had become a hub for butter trading. There, at the specially built Butter Market, the dairy equivalent of a corn exchange, the golden pats would exchange hands and begin their journey – at first by river, later by train – to the industrial cities of West Yorkshire. Low-quality butter – which the locals called 'grease' – went to the poorer districts, while the pats with a higher butterfat content inevitably ended up on gentlemen's tables. When the going was good, the Hickeses would have felt able to keep a generous share of their dairy produce for themselves. If a harvest was poor, or farm prices were low, most of it would have bypassed their breakfast bowls and gone directly to market.

Rapidly growing urban areas also, ironically, spent more money on milk than rural districts; both ends of the social spectrum drank it – poor working mothers often used cow's milk as a substitute for breast milk so they could return to the mill floor, while the well-to-do increasingly viewed breastfeeding as vulgar and lower class. Queen Victoria set the tone with her distaste for breastfeeding, bolstered by influential 'lifestyle' writers such as Jane Ellen Panton, who insisted, 'let me repeat once more, that in nine cases out of ten it is cruel and most unnecessary for a mother to nurse her baby herself. If carefully fed, the child flourishes just as well if the cow, and not the mother, provides its food, and I for one know no greater wretchedness than nursing a baby; it exhausts one to death, it makes one irritable, nervous, and old before one's time, and it ruins one's appearance, and I am convinced is of no good to the child.'[17]

Before the advent of the railway and, later, refrigeration, the only way for most eighteenth- and nineteenth-century city dwellers to get fresh milk was to buy not from a countryside farm but from an urban dairy. Far from the bucolic ideal, these pastureless milking factories required cattle to be tethered indoors day and night, in squalid conditions, and fed on the waste by-products of industry. Breweries and dairies often sat side by side, with cows enduring an endless diet of hot, steaming macerated grain from the brewing processes going on next door. The quality of the milk coming from the sickly cows was so poor that vendors often added chalk, flour and even alum to give the milk a thicker, more attractive consistency. While consumers regularly complained about adulterated milk,* few knew its deadliest secret. Tuberculosis

---

* Milk was just one of the many everyday foods that Victorians were suspicious of. In 1851 *The Lancet* commissioned a London doctor to investigate thirty common foods: he found that loose tea often contained nearly 50 per cent sand and dirt, along with traces of iron sulphate; lard was often cut with caustic lime; and coffee could contain mangel-wurzels, acorns or sawdust. Lead was also used as a colouring in chocolate, children's sweets, cheese and cocoa powder.

is a bacterial infection, spread by airborne droplets, and was the single biggest cause of death and disability in nineteenth-century Britain. A number of different strains of bacteria – all from the same family – cause tuberculosis in humans, including bovine TB or 'bTB'. Thanks to the unsanitary conditions of urban dairies, bovine TB was endemic among the cattle that supplied much of Victorian Britain's fresh milk, especially those poor creatures who spent their days in cramped sheds.

The statistics were horrifying; in the 1840s, Benjamin Phillips, assistant surgeon at Westminster Hospital, collected data from more than 130,000 children in charity schools, workhouses and factories across the country. Phillips found that over 30,000 of the sick children in the study displayed symptoms associated with bTB.[18] Something clearly had to be done. The Dairies, Cowsheds and Milkshops Orders of 1879 and 1885 gave local authorities the power to regulate the conditions in which urban cows were kept but did little to address similar conditions on country farms. Indeed, the overcrowding and poor hygiene that helped bovine TB spread remained common in many rural areas well into the twentieth century. Many farmers, landowners and politicians were reluctant to regulate the profitable trade in milk; at the end of the nineteenth century, country interests were still arguing over just how much of a problem bovine TB really was. In 1899, John's son, George Hickes, would have read with interest accounts of the debate in the *Yorkshire Herald*, some experts claiming that 'the risk from tuberculosis in milk was infinitely small' and that the whole controversy was a 'modern scare'.[19] Yorkshire farmers, however, could see the disaster unfolding for themselves. Only a few years earlier, in 1887, word was beginning to spread among the community that tuberculosis was not only a serious disease for animals but that 'it is at least probable that through them human beings suffer'. Worse still, farmers such as George were starting to realise that, more often than not, the disease didn't make itself known until it was too late and 'the painful hollow cough attracts the attention of the cowman'.[20] While it took another three decades for the British government to begin to test cattle for bTB routinely and reliably, new hygiene regulations introduced at the end of the nineteenth century started to make the Barn's cattle shed look outdated.

On mixed farms, like the Barn's, keeping dairy cows and pigs went hand in hand. Pigs were found on most farms; with their greedy, unfussy appetites, they were the ideal animal to feed on boiled kitchen scraps, potatoes, spent grains from brewing, and whey, the by-product of butter- and cheese-making.

Throughout medieval times, pigs had been allowed to wander freely. One of the most valuable common rights for villagers was 'pannage', the right to set pigs free to forage woodland floors, which were a rich source of acorns, beechmast and other fallen nuts. From the time of the Domesday Book, and even earlier, land documents had categorised the size of woodland by how many pigs it could support – entries would read *silva ad x porcos*, 'wood for x swine'.[21] Pannage was a way for everyday folk to fatten up pigs for slaughter for little cost. Even if the lord of the manor demanded payment of rent or, more often, a proportion of the pigs in return for pannage, the practice still brought villagers a decent return.

Enclosure, in the eighteenth century, had turned some of the last of the country's woodland over to commercial forestry or agriculture, while the early years of the Industrial Revolution also put huge demands on forests for charcoal production and timber for pit props, transport and building. As fewer people had access to woodland for pannage, farm labourers and other villagers turned to keeping pigs in their own back yards. The lucky ones might own their own pig, while others bought into a share of a communal pig or mortgaged a proportion of the meat in advance to the butcher. Those with even less money to spare might just help feed the pig, with peelings or rotten food, in return for some of the 'small bits' of the animal – its head, bones, feet or ears. Everything was used apart from the squeal.

Pigs were rarely kept for more than a year. They would be bought as piglets and then fattened up for killing just before winter arrived in order to provide a source of meat through the hardest months. Killing the animal in cold weather also meant its meat wouldn't go off as it was left to hang. The late pig's owners would then swap a ham or other cut for a new piglet, and the process would start all over again. Such was the value of the domestic back-yard pig that many a philanthropist of the day believed pig ownership could save a poor family not just from starvation but from social ruin. William Cobbett, in *Cottage Economy*, enthused: 'A couple of flitches of bacon are worth fifty thousand Methodist sermons and religious tracts. The sight of them upon the rack tends more to keep a man from poaching and stealing than whole volumes of penal statutes, though assisted by the terrors of the hulks and the gibbet.'[22]

When the Barn expanded in the 1870s, the new accommodation for livestock included not just cowsheds but pigsties as well. The pigs were housed just metres away from the back door of the farmhouse, the smell of manure clearly not off-putting enough to persuade John Hickes to place his porkers further down the yard. It was practical to keep swine near the house; pigsties were often placed near the kitchen or dairy to shorten the distance required for feeding. And although the aroma would have undoubtedly been eye-watering, its associations were good: a fat pig, rooting in its sty, meant a winter of plenty. On larger or more prosperous farms than the Barn's, the pigsties might have their own boiler house, for cooking up the swill, and chutes in the walls through which you could pour the pig feed directly into the feeding trough. Yorkshire was also famous for its 'poultiggeries' or 'hogbogs' – an ingenious combination of henhouse and piggery in one. The pigs lived and slept on the ground floor of the small hut while the poultry were accommodated, warm and dry, on the floor above them. The pigs not only kept the hens cosy with their rising heat, but provided a formidable deterrent against fox attack.

For many people, the pig occupied a curious place in household affection – a kind of edible pet. When the time came for slaughter, hearts had to be hardened. As Filmer Meadsen, the son of a Victorian stockman, recalled, his father rarely relished the occasion: 'When they had a litter o'pigs at the farm, there was always one small 'un they called the 'ant'ny',* and he always had that [...] And the butcher in the village here used to buy them off him when they were big enough to kill: but he only let the butcher have 'em on condition he never had any o' the meat.'[23] 'Pig killing day', when it

---

* An 'ant'ny' or 'tantony pig' was traditionally the runt of the litter. The name comes from medieval London, when small, weedy pigs – who were deemed unsellable at market – were donated to the Hospital of St Anthony and allowed to scavenge the streets for food. Each 'tantony pig' had a little bell hung around its neck and these itinerant creatures were well known for boldly following passers-by, squealing and begging for scraps.

came, was often a public affair; the owner and his family, butcher and other hangers-on would watch the gruesome entertainment, with a mixture of fascination, revulsion and the sheer excitement at the prospect of fresh meat. For many, it was cause for celebration: 'Oh yes, killing day was a great day!' recalled Mary Watson, daughter of a smallholder at the turn of the last century. 'It was November we generally killed one, and January or February the other: they were always killed in the cold weather, the dead of winter, because they had to keep.'[24]

The job was often undertaken by a butcher, but many other tradesmen added 'pig-sticking' to their list of skills – farmers, stonemasons, wheelwrights, even clergymen were involved in this bloody sideline: 'a country parson near Cricklade, Wiltshire was famed for his boxing and pig-killing. He boxed with the villagers... and killed the poor people's pig, gratis, with skill and despatch,' noted one rural historian.[25] The job wasn't without its expertise, as Jude the Obscure found out to his cost. In Hardy's novel, when the butcher failed to show, Jude clumsily attempted to perform the deed himself: 'Upon my soul I would sooner have gone without the pig than have had this to do!' he despaired. 'A creature I have fed with my own hands!'[26]

After the immediate trauma had passed, the spoils from pig-killing day were divided up. Anything that could be salted or smoked would be saved for the larder or, more often, sold, while some of the less salubrious remains had to be enjoyed before they spoiled. The modern fashion for nose-to-tail eating has nothing on nineteenth-century rural inventiveness when it came to pig organs and bones. Deep-fried intestines, blood sausage, roast backbone, trotter jelly, pig fry and pork blancmange from the smallest bits, fried tails – nothing was wasted.* Pig fat, or 'swine grease' as it was known in North Yorkshire, was also kept for smearing on the whetting 'strickle',† and used to sharpen the sickles at harvest time.

After a killing, there was often too much meat for one family to eat before it went rancid, and so many an impromptu dish of odds and sods would be shared among neighbours, with the tacit understanding that they would return the favour at a future date. Pig-keeping provided such a low-cost, accessible way of securing at least some protein, however

---

* The English language is full of ancient references to the nation's love affair with offcuts. In the expression 'punch someone's lights out', which is commonly mistaken to mean punching someone in the face, the 'lights' actually mean 'lungs', as they were always the lightest (in weight) of the meats. 'What a load of tripe' now means rubbish or nonsense but, for those of us who live in the north, tripe is still a popular dish of cooked cow's stomach. To 'eat humble pie', where someone has to publicly admit they were wrong, doesn't come from 'humble', as in being modest, but rather 'numbles', a medieval word for edible entrails.

† The strickle is an amazingly old tool – made from wood and shaped like a wedged door stopper, it was smeared with a mix of pig fat and sand to create an abrasive surface, perfect for sharpening sickles and other blades. The word comes from the Anglo-Saxon *strican* – to rub or pass lightly over. We get 'stroke' from the same word.

gristly, that pigs became a great source of pride and competitiveness among villagers. Weights were obsessed over, the bigger the better, a trend also followed by keen-eyed agricultural improvers – enthusiastic breeding and gluttonous feeding regimes ensured that Victorian prize pigs were some of the largest on record; 'The Yorkshire Hog', which belonged to Colonel Thomas Charles Beaumont of Bretton Hall, near Wakefield, measured nearly ten feet long (3 m) and weighed a knee-buckling 1,344 pounds (610 kg). Few modern breeds have ever matched it.

When the threshing section of the Barn was first built, in the 1780s, the pigs that farmers and villagers kept would have looked very different from the ones we're used to today. As Tuke was trotting around Yorkshire at the end of the eighteenth century, he observed that 'The breed of pigs, which prevails throughout the North Riding, has little to recommend it: they are chiefly of the old long-eared kind, with long legs, high narrow backs, and low shoulders; they are very slow feeders, and require good meat to keep them even in tolerable condition.'[27]

Indeed, most pigs in Britain up until the middle of the eighteenth century were rangy, lop-eared beasts with a narrow facial profile more akin to a wild boar than today's dish-faced porker. As the century drew to a close, however, a new, fatter, pointy-eared beast arrived from Asia and changed the face of British pig farming.* Tuke also unintentionally captured the moment when the world was introduced to the 'Yorkshire pig', an animal that has gone on to be one of the most numerous of all pig breeds and the most intensively farmed. 'A few individuals keep the Chinese kind,' he said of North Yorkshire farmers, 'which are much more kindly feeders than the first. In Ryedale, the Chinese breed are gaining ground, through the liberality of a gentlewoman lately resident in that neighbourhood, who, possessed of two or three excellent sows, has distributed several of their produce, both male and female, in the neighbourhood: they are larger than most of the Chinese breed I have seen; the old sow, as she ran about, would weigh sixteen or seventeen stones.'[28]

It was the commingling of native and Chinese pigs that formed the basis of all the well-known British breeds that dominated the national scene throughout the nineteenth and early twentieth centuries, until factory farming whittled it down to just three high-yielding varieties – the Welsh, the Landrace and the Yorkshire pig. The Yorkshire pig is no longer known by that name, except in the United States, where it was first imported in the 1830s. Across Britain it is

---

* In the late eighteenth century, many new pig breeds, which now form the backbone of some of the most successful commercial breeds, were created with the help of imported pigs from both China and southern Europe.

now referred to as the Large White pig and is the most widely distributed breed in the world.

now referred to as the Large White pig and is the most widely distributed breed in the world.

Unlike the lowly pig, perhaps the most respected animal in the Barn was the horse. We have already seen how, during the eighteenth century, new farming methods and innovations in machinery helped horses take the lead from oxen. Traditionally, oxen had excelled at the grunt work – pulling heavy ploughs through difficult soil – but with the invention of lighter, better-designed ploughs, two horses could race through the work of twice or three times the number of oxen. Another critical factor in the rise of the draught horse was the quality – and quantity – of food made available to them. Horses had worked alongside oxen for hundreds of years but only the larger, better-nourished horses could match the strength and usefulness of oxen. Britain's draught horses only really came into their own when farming started to produce enough high-quality grain, especially oats, to satisfy the considerable appetites of these very large beasts. The heaviest horse breeds – such as the English Shire or the Scottish Clydesdale – would consume several times the quantity required by a male human being, but the pay-off was clear: a horse would eat four kilograms of oats per day – enough to feed six adults – but in return it replaced the power of at least ten men.[29] It's no coincidence that the Barn acquired its

first stables at the same time as
the hayloft was built (to feed the
horses) and the threshing barn
was converted (to store additional
animal fodder). Grazing alone
would not have been sufficient to
feed the new horsepower behind the
Victorian farm.

While the mechanisation of farming in the nineteenth
century often reduced the need for manpower, the draught horse
enjoyed a long period of usefulness. Alongside pulling ploughs,
carts, waggons and seed drills, 'horse wheels' or 'horse engines'
(or gins) began to power much of a farm's machinery; horses,
walking around in a circle, would drive shafts, cogs and belts to
create energy that could be used to grind, thresh, pump or saw.
Even when the steam engine began to supplant equine power
in the second half of the nineteenth century,[*] horses were still
needed to drag the portable engines from farm to farm, or – in

---

[*] When inventor James Watt was marketing his new and improved steam
engine in the late 1700s, he needed to find a simple way to explain how
powerful it was. His steam engine was designed to replace the effort of
work horses – in industries such as coal mining – and so it made sense to
use a base measurement that his customers would understand. He worked
out that a powerful draught horse could pull around 330 lb of weight, 100
feet, in the space of one minute (the same as moving a mass of 33,000 lb
one foot in one minute). This is one unit of horsepower. Ironically, by basing
his measurements on big, muscular draught horses, Watt's horsepower is
actually an overestimate for the average horse.

the case of our farm – from the Barn out into the field. It was also horses that carted Hickes's produce to market and, even after the advent of the railway, from farm to train station and back again.

Country folk were fiercely protective of their horses' well-being, and they were keenly aware of the threat posed to them by those who used magical powers to evil ends. Belief in witches and their power to harm livestock, especially horses, was commonplace and many put their faith in amulets. One of the most common of these was the hagstone, a small pebble or flintstone with a naturally occurring hole in the middle. Until well into the twentieth century, rural workers would hang a hagstone in the stable wall or tie one around a horse's neck to prevent the animal from being 'hag rod'. Witches were thought to ride the horses during the night until they were exhausted and their manes full of tangles or 'hag knots', which the witch used as impromptu stirrups. The antiquarian John Aubrey, writing in 1686, described the custom: 'the Carters, & Groomes, & Hostlers doe hang a flint (that has a hole in it) over Horses that are hagge-ridden for a Preservative against it.'[30] Scarborough Museum, on the North Yorkshire coast, has an impressive haul of hagstones, most collected from farms around the Barn in the early twentieth century. While they were often dangled in stables, they were also nailed above cottage doors to keep witches away, hung on the horns of cows to prevent their milk from being spoiled, looped onto bedsteads to prevent nightmares, and taken on board fishing boats for good luck.

John Hickes would have bought his horses young, at just two or three years old. Draught horses by nature are gentle in temperament but it was thought that, after two or three years of hard agricultural work, a placid farm horse made the ideal candidate for pulling a coach or working in heavy industry. Agents would regularly tour out-of-the-way farms, looking for five-year-old horses who could cope with the noise and bustle of mining, brewing and the railways. Dealers also travelled to one of the many seasonal horse fairs searching for draught animals that were used to the harness and ready for a life on the road.

With large amounts of money exchanging hands for the right beast, there was plenty of scope for deception. One favourite trick was known as 'feaguing'; Francis Grose's *Classical Dictionary of the Vulgar Tongue*, published in 1785, defined the practice as follows: 'to put ginger up a horse's fundament, and formerly, as it is said, a live eel, to make him lively, and carry his tail well.' The practice was so widespread, the dictionary went on to explain, that 'a forfeit is incurred by any horse-dealer's servant, who shall shew a horse without first feaguing him'.

Another common fraud was to pull out the baby teeth of a young horse prematurely. Once this had been done, the horse's adult teeth would come through sooner and make 'three or four year old horses have the mouths of those of five',[31] enabling the farmer to sell an immature horse as if it were an adult one. In 1800, a three-year-old horse would sell for £14 but a five-year-old might fetch as much as £22. A profit of £8, however dubiously obtained, would have bought the farmer an extra cow or allowed him to employ a skilled tradesman for nearly two months. But the outcome for the horse wasn't so rosy. Three- or four-year-old ex-farm horses were then 'taken into immediate work, either for the coach or saddle; and in a few months, many of them are completely destroyed by this premature and too severe labour'.[32] Practices such as tail docking, in which the horse's tail was cut off leaving just a few inches of bone so it wouldn't get caught up in the harness or vehicle, and 'nicking' – cutting the tail's tendons so it didn't swish about – were also part and parcel of making up a working horse for sale. Attitudes to draught horses were neatly summed up by the character of Nicholas Skinner in Anna Sewell's 1877 novel *Black Beauty*, who boasted: 'my business, my plan is to work 'em as long as they'll go, and then sell 'em for what they'll fetch, at the knacker's or elsewhere.'

Horses were also easier to steal than any other farm creature, provided you could ride one. As with twentieth-first-century car crime and joyriding, it wasn't unusual for children to have a go if they were comfortable in the saddle.

An audacious account from the high days of the Barn describes one young lad's adventures: 'A most extraordinary case has been brought to light by Superintendent Metcalf, of Malton, who apprehended a lad named Richard Robinson, who said he was 11 years old, for horse stealing. The prisoner came from Brandsby, and on Tuesday week he had gone to the stable of Mr Cattley, a farmer there, at noon, saddled up and mounted a mare, and rode away with it.' As if he had all the time in the world, Robinson 'called at a smithy and got a shoe fastened, and then rode across the country to Wass, where he put up at a farm where he was known. Later on he proceeded to Stonegrave, where he called at the inn, got a cigar and something to drink, and then started off to Malton. On the road he met two horse-dealers, to whom he offered the mare for £20. At night these gentlemen found the youngster at an inn in Malton and, after conversation, were convinced he had stolen the mare and said so. This alarmed the young rascal and he bolted, leaving the mare in the stable.'[33] Robinson was eventually discovered hiding in a nearby field and arrested. Despite his young age, he was sentenced to three months in prison and five years at a reformatory. He was fortunate not to receive a more severe punishment – only a few years after the horse incident, a young man called Thomas Robinson was convicted of pilfering a pair of socks from a cottage in Stonegrave and sentenced to eighteen months' hard labour.[34]

When the Barn's horses were first put to work, in the 1850s, horse theft was a serious crime, but few farmworkers would have worried about being accused of animal brutality, however hard the beasts were made to work. Cruelty to animals, especially horses and donkeys, barely raised an eyebrow. Whether it had always been that way was a matter of debate. William Cobbett, in the 1830s, laid the blame firmly at the feet of politicians and the dislocation of the rural classes from their land:

'I should be very loth to intrust the care of my horses, cattle, sheep, or pigs, to any one whose father never had cow or pig of his *own*. It is a general complaint, that servants, and especially farm-servants, *are not so good as they used to be*. How should they? They were formerly the sons and daughters of *small farmers*; they are now the progeny of miserable property-less labourers. They have never seen an animal in which they had any interest. They are careless by habit. This monstrous evil has arisen from causes which I have a thousand times described; and which causes must now be speedily removed; or, they will produce a dissolution of society, and give us a *beginning afresh*.'[35]

While Cobbett's views were surprisingly enlightened for the time, it's hard to find an era in history when animals weren't badly treated by humans. From medieval animal trials, in which creatures were tried and executed for crimes such as murder and criminal damage, to early vivisection and blood sports, cruelty to animals has a lengthy and consistent pedigree. There had been some early forays into animal welfare. 'An Act against Plowing by the Tayle' was passed in Ireland in 1635. Since Saxon times, subsistence farmers, if they couldn't afford a harness, had attached their ploughs to the tail of the horse. The system wasn't a comfortable one for the horse, who would feel every rock or impasse as a sharp, painful tug. But the Act was a rare example of consideration being shown to animals, and few people concerned themselves with their plight. Animals were viewed as either personal chattels, no different from a plough or a piece of clothing, vermin to be controlled, or objects for entertainment and torment.

As the nineteenth century progressed, however, society saw a shift in attitudes towards animal welfare. At first, minds needed to be changed – the public had to be persuaded that animals could experience pain and suffering. Only then could lawmakers have any chance of passing effective legislation. In 1824, a group of illustrious and powerful animal welfare campaigners (including the MPs Richard Martin and William Wilberforce, and Reverend Arthur Broome) met in the deliciously named Old Slaughter's Coffee House in London to set up a new organisation, dedicated to preventing cruelty to animals.

The world's first animal charity was born and named the Society for the Prevention of Cruelty to Animals (SPCA), soon after to become the RSPCA thanks to Queen Victoria's royal stamp of approval. The charity began an enthusiastic and high-profile campaign to bring incidences of horse cruelty to light. No one was immune from criticism. In 1854 the finger of animal cruelty was pointed at an individual working for Queen Victoria herself: 'One of the worst cases was that of Mr. Robert Cheal. He is carrier to her Majesty, and it was while drawing a wagon heavily laden with wine for the royal cellar, that one of his horses was perceived in a most deplorable condition. An officer deposed to seeing the cartman, Thomas Perren, standing at the horse's head, and lashing the poor beast most unmercifully [...] The wagon was stated to have contained 54 dozen of wine, a heavy load even for a horse in good condition.'[36]

In 1883, a Stonegrave resident found himself in the RSPCA's sights. James Swales, a hawker from the village, was charged with horse cruelty by the newly formed organisation. In an attempt to escape from the police, Swales – a local menace who was regularly in trouble across the county for hare coursing, gambling, drunkenness and fighting – 'unmercifully beat and overdrove his pony, which had a large sore upon it'.[37] The RSPCA had its day in court and won, Swales being made to pay 16 shillings or face seven days in gaol. It perhaps says something about Victorian priorities that the National

Society for the Prevention of Cruelty to Children wasn't formed until 1884.

⊕

Not all horses were mistreated, of course. Farm horses, despite their tough lives, were also often the object of great affection from the men and boys charged with their upkeep. The job of a waggoner was seen as prestigious, with a defined period of apprenticeship and strict hierarchy. George Ewart Evans, who collected oral tradition in the East Anglian countryside in the middle years of the twentieth century, discovered that 'The farm revolved around the horse [...] and the care and attention which the old type of farmer and his men bestowed on his horses and on their breeding was a recognition of their importance.'[38]

Depending on the type of farm, the role of the waggoner varied in status. On a small hill farm with just two horses, the lone waggoner* may have had to chip in with other duties around the farm, while a large-scale arable venture might need as many as twenty or more large horses, and a team of waggoners, with their second- and even third- and fourth-in-commands, to manage them. Regiment and respect for order were everything. One Lincolnshire

---

* There are lots of regional variations for the job title – horseman, carter, ploughman, teamster, wagoner, waggoner, hind.

waggoner remembered: 'The waggoner would do everything first, then the second chap, then the third chap. As soon as the waggoner had put the collar on, then you could put a collar on [...] And he'd be first if you was doin' road work – you had to keep your place.'[39]

The daily routine of a waggoner and his team was a full one. Life in the moorlands of North Yorkshire, looking after horses, was a non-stop cycle of feeding, grooming, harnessing, breaking in and attending births. The waggoner's day started before that of any other labourers or servants on the farm; the 'horses were fed at 5.30am. They returned from the fields at dinner time, and afterwards a second pair was brought out. By the time they had been stabled and fed, the harness cleaned and other stock attended to, it might be 8pm. Then all the horsemen round about met at a stable and played cards or merrills* on the corn bin by candlelight.'[40]

In the early 1890s – by which time John Hickes was dead and his son George had taken up the reins – the horse was still integral to life at the Barn. Despite the ubiquity of steam engines in farming by this time, George still needed to employ a foreman, William Dennis, a waggoner, John Harwood, and

---

* Merrills, also known as 'Nine Men's Morris', is a two-player board game with counters that has been played for at least two thousand years. Like a cross between draughts and Connect 4, the aim is to get as many three-in-a-rows as possible. The Romans called it *merellus*, a slang term for 'counters', and the game was often played in impromptu settings – carved into church pews, for example, or drawn into the dust with pebbles for counters.

an under-waggoner, Arthur Dixon, all of whom lived in, above the scullery. Even though William was only twenty-six, the foreman was a position of considerable responsibility that paid a decent wage. He would have overseen the day-to-day running of the farm but also had the role of head horseman, exercising a supervisory role over the stables – providing care if the animals were sick, helping with foaling and breaking in the young horses.

The waggoner, John, was next in rank. The waggoner's role was also a respected one, and usually went to a man of experience in his twenties. In his study of horsemen in rural East Yorkshire, the historian Stephen Caunce found that the head waggoner was a heroic figure to the younger boys, and the strongest, most capable man in the stable: 'When he issued instructions, boys were expected to respond instantly, or a liberal helping of boot-toe was likely. Whenever a delivery or collection off the farm had to be made, he went, sometimes sitting up half the night to prepare the harness. The waggoner was normally the oldest and the ages of the rest conventionally reflected their positions, though a big lad, or a skilful one could advance ahead of his years at times.'[41]

Unusually, George Hickes had employed a young lad as a waggoner at the Barn; John Harwood was just seventeen and Arthur Dixon, his under-waggoner, a year younger. Whether the Barn had rising stars in its stables or George had simply employed anyone the local hiring fair could muster, however young they were, is impossible to know, but from local reports it seems good workers were getting increasingly hard to come by. The lure of industrial wages from big cities, or the promise of a new start abroad, was having a tangible effect on the numbers of rural workers seeking work at hiring fairs. Girls were also notable by their absence, especially as demand for domestic servants in towns increased. In 1890, the year George Hickes had tried his luck at Helmsley hiring fair, where he employed John and Arthur, attendance was dismal: 'Helmsley Martinmas hirings were held yesterday in dull and threatening weather, and the attendance was smaller than usual.' Reduced crowds meant that those servants and labourers who did attend could haggle their rates upwards: 'Servants were fairly well hired up. Men were £2 to £4 a head more than last year, and boys in proportion. Girls very scarce, and readily hired up.' Remarkably, the Helmsley hirings weren't seen as an unqualified disaster and were even 'an improvement on late years'.[42] The pride among horse lads, who must have been beginning to sense their value, was evident in the clothes they wore for the hirings – boys and men would don 'gaudy neckties, moleskin jackets, sometimes fastened by a length of chain, corduroy trousers slit up at the bottoms and decorated with rows of pearlies'.[43]

The arrival of the railways, as we shall see later, didn't spell the end for the draught horse. Rather, the number of horses employed in land work continued to rise; by 1900 there were still an estimated one million farm horses working in British agriculture. When the First World War broke out, in 1914, the British army had fewer vehicles in its ownership than the average suburban car dealership would have today. With just eighty motorised vehicles to its name, the army knew it would have to rely on horses not only for the cavalry but also to move guns, supplies and ammunition, and put out a call for 25,000 horses. It soon became clear that this number was a gross underestimate and urgent action was needed to impress privately owned horses and horse-drawn vehicles for the war effort. In no time, market squares across the nation were filled with working horses – requisitioned from farmers and local businesses – destined for the Western Front. Only a few miles from the Barn stands a reminder of just how central horses and horse lads were to the conflict and how many of them failed to return; the Wagoners' Memorial * in Sledmere

---

* Waggons or wagons? Most of the Northern European words for a wheeled vehicle come from the pre-Roman early Germanic *wagna*. The English corrupted the word to produce *wain*, which was in popular use until the sixteenth century, when the Dutch brought over both their own version of a four-wheeled vehicle and the corresponding word *wagen*. *Wagen* became *wagon* but was also spelled *waggon* – neither was incorrect – until the middle of the eighteenth century when *waggon* became the more common spelling in Britain and *wagon* the American version. There are, however, still regional variations – in East Yorkshire, *wagon* is still correct.

commemorates the bravery and losses of a corps set up by the local landowner, Sir Mark Sykes. During the Boer War, Sykes had witnessed at first hand the challenges of supplying an army at the front line and believed that a crack reserve team, made up of experienced waggoners drawn from his 30,000-acre estate in the Yorkshire Wolds, could be just what the country needed should hostilities break out again.

Sykes invited the War Office to come and see the waggoners in action at the annual Sledmere agricultural show; military officials were dazzled to see the men and their horses glide through tricky obstacle courses, dismantle and reassemble wheels and axles, and load and unload heavy sacks in double-quick time. By 1913, a near 1,200-strong 'waggoners unit' had been created, with each reserve being paid a retainer (a sovereign for a waggoner and two for a foreman – some called it 'the silly quid' since it seemed like payment for doing nothing[44]). The War Office soon got its money's worth; in the summer of 1914, the waggoners – many of whom were still harvesting the fields – were handed their mobilisation papers and a fortnight later found themselves on ships bound for France.

Horses suffered terribly in the trenches, and both farmers and their families grieved the loss of both a farm asset and, in some cases, a family pet. Between 1914 and 1918, around 8 million horses, mules and donkeys are thought to have been killed in the Great War. It's a staggering number and yet, remarkably, the loss of so many animals wasn't the decisive blow to horsepower that many believe. In fact, numbers of horses in British agriculture actually rose. In 1910 the country had 1.18 million working horses. Ten years later, this figure had climbed to 1.2 million.[45]

During the First World War, many of the farmers who had lost horses through requisitioning found they could buy replacements from abroad or start breeding their own. Other farmers discovered that they could pick up a bargain by repurchasing one of the thousands of battered and bruised former warhorses that flooded the market after the conflict was over. The First World War did nonetheless hasten the eventual demise of horses on farms, although this was not down to the physical numbers of horses that were lost but was the result of technological and engineering improvements that were fast-tracked during the conflict.[*] In 1917 the first mass-produced tractor – the Fordson – was introduced by America's great industrialist Henry Ford, and soon accounted for half of all global tractor sales. Machines that could do the work of a whole group of men, and their horses, filled the void left by the hundreds of thousands of agricultural workers killed or maimed at the Front. Between the 1920s and the 1960s, every decade that passed saw the number of

---

[*] After the war, the British army had gone from owning just eighty vehicles to nearly 60,000 lorries and tractors, over 20,000 light road vehicles and 7,000 ambulances.

draught horses drop, with a concomitant rise in numbers of tractors. By 1960, fewer than 100,000 horses remained in the rural workforce, compared to 500,000 shiny new tractors. Ten years later, the working horse was – to all intents and purposes – a museum piece.

Horses were also replaced as a means of personal transport. In 1900, at the Malton Agricultural Show, local MP and horse enthusiast Grant Lawson had made a stirring speech to anxious breeders, worried that a novel invention – the motor car – might jeopardise their business. The car will never catch on, he assured his assorted chums, because 'deep down in every Englishman's constitution was the germ of the desire to own a horse, and it only wanted favourable circumstances for that germ to come into active life'.[46] Only seven years later, a member of Lawson's audience, Lady Worsley of Hovingham Hall, had the peculiar privilege of being involved in one of North Yorkshire's very first car crashes, only two miles from the Barn. Lady Worsley's friend, Mr Hunter of Gilling Castle, had treated himself to the 'latest novelty' and invited his wealthy friends along for a ride. The ensuing accident even made the pages of the *Manchester Guardian*: 'While descending the steep hill leading from Gilling Castle [...] a motor-car containing five people got out of the driver's control and in the end upset. The occupants of the car were

Colonel and Mrs. Anstruther, of London; Lady Worsley, wife of Sir William Worsley, of Hovingham Hall; Mrs. Marriott, a relative of Lady Worsley; and the chauffeur. The two last-mentioned escaped with slight cuts and bruises, but Lady Worsley's wrist was broken, and Colonel Anstruther sustained severe injuries to his back.'[47]

The poop-poop, 'Toad of Toad Hall' view of the dubious driving skills of early users of the motor car was not entirely without foundation – carefree and unqualified early motorists regularly came to blows with farmers, the steady-as-she-goes drivers of horse-drawn vehicles. Only a few months after Lawson's blithe dismissal of new-fangled motor cars at the Malton Agricultural Show, Helmsley District Council was voting on whether they needed police assistance to curb the worst excesses of this new form of transport. Cars, demanded one councillor at the meeting, are 'a terror to anyone meeting them with horses. There was no warning given, and the terrific pace they travelled was appalling.'[48]

When motor cars first made their appearance on the road that passes the Barn, the few wealthy owners who drove them also seemed to take great delight in testing their vehicles to their limits. West of the Barn, where the Hambleton Hills descend to the Vale of Mowbray, the road takes travellers a long mile down the slope of Sutton Bank, one of the country's steepest escarpments. Sutton Bank has a maximum gradient of a buttock-clenching 1 in 4, plus two hairpin bends thrown in for good measure. Early motorists took the dramatic drop as a challenge, and not always with success. As early as 1899, locals despaired of the number of foolhardy drivers who had attempted the descent, despite there being a clear warning notice at the top. On one occasion, according to the *Yorkshire Herald*, 'the drivers had to get out and engage several farmers, their wives and daughters to hang back on a rope at the rear of the car during the descent. A more daring descent was made recently, when a motor car came down without the drivers getting off the boxes.'[49] These feats of bravado made Sutton Bank famous in motoring circles. In the early 1900s, the Yorkshire-based motor manufacturer Jowett Cars* had set their sights on creating the world's first affordable car – one that would run 'at a penny a mile'. By 1910, the design was established and had been tested not on a racing circuit, but up and down the western escarpment of the Hambleton Hills. The result, boasted the literature, was a 'real hill climber, making short work of such steep gradients as Sutton Bank, a notorious climb'.[50]

* A few years later, Jowett branched out into sports cars and caught the attention of early motorsport enthusiasts, including one of the country's best female racers, Victoria Worsley. Victoria began her motorsport career in 1928, when few women were behind the wheel, and she excelled in both gruelling long-distance and high-speed trials. It's not a little ironic that Victoria was the youngest daughter of Lady Worsley, who had, twenty or so years before, herself been hurtling down a hill at breakneck speed at Gilling Castle, only with less happy results.

On farms like the Barn's, the motor car made little impact until the arrival of an affordable and competent 4x4. Land Rover, the off-road car now synonymous with rural living, started life after the Second World War, when the bottom had fallen out of the market for luxury cars. Maurice Wilks had spent the war working on gas turbine engines for fighter planes. After the conflict was over, he returned to his Anglesey farm, where he would drive about in a battered old Willys Jeep, one of many that had ably served the US army during the conflict. Spare parts for the jeep were extremely difficult to get hold of in the UK, and so Wilks decided to come up with a design for a new home-grown vehicle aimed at a fresh sector of the market – farmers – and which combined the might of a tractor with the drivability of a car. In 1948, the 'Series I' Land Rover was launched, resplendent in light green aircraft paint – one of the many gluts of military surplus left over from the war. In the same year, *Autocar* magazine gushed that the 'Land Rover is a mobile power station, which will tow or do a variety of useful work on the land over rough ground. It can drive a large circular saw and cut up timber for firewood. It can be used with trailers to transport loads over ploughed fields or other hard going terrain. As a mobile power-source it takes the power to the job and, with the power-take-off, it can be harnessed to drive a threshing machine, an elevator or a chaff-cutter, draw a plough, and most other farm implements.'[51] In reality, the Land Rover didn't present any real competition to the tractor in terms of pulling power, but the versatility and robust engineering of the vehicle made it a winner with farmers. By 1951, the company had sold a quarter of a million Land Rovers and forever fixed the car as an icon of rural independence. The stables in the Barn were no longer needed. A place that had once been the hub of life at the Barn, full of the noise of whinnying and jingling, fell eerily silent.

Not all animals were as welcome on the farm as the horse. During the entire length of the Barn's life, the Hickeses and their labourers would have battled, mostly fruitlessly, against 'vermin' – the rodents, rabbits, crows, deer, pigeons, moles and other creatures who made the North Yorkshire countryside their home. It's not unusual, in stone farm buildings like the Barn, to find 'owl holes', small ventilation openings that were deliberately built into the gable end or under the eaves of granaries to attract barn owls to roost inside. The relationship between farmer and owl was one of mutual benefit – the farmer's valuable cereal grains were protected from rodents and the owl not only had somewhere warm and dry to nest but also could hunt indoors when the weather was bad.

However, few human–bird relationships were so happily symbiotic. Grain-eating birds were hunted down relentlessly, and sparrows were a particular favourite for slaughter, especially when anxieties about grain shortages were at their most acute. Children were often employed as vermin catchers, as one farmhand remembered of his childhood: 'There was sparrow-money, and rat-money. You'd git ha'penny a sparrar killed, and penny a rat-tail. Years ago, there used to be a lot o' straw stacks when they'd thrashed, and sparrars would sleep in there. And when it was gitting dusk, we used to go round with a big old sieve, and clap it on the side o' stack, and they sparrers would come out into it: then you could put your hand in and get 'em.'[52]

In the hungry last decades of the eighteenth century, just as the threshing section of the Barn was being built, bounties for sparrow killing reached their zenith, with millions of birds and their eggs destroyed. In the period of fifty years or so that straddled the end of the eighteenth century and the beginning of the nineteenth, one tiny parish alone paid out on the heads of 250,000 sparrows; 5,000 birds per year over a sustained five-decade campaign. In 1755, a book had been published that was aimed at farmers and housewives alike. *The Vermin-Killer*, which described itself as a 'compleat and necessary family book shewing a ready way to destroy', provides an exhaustive list of all the creatures that might irritate an eighteenth-century country dweller, including: 'Adders, Badgers, Birds of all sorts, Earwigs, Caterpillars, Flies, Fish, Foxes, Frogs,

Gnats, Mice, Otters, Pismires,* Pole-cats, Rabbits, Rats, Snakes, Scorpions, Snails, Spiders, Toads, Wasps, Weasles, Wants or Moles'. Some of *The Vermin-Killer*'s suggestions for how to deal with animal pests were bizarre in the extreme. For foxes, it was recommended: 'Anoint the soals of your shoes with swine's fat a little broiled, and coming from the wood, drop here and there a piece of roasted swine's liver dipt in honey, drawing after you a dead cat, and he will follow you so you may shoot him.'[53]

The widespread antipathy towards wildlife seems to have its roots in the sixteenth century, when the first English legislation targeting vermin was enacted. During the Tudor period the population of England and Wales nearly doubled, from just over 2 million to 4 million people. Greater pressure on food supplies, a series of bad harvests, price rises and tax hikes, and the increasing amount of farmland being converted to sheep pasture for wool meant that a large part of the population went hungry. In response, the government turned its attention to anything they thought might be competing with farming and food supplies. Following the 1566 Acte for the Preservation of Grayne, local parishes encouraged men, women and children to tackle the problem of 'vermin' head on; a long list of nuisance animals was drawn up, despite the fact that many of them didn't eat arable crops: 'Various bird

* An old name for ants.

species, foxes, hedgehogs, otters, moles, polecats and badgers found themselves reclassified in these unflattering terms – and with a fixed price on their heads.'[54]

Villagers were paid for each animal they killed or the eggs that they destroyed. With prices ranging from a penny for a raven to a dizzying twelve pence for a badger or a fox, it's not surprising that many an impoverished villager took to the task with gusto. Villages that failed to kill enough animals were sometimes even fined. The definition of which animals constituted vermin had little basis in fact. Hedgehogs, for example, were targeted on the false belief that they suckled milk from cows' udders and stole windfall apples by rolling over them and spearing them with their spines, while kingfishers, woodpeckers, barn owls, cranes and other benign birds with no interest in eating arable crops were also targeted.

Animal poisons were easy to obtain and so, not surprisingly, were also employed for yet darker deeds. A case of mass poisoning in Stonegrave, in 1865, was serious enough to make headline news in the London newspapers and even reached the *Sydney Morning Herald*. The Hickeses and their employees would have known the intimate details of the plot, not least because two of their farm labourers and two child workers lived in the village and walked to the Barn every day. 'WHOLESCALE POISONING OF ANIMALS' screamed the *Leeds Mercury* headline:

'A rascally business has been perpetrated a few nights ago at the village of Stonegrave, about twelve miles from Malton, where someone has strewn wholesale pieces of poisoned beef, the poison being strychnine. It is said that most of the sheep dogs in the neighbourhood, with various other animals, are poisoned. Some of the inhabitants have searched the hedges, &c., and have found many pieces of the beef, about two inches square, just such pieces as a dog would pick up and swallow off hand. Some uneasiness is felt from a belief that some of the poisoned beef was dropped into a draw well. The police are believed to have a clue to the offender.'[55]

The residents of Stonegrave, it seems, had had a narrow escape. Strychnine was used as rat poison and, in the heyday of the Barn, could be bought for a few pence over the counter. If ingested or absorbed into the skin, however, you could expect a spasmodic, frothy-mouthed death, so it was a favourite among Victorian miscreants and murderers. The middle decades of the nineteenth century were to prove the 'high-point in English criminal poisoning', with hundreds of people dying every year. *The Times* newspaper noted that England had '500 or 600 persons... die by poison every year ...; besides the cases of poisoning which are never detected.'[56] In the years leading up to the Stonegrave incident, strychnine poisonings regularly made Yorkshire headlines, including a domestic servant in South Yorkshire who had been convicted of lacing her mistress's morning tea, a Leeds husband who poisoned his wife, and a young North Yorkshire labourer's wife who murdered her elderly uncle. No doubt the free and cheap availability of poisons, many designed to tackle the growing problem of vermin in both rural and domestic settings, contributed to the grim total and allowed perpetrators to go undetected. The poisoner of Stonegrave was never caught.

Once the wheels were set in motion in the sixteenth century, the destruction of wildlife continued unabated for the next three centuries and beyond. Surges in vermin control often coincided with food shortages, failed harvests or periods of particularly low wages; poor families found they could boost their income by killing wildlife, a job that could be done by even the smallest of children. Ironically, one of the only animals not included in the Tudor Act was the rabbit; at the time the legislation was passed, rabbits were only supposed to be kept by gentlemen, in 'coney* garths' or private warrens. Wild populations existed but the explosion in rabbit numbers came during the eighteenth century with the acceleration of

* Coney was the old word for rabbit. It first appears in the English language around the thirteenth century, probably from the French *conis*, but was supplanted by 'rabbit' in the fourteenth century. The word 'rabbit' used to refer only to the young of the species but replaced 'coney' in polite society when the British started to use coney as punning slang for 'cunny', or female genitalia.

agriculture. It's a depressing irony that rabbits – which are now classed as an invasive species by farmers – proliferated largely as a result of our constant and energetic persecution of predators such as foxes and wild cats.

For more than three hundred years, parishes carried on paying for the legal destruction of wild birds and mammals; the 1566 Acte for the Preservation of Grayne was finally repealed in 1863. Unfortunately for Britain's wild bird population, that wasn't the end of the story. The Georgian obsession with vermin control was replaced with an equally ardent Victorian passion for egg collecting and avian taxidermy. Many a country home was furnished with glass cabinets and collector's drawers, filled with a dazzling array of both rare and common birds and their eggs. Collecting eggs and shooting birds offered cash-strapped rural workers a quick way of earning extra money. Egg collectors used the services of gamekeepers or other rural workers to kill birds for stuffing and to obtain specimens of their eggs; a shepherd might find himself paid as much as half a crown for a rare bird or its eggs.[57]

On the Yorkshire coast, at Bempton Cliffs just north of Flamborough Head, 'climmers' helped themselves to handfuls of seabird eggs. Men had been harvesting seabird eggs on this short stretch of cliffs since the sixteenth century, lowering themselves precariously over sheer drops on home-made harnesses. At first the eggs were eaten locally, but by the nineteenth century climmers 'quickly came to recognise the gleam in the collector's eye and their insatiable passion for particular eggs'.[58] Sam Robson, a climmer working at the beginning of the twentieth century, remembered the tussle for prized eggs:

'You went by colour a lot, for collectors' eggs: if you saw an unusually marked one, you'd take care o' that, and wait 'till these collectors came. In them days, eggs was same as coin-collecting or summat: they'd get the set, and they used to trade 'em or flog 'em. They used to come all together did collectors: you'd get as high as four or five staying in the village. It was their profession to collect eggs, and sell 'em: a lot of 'em was dealers for other collectors ... So it was more or less like an auction at the cliff top, sometimes ... It was a gamble, what they would pay: you demanded so much and they'd barter you if they could, to beat you down. We took what we could get, because we wanted rid on 'em: we didn't want eggs, we wanted money.'[59]

Pressure on the seabird numbers at Bempton increased with the arrival of the railways in the middle of the nineteenth century. When climmers weren't busy filling their baskets, down in the water holidaymakers were enjoying the new, thrilling pastime of taking potshots at seabirds from the comfort of a boat. Numbers of birds plummeted. Not only were tens of thousands of eggs being taken every year, but shooting parties, bobbing up and down in the waves, were injuring and killing birds in their droves. As the panicked seabirds took to the sky for safety, they also often nudged their eggs off the rock ledges, sending them crashing onto the rocks below. It is estimated that at the height of the egg-collecting mania, around 100,000 eggs were being taken from Bempton every year. Pressure brought to bear by campaigners in East Yorkshire, including clergy, a local MP and a group of naturalists, resulted in the passing of the Sea Birds Preservation Act of 1869. While this curbed some of the excesses of the egg-hunters, by establishing a 'closed season' that ran from 1 April until 1 August, it wasn't until the Protection of Birds Act of 1954 that seabirds enjoyed any consistent protection. By then, fewer than 10,000 eggs could be found on the ledges at Bempton Cliffs.

When the threshing barn was first built, one of its novel features was a mezzanine floor. Before that time, most threshed grain in the locality would have been kept in a villager's house.* Corn yields before the threshing barn

---

* The exception to this was the 'tithe barn', the name often given to medieval buildings where the entire tithe from a parish was stored. While some of these were genuine tithe barns, in that they stored the Church's allocation of grain, many are simply great barns designed to store the produce of a large monastery or lord's estate.

were also small. With the increase in grain production that came with enclosure and farming improvements, the rector would have needed to build somewhere to store a generous amount of grain. The mezzanine floor in the Barn would have been particularly useful; not only did it utilise an otherwise redundant space above the threshing floor but, more importantly, it protected the sacks against a new and potentially devastating creature – the brown rat, also known as the 'sewer rat'.

Since Roman times, Britain had played host to the black rat or 'ship rat', an animal that presented an irritation to anyone who farmed but rarely threatened his entire livelihood. Despite its nickname, the ship rat didn't swim willingly, it couldn't gnaw through timber, and although some nibbling was inevitable if the black rat found its way into a grain store, infestation was usually controlled by the constant vigilance of barn owls, farmyard dogs and feral cats. But in the early years of the eighteenth century, a new rat scuttled onto British shores from Baltic ships – the brown rat or 'sewer rat'. Like a commando of the rodent world, the brown rat proved not only impervious to traditional recipes for rat poison, but could also swim proficiently, eat through building materials, burrow furiously, reproduce energetically and devour grain with ardour. Any farmers who didn't quickly adapt the way they stored grain, by lifting it high off the ground, faced major losses. In 1788, William Marshall noted the gravity of the situation in North Yorkshire in his *Rural Economy of Yorkshire*: 'Should their numbers continue to increase with the same rapidity they have done since the present breed got a footing in the island, they will in no time become a serious calamity.'[60]

By the 1770s, on the country's farms, the indigenous black rat had been all but displaced by the brown rat. Farmers and landowners, including Reverend Thomas Mosley, were having to create ever more ingenious ways to protect their grain. 'In farm-homesteads situated near water,' warned William Marshall, 'it is almost impossible to keep down their numbers.' The Barn was particularly vulnerable; through its fields runs Holbeck,* a narrow brook that meanders east to west along the valley bottom. Across Ryedale, where limestone barns prevailed, the easiest solution was to build a mezzanine floor to keep the sacks aloft. In other parts of the country, with their timber-framed vernacular, wattle and daub infills on timber barns were quickly bricked up and new grain barns built on staddle stones† to raise them off the ground.

The brown rat proved indomitable. By the middle of the nineteenth century, despite the enormous effort and manpower it took to haul tons of grain to an upper storey, most granaries were being built at first-floor level. When the Barn was expanded in the 1850s, the granary was constructed

---

* In old Norse, 'Hol' refers to a hollow, 'beck' is the stream. Holbeck is the 'stream in the hollow'.

† Staddles (or steddles) are often mushroom-shaped stone or timber supports.

over the cart shed – a deliberate attempt to protect the grain from attack. The only way to access the granary was by a removable ladder, so that rats couldn't climb the rungs. A permanent set of external stone steps wasn't a good idea as it was found that brown rats could clamber up them with ease; the only way steps could work was if they were built to finish deliberately short of the granary door, or with a gap between free-standing steps and the barn wall, so rats couldn't make the last daring leap. Many a desperate farmer even built a dog kennel into the granary steps to house a keen ratter or knocked a cat hole through one of the barn doors.

For an animal that now outnumbers humans on the planet by a ratio of three to one, chickens have spent most of their lives living in relative obscurity. And although the bird now constitutes 23 of the 30 billion of the world's current population of livestock, until the early twentieth century, most farmers – including the Hickeses – wouldn't have given chickens a second glance.

Chickens were viewed, primarily, as 'women's work', a way for the farmer's wife to earn a little pin money or boost the kitchen's store cupboard. In fact, poultry were so ignored as a potential profit-maker for the eighteenth- and nineteenth-century farm that, when Tuke carefully penned his 'Livestock' chapter in his *General View of the Agriculture of the North Riding*, he missed them out entirely. Fifty years on and the situation remained unchanged. 'On most farm houses', explained one mid-nineteenth-century how-to book on British husbandry, 'there is but indifferent accommodation for poultry, as the rearing of a greater number than can subsist by picking up waste grain is considered unprofitable by those farmers whose wives will not be at the trouble of carrying them to market.'[61]

The Barn was no different. John Hickes's wife, Jane, would have kept a small clutch of chickens, with their coop placed near the kitchen door for convenience. Jane's hens would have kept her six children in fresh eggs, but throughout the nineteenth century, few male farmers viewed poultry as a serious business concern, either as meat birds or layers. The idea of eating chicken wasn't unusual – it just wasn't particularly economic.* Birds were more useful as egg layers – and only eaten when that function was exhausted or, in the case of cockerels, non-existent. Chickens were a quaint bonus to the family coffers – as one land agent noted in 1899: 'The busy farmer himself pays

---

* The practice of keeping chickens for reasons other than eating them is not new. Evidence suggests that they came across to Britain sometime around 500 BC but may have been kept initially as fighting birds or status symbols, or as a focus for worship, rather than a fine roast dinner. When Julius Caesar scribbled down his thoughts about Iron Age tribes in *De Bello Gallico*, he noted: 'The Britons consider it contrary to divine law to eat the hare, the chicken, or the goose. They raise these, however, for their own amusement and pleasure.'

little attention as a rule to the feathered tribe, but a thrifty wife knows too well the profit attached to them.'

Indeed, poultry-keeping was seen as such a trifling 'feminine' pursuit that many middle-class women were encouraged to keep a few chickens as an amusing and wholesome pastime. *Farming for Ladies*, published in 1844, implored women of high standing to embrace the habits of their rural sisters and rise with the larks to feed their hens. Keeping chickens would not only, it seemed, provide fresh eggs every morning but, importantly, keep moral slips and temptations at bay: 'Active habits are the great means of health; and among these, early rising is one of the greatest. To a man of business it is indispensable; and to the mistress of the family it is equally important. Independently of the health, and consequent longevity which it almost invariably ensures, the contrary system, of indulgence in bed, destroys that elastic vigour which should brace the nerves to all the purposes of our being.'[62]

One of the barriers to commercial success was that raw chicken, unlike fattier meats such as beef and pork, didn't lend itself to smoking or salting and so didn't keep or travel well. The chickens that scratched around in the dust at the Barn would have also been lean and scrawny birds, with little meat to speak of and a weight of less than half that of a modern breed. If rural folk wanted to eat poultry, their preference was goose, not chicken; geese were traditionally bred to be eaten at two times of the year: in early summer when they were very young or, more commonly, in winter when the birds had spent the entire summer and early autumn foraging on the same wheat fields picked over by the gleaners. Indeed, many people believed that goose was only good to eat once the first frosts had arrived and the bird had had a chance to develop a generous layer of post-harvest body fat.

Commercial broiler chickens – birds bred specifically for meat production– only took off in the early twentieth century with the advent of widespread refrigerated transport. Hens usually stop laying in winter but the development of all-year-round hybrid breeds, and the introduction of artificially lit sheds, ensured a 365-day supply of eggs. Chickens also need natural light to synthesise Vitamin D – keeping large numbers of birds indoors wasn't possible until chemists worked out how to fortify chicken feed with vitamins and antibiotics. Once they'd achieved that, our feathered friends could look forward to a future of cramped, windowless living and burgeoning body weights.

It's interesting that the Hickeses didn't attempt to become sheep farmers. Wool had made medieval Yorkshire rich beyond its wildest dreams and many of the monasteries close to the Barn – Rievaulx, Byland, Kirkham – had made a roaring success of the business of growing, shearing and selling sheep fleeces. On a smaller scale, villagers also kept sheep for their own use. A handful of beasts, grazing on common land in rotation, would have provided a family with wool, milk, manure and, when the sheep were no longer productive, delicious mutton.

As the eighteenth century progressed, business-minded agriculturalists turned their sights towards farming sheep for meat. In the same way that he had supersized cattle, livestock breeder Robert Bakewell transformed the Leicester sheep into a behemoth of mutton, taking a sleepy, long-woolled relic from Roman occupation and mutating it into an early-maturing, rapid-weight-gaining icon of modern sheep breeding. This new propensity for fast body growth, combined with more generous feeding regimes, resulted in 'improved sheep' ballooning to nearly three times their original size – records from Smithfield Market in London, the destination for much of the country's meat, showed that between 1710 and 1790 the average sheep carcasses swelled from 13 kilograms to 37 kilograms.[63]

Bakewell's prize rams were monstrously expensive to hire out for breeding, and way beyond the reach of a typical, modest farm. In 1780, most of Bakewell's rams had cost under ten guineas to lease for a season. But by 1786, Bakewell was making £1,000 from hiring out just twenty rams, and three years later he could command 3,000 guineas for a mere ten of his best.[64] In Nunnington, one of the Barn's closest villages, the agricultural improver and local landowner Edward Cleaver (the same man who had been the first to buy a threshing machine) had been lucky enough to get hold of some of Bakewell's Leicestershire breeding stock: 'We have been endeavouring for sixteen or seventeen years', Cleaver noted in 1800, 'to get as much Leicestershire as we can. The first cross I made, with a mixture between the Tees-Water and Leicestershire, advanced my stock 12s. per head in one year.[65] For Cleaver, his society connections and deep pockets allowed him to improve the value of his sheep from 32 shillings to 45 shillings in one year alone – an increase of nearly 30 per cent. Just a few years later, the Leicester breed had caught the attention of another successful farmer, John Reed, in Stonegrave, who soon perfected the art of 'fattening up'. The weight gains achieved beggar belief; writing about one ram under John Reed's care, a local journalist was astonished to note: 'On the 19th of March he was first weighed, and again on the 7th May, being an interval of seven weeks, during which time he gained 3st. 7lb.'[66] The poor ram continued to be stuffed to the eyeballs and by July weighed a mighty 30 stone (190 kg), but, as the writer took great pains to note, 'remained remarkable active'.[*]

Great things clearly awaited the Stonegrave sheep with

---

[*] To give you a comparison, 70 kg (11 st) is considered a large sheep by modern standards.

a hearty appetite – he was quickly snapped up at the local agricultural show by an eminent breeder from Devonshire and whisked off to spend a season of unfettered mating in the south-west. 'Improved breeding' made celebrities of animals and, crucially, consolidated the family fortunes and social standing of the few farmers lucky enough to buy into the idea. Our Stonegrave ram-feeder, John Reed, soon became a skilled breeder of both pure-bred Leicester sheep and Shorthorn cattle, the two pin-ups of the nineteenth-century improver. Reed also became a key member of local society; by the time of his death in 1864, John had also held the position of High Constable for Ryedale for nearly half a century. High farming had many rewards.

4

YAN MUD AS GOOD STOP AT YAM

YAN MUD AS GOOD STOP AT YAM
You might as well stay at home

In late spring, sparrows sit in the gutters above the cart shed and shout at each other across the orchard. The Barn's walls are rich with crevices, which the birds stuff tight with hay. There's also a thick quince hedge growing up along one of the walls, which makes a good second choice for a nest when all the limestone gaps have been taken. Few things bother the sparrows sitting on their speckled eggs; for most of the time, the cart shed is still. It's an artist's studio now and a quiet one at that.

The constant clatter of metal-rimmed wheels and clinking harnesses would have been a familiar sound in this corner of the Barn. It's a lovely, dry spot – the cart shed's open doors are sheltered from the weather and face directly east. The waggoners and horse lads – who always rose with the larks, before everyone else – would have seen the sun rise and watch it move across the top of the farmhouse before their first bite of breakfast.

Once the horses were hitched, the cart could set off for the day. When the grass grows in one of the far fields, its differing heights reveal the line of an old track heading out into the valley. Layers of compacted earth, topped with broken limestone, have left a shallow causeway along which the sheep faithfully wander back and forth. To gather any crops on the sloping fields, however, or to join the main road, the horses and cart would have had to brace themselves for an uphill pull. I'm not sure which would have been worse – the slow heave upwards with sacks of grain, or the coming back down, hooves skidding under the weight of a cart full of limestone.

A good deal of farming, even today, is about moving great quantities from one place to the next. Whether it's dragging muck-loads of manure onto the fields, bringing the harvest home, spreading fertiliser, taking produce to market, collecting feed for livestock, or visiting other farms, the ability to get places has always mattered. When the Barn was extended in the 1850s, the construction of a cart shed would have been critical to the success of the rector's venture into modern farming. It also went on to house what was the second most important farm asset after the horses in the stables – the Hickeses' wheeled transport.*

* Carts have two wheels, waggons have four. They both made their first

For the farmer, two-wheeled carts were the ultimate zippy vehicle – the equivalent of a small runabout car. Their diminutive size and carrying capacity made them ideal for short distances both around the farm and in the fields, and for trotting into town. If the cart needed to increase its capacity, say at harvest time, temporary  'ladders' or wooden side panels could be added. With just two wheels, and one horse (or mule or ox) needed to pull it, the cart was cheap, quick to harness and very manoeuvrable. Even as late as the 1950s, carts were a common sight in the countryside around the Barn. They were also central to the farming community, not only in a practical sense, but also by being part of the cultural vocabulary of rural life. The 'bridewain', for example, was a key part of the marriage pact from medieval times up until the late nineteenth century. The father of a bride-to-be provided his daughter with a bridewain, a cart full of all the chattels and domestic bits and bobs a new home would need. As the cart trotted from the daughter's family home to her new marital home,

appearance in the Middle East around 3500 BC and quickly trundled across Europe and Russia via trade and contact between different cultures. It's not clear which came first – the waggon or the cart – but they had slightly different uses and so, logically, probably developed side by side.

neighbours gathered in the lanes to wish her well and added gifts of their own as it drove past.

Waggons were for larger loads – the HGV of the pre-combustion era. A section of the eleventh-century Bayeux Tapestry shows a four-wheeled waggon, loaded with wine and weapons, being laboriously dragged along by two men. However, while we can safely assume that four-wheeled transport has been in Britain for a thousand years, it's not clear how useful it was for the ordinary farmer. Early waggons had issues with their turning circles; the short distance between the front wheels and the body of the waggon was often so small that the waggons needed large areas to turn around in. It wasn't until improvements in the design of the front axle, in the seventeenth century, that the waggon could really come into its own. Large corn-producing arable farms tended to keep waggons, but farmers like the Hickeses, with their modest mixed farm, would have managed perfectly well with two-wheeled carts. Even if the Hickeses had wanted a waggon, the steep slope up and out of the farm and onto the main road into town would have made life extremely difficult for horses pulling a full load.

The fact that the Barn's cart shed has three bays doesn't necessarily mean that the Hickeses had three carts. The open-fronted building also stored farm implements, such as ploughs, and perhaps a pony trap – a sporty two-wheeled, two-person carriage perfect for smaller horses. One or two of the cart shed's bays may have also had doors to keep their contents dry. Under the tenancy of the Hickeses, the Barn also had its own small smithy. The blacksmith would have been called upon to reshoe the horses, repair harnesses and mend tools but also make running repairs to any of the Hickeses' wheeled vehicles. It's telling that Stonegrave and Hovingham had three blacksmiths between them, and Helmsley had a further four, plus two wheelwrights. There was clearly plenty of work to go around.[*]

Cart sheds were always built near the stables, to make harnessing up easier, and were often orientated so neither horse nor cart had to wheel through a muck-filled fold yard to get out. The cart shed at the Barn is no different and sits right next to the farm track, giving the driver easy access to the fields and up the steep slope to the main road. Above the cart shed is the granary. As we already know, first-floor grain storage was a necessity for the Victorian farmer, but its position above the cart shed added an extra layer of convenience. As with many cart-shed-granaries of its age, the Barn still has openings in its wooden first floor – these allowed sacks of grain to be dropped directly into the cart

---

[*] Up until the First World War, most villages had their own wheelwright or blacksmith – when not making and repairing wheeled vehicles, they would turn their hands to other projects such as hurdles, tool handles, gates, house repairs, even coffin-making. Some wheelwrights worked alongside blacksmiths, others combined the two skills, but with the rise of motorised transport in the twentieth century demand for both crafts began to wane.

below and whisked off to market. Whether the cart would make it there intact was a different matter.

At four o'clock on a December afternoon in 1879, across the Barn's quiet valley the light was fading as a young servant girl named Beatley Richardson set off from her master's house to post a letter. The journey was a short one – just two miles from Cawton hamlet to Gilling village – but not long into her walk Beatley was offered a lift. Hezekiah Coates, groom to the local vicar, invited Beatley to join him on his horse-drawn cart and she climbed up.

Two hours later, the young girl had not returned and neither Coates nor his cart were anywhere to be seen. A farm servant and friend of Beatley's was dispatched on horseback, in the dark, to find her, and on his way to Gilling he met two other men, who had been sent out to locate the groom. The three of them searched the entire length of the track and finally, only a few yards from Cawton, they located the cart, upside down in the ditch that ran alongside. Holding his lantern towards the upturned vehicle, one of the men saw to his horror that young Beatley lay trapped underneath the shaft. The cart had landed on her neck and killed her. Two hundred yards away, Coates was also discovered – alive but unconscious.

What should have been a simple journey had turned into a tragedy. Somewhere along the way, the horse had been spooked by something and - with the track being so uneven and poorly maintained - the cart had been flipped like a coin, trapping the poor servant girl underneath. Beatley wasn't killed instantly and, according to Coates's later testimony, he was in the process of trying to free her when the horse headbutted him. Badly dazed, Coates had set off to raise the alarm but lost his way in a field and then passed out. Rumours flew that Coates had been drunk at the time - two witnesses swore they had seen him stumble out of the Stonegrave inn - the wonderfully named 'Wings of Liberty' - a little 'fresh', earlier in the day. The pub, it seems, had a dubious reputation - only a few years back, its landlord had been charged[1] and found guilty of keeping a disorderly house* - but in the end, Coates was found not guilty. In the case of the fatal accident of December 1879, while Coates was slapped on the wrist for not exerting 'himself sufficiently to rescue the deceased', the jury settled for a verdict of accidental death. As an afterthought, they also suggested that someone might fence off the track from the ditch.

Accidents like these were commonplace on the tracks and

---

* The crime was a serious one: in English criminal law, for a landlord to be found guilty of running a 'disorderly house' the conduct of the people drinking there has to be so bad as to constitute a public nuisance, outrage public decency, or be deemed corrupt or depraved.

roads that connected the Barn to local villages and towns. William Marshall, writing a hundred years before the Cawton accident, had despaired at the state of the county's roads and the dangers they posed to the unsuspecting traveller. In an almost prescient rant, he had warned: 'But who possessed of common prudence would rise upon the tender brink of an unguarded ditch?'[2] Or, as a local might have said in the dialect of the area: 'Yan mud as good stop at yam' – you might as well stay at home.

It's almost impossible to overstate just how terrible most of Britain's roads were until well into the late nineteenth century and, in some cases, even the twentieth, especially in rural areas. Before the early eighteenth century, the responsibility for road construction and maintenance belonged to individual parishes. The Highways Act 1562 required that parishioners had to give six days' free labour every year to help look after their own local roads, and that two 'honest persons' should be elected to supervise the work. Every person's commitment to road maintenance was based on a rough sliding scale of affordability – the rural peasant might just give his labour, while the lord of the manor would be expected to loan the use of his carts and offer extra labour. It was a good idea in principle, but the reality often fell far short – only fifteen years after the 1562 Act, clergyman William Harrison, in his *Description of England*, observed that 'the rich do so cancel their portions and the poor so loiter in their labours that of all the six, scarcely two good days' work are performed'.[3]

There was no real incentive to make roads any more than rough tracks. One of the most obvious flaws with parochial maintenance was that parishes couldn't impose charges on people who used the road but hadn't helped to maintain them. Through traffic, on its way to market towns and cities, caused significant wear and tear to a road – rural villages on the routes into these busy areas would have to stump up the costs of road maintenance and see little benefit in return, apart from perhaps the owner of the local inn. At other times, locals had to put up with nuisance neighbours obstructing ancient rights of way. One now lost medieval village called Thornthorpe, not far from the Barn, had trouble with the antisocial antics of John Boneyfayth in the 1360s. Not content with letting his cows constantly trample over other people's crops, Boneyfayth had wilfully blocked up the road with two pairs of gates and a wall. In case any parishioners felt bold enough to try to pass through the gates, the bloody-minded Boneyfayth had also parked his carts in front. No one had dared tackle Boneyfayth and his obstruction, for fear of retribution from his extended and, by all accounts, an alarmingly unpleasant family.[4] Similar incidents throughout the centuries demonstrated the problem of maintaining long-established rights of access.

Most people had, for centuries, travelled on foot and many goods were carried by packhorses or donkeys following packhorse trails. Many of these were informal trackways, little more than trampled pasture. The land around the Barn, however, has a rare survivor of a more permanent type of walkway – the 'trod'. Kirby Bank Trod is a remarkably well-preserved, half-kilometre stretch of paved footpath thought to have been constructed in the twelfth or thirteenth century by the monks at nearby Rievaulx Abbey. These stone-flagged paths are thought to have once criss-crossed the region, covering long distances and linking farms to farms, settlements to settlements and built by abbeys to exploit their far-flung holdings. The amount of time it would have taken to lay miles of heavy York stone flags – most of them around half a metre across and around 15 centimetres thick – is testament to the wealth and manpower available to medieval landholders such as Rievaulx.

Meat was moved while it was still alive – cattle, sheep and geese with tarred feet were walked to market along drovers' roads. And while horses and oxen were asked to pull carts and waggons, they would often find rutted road surfaces and quagmires scuppered their progress. In winter, many roads and tracks simply became impassable.

Personal travel was no more comfortable. The waspish historian Edward Gibbon described an excruciating journey to see his surgeon in 1794 along the rough tracks of rural East Sussex. He complained he was 'almost killed between Sheffield Place and East Grinstead by hard, frozen, long, and cross ruts that would disgrace the approach to an Indian wigwam'.[5] The wretched author of *The Decline and Fall of the Roman Empire* was certainly not exaggerating his levels of physical discomfort; he had been bounced along the trackways of the Sussex Weald while suffering from a chronic and agonisingly extreme case of scrotal swelling. He concluded, no doubt with tears in his eyes, 'I reached this place half dead [...] What an effort! Adieu, til l Thursday or Friday.'[6] The poor man expired a week later.

Even the shortest journeys over ancient tracks needed careful planning. 'What a time people took formerly in travelling over old roads!' wrote the Devon-based priest, hymn-writer, antiquarian and astoundingly prolific author Sabine Baring-Gould in his *Old Country Life*, in 1889. 'There is a house just two miles distant from mine, by the new unmapped road. Before 1837, when that road was made, it was reached in so circuitous a manner, and by such bad lanes, and across an unbridged river, that my grandfather and his family when they dined with our neighbours, two miles off, always spent the night at their house.'[7] Near the Barn, roads were so flooded over winter that there was little chance of any post getting through. Worse still, some of those who tried to navigate the tracks perished in the attempt. Local roads might go through periods of passability, followed by years of neglect, all depending on how much energy a parish could muster to keep its tracks in a decent state; in 1609, the North

Riding justices were so irritated by the poor state of the Barn's road that they took Stonegrave parish and its rector to task. The judgement confirmed 'that beyond living memory this had been a highway for cart and carriage, yet the inhabitants of Stonegrave were mending it only enough for a horse way'.[8]

As trade gathered pace in the late seventeenth century, the need for decent roads to carry both long-distance travellers and waggons became cripplingly apparent. The transportation of goods and raw materials to and from places of industry was being stymied, especially that most essential of fuels, coal; 2 million tonnes of it were being moved around Britain, often in deeply frustrating circumstances. Relying on local populations to maintain an increasingly national network just wasn't working. Parliament decided it was time to legislate and passed the 1706 Turnpike Act. It allowed private enterprise, in the form of trusts, to build and maintain roads in return for charging users a toll. Each turnpike trust would nominate a board of trustees – usually local gentry, clergy and businessmen. And while the trusts were, in principle, not-for-profit, the trustees could expect indirect benefits from the roads, such as lower transport costs or increased rental income in villages along the route.

London's radial routes were quickly turnpiked and a few decades later, in the period between 1750 and 1772, 'Turnpike

Mania' took hold and newly formed trusts covered more than 11,500 miles of road across the country. By 1840, around a thousand turnpike trusts had created 20,000 miles of road, drastically improving both travel times and the cost of moving goods.[9] In 1750 it took ten days to travel by stagecoach from Edinburgh to London* and, because of the state of the roads, the average speed of the journey was a painstaking five miles an hour, not much quicker than a brisk walk. By 1775, thanks to the introduction of turnpiked roads, the journey between the English and Scottish capitals had shrunk to four days and by 1840, on the eve of the railway revolution, just forty hours. National perceptions of distance would never be the same again.

One of the most important, and unlikely, heroes of this period of road engineering was a North Yorkshireman. John Metcalf was born in 1717 to a poor family in nearby Knaresborough, a market town about 30 miles south-west of the Barn. At the age of six, he contracted smallpox, which left him totally blind. Undeterred, Metcalf proved himself worthy of the pages of a *Boy's Own* adventure story: by the age of fourteen he had learned to swim and was being paid to retrieve drowned corpses from the River Nidd; at fifteen he was playing the fiddle professionally, horse-trading and

---

* Stagecoaches were so called because the journey had to be broken up into small stages, perhaps ten or twenty miles at a time; each stop would need a change of horses.

cockfighting; and by his late twenties Metcalf had joined the Yorkshire Blues, a provincial corps, during the Jacobite Rebellion. Most impressive, though, was his knowledge of local roads and horse travel, experienced only through sounds and memory. From the age of twelve, 'Blind Jack' was guiding nervous travellers along North Yorkshire roads on horseback and later ran a business hiring out horse-drawn coaches and carrying goods. His knowledge of the state of local tracks was unsurpassed and so, with no previous experience, Metcalf – with typical Yorkshire 'brass neck' – decided to bid for the contract to build a three-mile section of turnpike road between Ferrensby and Minskip on the Harrogate to Boroughbridge road in North Yorkshire. Metcalf had his critics, but he was an instinctive engineer who used sound methods – his road had a strong foundation and a cambered surface to allow water to drain off – and soon other contracts poured in from Yorkshire and beyond. In the end, between 1765 and 1792, 'Blind Jack' Metcalf built around 180 miles of turnpikes across Yorkshire and Lancashire and is credited as one of the fathers of the modern road.

Turnpikes, however, only usually covered busy arterial routes. At their height they snaked along only one-fifth of the entire road network and most minor roads were still maintained at a parish level. A new building, landslide, fallen tree or flood might divert the course of an old road, while road maps were often worse than useless. Reverend Sabine

Baring-Gould, who penned such Victorian flock-pleasers as 'Onward, Christian Soldiers', was indignant to discover a group of young boys accidentally trespassing: 'One day I found school-boys in my walled garden eating my Bon-chretien pears. I ordered them off, threatening them with vengeance. "Please, sir, we did not know we were doing wrong. On the map we saw that this was a high-way, and we thought we were at liberty to take anything that grows on the road." Bad maps and over-education had robbed me of my Bon-chretien pears.'[10]

Many people also felt aggrieved at suddenly having to pay to use a track that had, for centuries, been free of charge. The road that runs past the Barn is undoubtedly an ancient one – it has been in use at least since medieval times but is perhaps even older, especially given that it cuts directly through Saxon Stonegrave and Roman Hovingham. In 1768, in the grip of 'Turnpike Mania', the great and good of the region established a 20-mile-long turnpike between York and Oswaldkirk, a village only a mile west from the Barn. The trustees read like a *Who's Who* of the landed nobility of the area, peppered with wealthy merchants and clergy, including Laurence Sterne, local vicar and author of the wonderfully peculiar novel *The Life and Opinions of Tristram Shandy, Gentleman*. Initially, the York and Oswaldkirk turnpike road was considered a success and so, emboldened, in 1786 the Trust decided to extend the turnpike to include a section of the Barn's main road. The threshing barn had just been built and Reverend Thomas Mosley suddenly faced new road tolls if he wanted to take a cart of produce west along the main road. 'A petition of several Gentlemen, Freeholders and others' was hastily sent to Parliament, complaining that the Trust unfairly 'stopped up part of the ancient course of the said road' and was demanding money from anyone who wanted to pass. They continued: 'The inhabitants [...], although they make use of the road so taken under the care of the said trustees for the space of only about 480 yards, are charged at the said turnpike with tolls for their cattle, and with the like tolls for their carriages, as persons who pass the whole extent of the said road (which is upwards of twenty miles).'[11]

Locals had every right to be worried. It now cost one shilling every time someone needed to drive a herd of twenty cattle (about £4.50 in today's money) through the short stretch of road and one shilling and six pence (about £6.50) for a waggon and four horses or oxen. Anyone wanting to drive a coach and six horses along the 480-yard stretch was stung for three shillings (a hefty £13). In the end, local residents took the Trust to court and remarkably, given who ran the Trust, they won. The Trust was also ordered to take down the toll gate and demolish the toll booth, and to move the whole operation several miles back down the original route towards York. Thanks to local vigilance, future farming families, including the Hickeses, would be allowed to travel to and from market without having to put their hands in their pockets.

Trusts were also accused of corruption and failure to maintain the roads, despite the hefty tolls being charged. The York-Oswaldkirk Trust sacked three of its own surveyors for dishonesty or incompetence. In 1829, Reverend Sydney Smith – wit, cleric and one of the turnpike trustees – wrote a bitter resignation letter to his fellow turnpike colleague Jonathan Gray. His cheerful tone barely disguised the frustrations of his tenureship; the Reverend wished for the prosperity of the road and for the committee all the things that had clearly been in short supply:

'Nobody can more sincerely wish the prosperity of the road from York to Oswaldkirk than I do. I wish you hard materials, diligent trustees, gentle convexity, fruitful tolls, cleanly gutters, obedient parishes, favouring justices and every combination of fortunate circumstances which can fall to the lot of any human highway. These are my wishes, but I can only wish [...] Perhaps you will have the goodness to scratch my name out of the list of trustees [...] I shall think on the 15th of my friends at the White Bear, Stillington. How honourable to English gentlemen that once or twice every month half the men of fortune of England are jammed together at the White Bear, crushed into a mass at the Three Pigeons, or perspiring intensely at the Green Dragon!'[12]

It was fortunate that the kerfuffle caused by the Oswaldkirk toll booth and turnpike did not end in bloodshed. Across the country, turnpikes were a cause of deep resentment, with farmers and other rural dwellers up in arms at the high fees being levied on routine journeys. In West Yorkshire, residents had violently opposed the new turnpikes, including one on the Harewood estate, home to Lord Lascelles, but the most famous of all the turnpike incidents were the Rebecca Riots, a series of attacks between 1839 and 1843 on the toll roads of West Wales. The protestors were impoverished farmers and other rural workers, disgruntled at the financial burden being placed on them, not only by the road tolls but also the high farm rents from wealthy landlords and punitive tithes demanded by the Church. And while the harvests of 1837 and 1838 were dire across Britain, the following two years saw wet weather and failed crops hit western parts of Wales even harder. The relationship between Welsh growers and the gentry, many of whom were also turnpike trustees, was at an all-time low. Small tenant farmers felt the force of the tolls more acutely than anyone, especially if they had to travel on a road that was owned by several different, consecutive trusts. Anyone wanting to transport grain or livestock to Carmarthen, for example, had to run the rapids of eleven different turnpike trusts, each charging its own toll. It was said that the cost of fetching a waggon load of lime, which farmers needed to fertilise their fields, cost ten times as much in road tolls as it did in raw materials.

The Rebecca Rioters' strategy was unusual. During an attack, the men would dress up in women's clothes, wearing masks or with blackened faces. Burly farmers, clad in frilly petticoats and pretty bonnets, called themselves 'Rebecca and her daughters', a biblical allusion from Genesis – 'may your offspring possess the gates of their enemies' (Gen. 24:60). One man would play Rebecca, the others her followers. In the dead of night, the group would approach toll gates and begin a dramatic pantomime. Rebecca would turn to the assembled masses and ask, 'What is this my children? There is something in my way. I cannot go on.'[13] And with this, the toll gates would be smashed to great cheers. While the image of men dressed in drag now raises a wry smile, the symbolism wouldn't have gone amiss on local villagers. *Ceffyl pren* (wooden horse) was already a well-established rural practice, a kind of mock trial where locals accused of domestic violence or infidelity were paraded up and down the village lashed to a ladder or pole (*riding the stang** was North Yorkshire's version of this

---

* Riding the stang was medieval in origin, and was meted out to husbands and wives who had mistreated their partners or been unfaithful. The 'stang' was the pole and the humiliation was carried out in one of a number of ways: an effigy of the adulterer was sometimes tied to the pole and carried around the village before being burned; if they were really unlucky, the guilty party would be tied to the pole and dragged around the village; or sometimes the

public punishment). To add to the humiliation, the rest of the men in the village would accompany the 'wooden horse' dressed up in women's clothes and paint their faces black, to symbolise a 'world gone awry'.[14] Rebecca and her daughters would have appealed to the notion of commoners taking the law into their own hands, a way of delivering rough justice in a pantomime of resistance when the system had failed them.

Unlike the Swing Riots in England, just a decade earlier, the Rebecca Riots are considered – by modern historians – to have been an effective protest. The 1844 *Report of the Commissioners of Inquiry for South Wales*, which was established to look into the reasons behind the riots, found that the turnpikes and their mismanagement, along with the crippling tithes and other government fees, had precipitated the unrest. As a result of the report, tolls on lime were cut by half, and other tolls standardised to reduce profiteering. County Road Boards were also set up nationally to take control from the private turnpike trusts.

The quality of turnpike roads varied enormously. Nearly a century after the first Turnpike Act, the condition of most of the tracks around the Barn was still treacherous. In 1799, when the threshing barn was in full swing, Tuke wrote a blistering criticism of the local roads: 'the parochial roads

pole was carried by two men with the 'stangmaster' sitting upon it, banging a pan and shouting a rhyme that detailed the crime.

are in as bad a state as possible: good materials are scarce in some districts, but care and attention, much more so in them all. Many of these roads are built upon the natural soil, and in winter not passable without great danger and difficulty, if passable at all. No part of England produces worse roads, either turnpike or parochial.'[15] One of the problems was that the materials for constructing turnpikes were starting to run out. Much of the easily available local stone had been used up in the first flurry of road building and contractors were having to resort to dragging materials from long distances across the North York Moors or grabbing redundant stone from historic ruins. A good deal of building stone from Marton Priory, a glorious twelfth-century monastery ten miles south-west of the Barn, for example, was pilfered to provide foundations for the York–Oswaldkirk turnpike. Tuke also despaired of local engineers who, instead of taking a slightly longer but less steep route around a hill, insisted on driving a road over the top. While the 'straight line afforded little inconvenience to a carriage scarcely bigger or heavier than a one-horse cart,' he complained, it 'is an almost insurmountable obstacle to a modern broad-wheeled waggon'. He went on: 'A striking instance of this want of attention, or knowledge, is exemplified in a turnpike-road carried across the moors, from Saltergate to Whitby, where, for above eight miles, the road is one continued steep ascent.'[16] Any horses that did attempt the long pull must have only been fit for the knacker's yard by the time they reached the coast.

✻

Forty years later, little had changed. Charlotte Brontë's *Jane Eyre*, published in 1847 and set partly in North Yorkshire, described a 50-mile journey taking from six o'clock in the morning until well after nightfall. 'I remember but little of the journey; I only know that the day seemed to me of a preternatural length, and that we appeared to travel over hundreds of miles of road. We passed through several towns, and in one, a very large one, the coach stopped; the horses were taken out, and the passengers alighted to dine [...] Here I walked about for a long time, feeling very strange, and mortally apprehensive of some one coming in and kidnapping me; for I believed in kidnappers, their exploits having frequently figured in Bessie's fireside chronicles.'

Passengers like Jane had every reason to fear kidnap and highwaymen. While the eighteenth century had been the 'heyday' of the highwayman, robbers on horseback still plagued parts of rural North Yorkshire well into the nineteenth century. The crime had burgeoned in the eighteenth century – the country was rapidly expanding in both long-distance trade and population but had little in the way of an effective local police force. A stagecoach's painfully slow pace made it a sitting duck, and once the crime had been committed the highwayman could easily dissolve, with a clatter of hooves, into the wilderness. Turnpikes, with their toll booths and closed gates, drastically reduced the amount of getaway robberies on major routes, but rural tracks and the people who travelled on them remained fair game across the country. Every county had had its dazzlingly brazen horse-riding delinquents. Dick Turpin, who was found guilty and hanged in York, was undoubtedly Yorkshire's most famous, but others also tried their luck. A now almost unknown North Yorkshire highwayman – George Cutterman – was still riding high in 1815. While the details of his exploits are largely lost, it seems he swashbuckled his way to the last; after being caught and taken by coach to York for prosecution, he somehow managed to cajole his hapless guards into removing his handcuffs. Freed from his shackles, Cutterman sprang from the vehicle and disappeared into the night, never to be seen again.

Fortunately, roads weren't the only means of getting produce or people around. As Tuke noted at the end of the eighteenth century: 'nature had afforded the North Riding navigable water on half, at least, of its circumference.'[17] The River Rye meanders close to the Barn but, for most of its length, is neither navigable nor safe. It zigzags, like an amusing drunk, taking a delightfully long time to cover any ground. As the crow flies, the distance from the Barn to Helmsley, the closest market town, is about four and a half miles – if you attempted to paddle there on the Rye, it'd be more like ten.

The Rye is also petulant. Significant breaches over the decades have left farms flooded and fields wrecked. On one particularly memorable occasion, on Bonfire Night in 1754, the river burst its banks with such ferocity that it made headline news. A Helmsley woman, who was sick and bedbound, was carried half a mile downstream until she, and the bed, came to rest in a farmer's field. The same night, fourteen haystacks were washed a mile down the river, with a six-month-old cow balanced precariously on top of one of the stacks. To everyone's amazement, the calf kept its footing, albeit wobbly, and was lifted off alive at the other end.[18]

Farmers with an interest in transporting goods by river also had to contend with the other people who relied on the river. Millers, for example, often erected weirs to drive their waterwheels, while fishermen used all manner of ingenious static structures to direct and trap fish, all of which made progress by boat impossible.

If a local farmer could manage to get his produce to the larger town of Malton, 12 miles east of the Barn, he could join up with the River Derwent. The Derwent had been carrying goods for hundreds, if not thousands of years, albeit intermittently. Some of York's most ancient buildings, and parts of Roman Malton, are thought to have been built using blocks quarried in the Howardian Hills and floated either up or downstream.[19] Rivers are changeable beasts, however. They can silt up, drop their levels, alter their route, even dry up – and so for any kind of consistent travel arrangements, a river often needs improving and maintaining.

At the same time as turnpike trusts were busy trying to upgrade Britain's woeful roads, other Acts of Parliament sought to allow for some kind of strategic river improvement; after all, a horse-drawn boat could carry many more times the load than a waggon or cart, even with the flattest, best-maintained road. At a steady walking pace, a horse could pull – on water – up to forty or fifty times as much weight as it could on land with a wheeled vehicle. The economics of water travel couldn't be ignored.

In 1702 the government passed a Bill that allowed a group of local Ryedale landowners and merchants, called 'undertakers', to make the Derwent permanently navigable downstream from Malton to where it meets the River Ouse, another major river for trade, near York. In practice, this meant widening sections of the river, improving the banks, dredging certain parts, adding towpaths, creating new locks, and building wharves and warehouses to store goods at either end. To finance the river improvements, the undertakers were authorised to levy tolls on cargo carried on any part of the route. At first progress was slow, but by 1730 the river or 'Derwent Navigation' had become the major transport artery for the entire region, with hundreds of vessels sailing up and down its waters every week. By the early nineteenth century, some of the larger local farms were producing enough grain not only to satisfy home demand but also to have a surplus to send on to national markets. The rector of Stonegrave, with his new purpose-built threshing barn and neatly apportioned fields, would also have been deliberately growing a surplus to sell. Now, thanks to the newly improved river, Malton and its hinterland could send the region's grain, butter and bacon – and anything else that could stand a period in transit – downriver to York, and from there to the mill towns of West Yorkshire or even, following the Ouse and then the Humber, as far as Hull to be shipped around the coast. Back up the river came salt, sugar – or anything that the area needed but couldn't produce for itself. Chief among those items was coal from Newcastle and woollen cloth from West Yorkshire.

When the entire Borough of Malton was bought by the fabulously wealthy Wentworth[*] family in 1713, the Derwent

---

[*] The Wentworth family are best known for Wentworth Woodhouse, South Yorkshire. It was once the grandest country pile in England, larger than Buckingham and Blenheim palaces combined. It's an architectural colossus – with more than 300 rooms and a 606-foot façade. Its five miles of passageways often proved confusing for guests – one, Baron von Liebeg, was said to have laid a path of crumbs from his bedroom to the dining room so he could find his way back. The family were one of the greatest Whig dynasties of the eighteenth century – Charles, the 2nd Marquess, was prime minister *twice* but died childless and so, on his death, the estate passed to the Fitzwilliam family.

Navigation was included in the purchase, along with the right to collect money from anyone using the river. For almost a century, the responsibility to collect river tolls was leased out to other businessmen, but in 1807 the 2nd Earl, who had inherited the Wentworth estate, took control of the Derwent Navigation back under his wing. On the face of it, the decision was a business one. But, as with all matters of money, politics wasn't far behind. A short time before, the earl had put forward nominees for two members of Parliament to run for Malton, expecting the unequivocal support of those few people in the borough who were, at that date, allowed to vote.* At the time, only 500 men qualified for the franchise: '250 were direct tenants of the Earl Fitzwilliam; 48 were undertenants of his property; 140 were holders of land or houses of his tenants, so that only 62 might be considered "independent" of his influence.'[20] It was a system that was, to all intents and purposes, semi-feudal – paternalistic responsibility for the borough was rewarded with rent, political support and social deference.

The earl was blindsided, however, when the locals – dissatisfied with how the town was being run – elected the opposing candidate and outsider Lord Headley, who was also backed by the anti-slavery campaigner and Yorkshire

* In 1831, for example, only 4,500 'men of property' could vote in parliamentary elections, out of a population of more than 2.6 million people. (Source: The National Archives)

MP William Wilberforce. The earl, incensed at the treachery, exacted swift reprisals, evicting any tenants who had not shown loyalty and forcing supportive tenants to turn off any of their own subtenants or workers who had gone against his wishes. Fitzwilliam also took the business of collecting river tolls back in hand so he could nearly double the rates for any merchants who had failed to support his campaign. A petition was hastily gathered together by his supporters, charging Lord Headley with corruption, and the earl further reinforced his position by snapping up even more property in the borough. Supporters of Fitzwilliam's position wrote letters to local newspapers, accusing Malton voters of 'folly and ingratitude'.[21] The campaign worked: 'the electors of the Borough had learned their lesson; at the ensuing by-election they returned the Earl's candidate. Fitzwilliam, magnanimous in victory, thereupon restored the tolls to their previous level.'[22] But the days of the Derwent were numbered.

✳

In 1845, a train station opened at Malton. The York to Scarborough seaside line had launched to much 'gaiety and festivity' just a few months before and, it was predicted, would provide 'a ready and easy access to one of the most delightful and pleasant watering places in the kingdom'. The 1840s was a decade of unprecedented and often blindly enthusiastic investment in railway building – a time when 'people had more money than sense'.[23] At the beginning of the decade, Britain's railway lines were small and widely scattered – just a few lines on a blank page – but within ten years those tracks had become a virtually complete network, connecting almost every town and, in many cases, tiny, unknown villages with the rest of the country.

The business model was one of Wild-West-like speculation. Almost anyone could form a railway company and propose a new line. A prospective company would have to put together a proposal and a list of investors, often bolstered by the names of influential supporters – such as George Hudson,* the 'Railway King' – who 'lent their prestige but not always their cash'.[24] Each soon-to-be company would also include locally influential people – both investors and landowners, the latter always compensated for any disruption caused by the building of the new line. Such was the excitement about the profit-making potential of the railways that hundreds of

---

* Few rags-to-riches stories are as dramatic as George Hudson's. Born in 1800, in the village of Howsham only ten or so miles from the Barn, George had a traumatic start in life. By the age of six his mother was dead, by eight his father too. Briefly cared for by his gruff brothers, George was sent away at fifteen to join a firm of drapers in York as an apprentice. Business clearly suited him. By the time he was twenty-one he had a share in the company and had married the owner's daughter. Soon after, George inherited a life-changing amount of money from a great-uncle – £30,000 (about £2 million in today's money) – and began to buy shares in a new venture to build a railway line from York. By his early forties George owned more than a thousand miles of railway and was so wealthy he could buy not one, but two large country estates.

companies were quickly formed, all vying to lay down the country's tracks. Within weeks of the York to Scarborough line's inauguration, yet more new routes were proposed, including a track that would change the fortunes of the Barn. Local investors had expressed an interest in creating a new railway line that ran between Thirsk and Malton, a 23-mile stretch dashing across North Yorkshire. At the Thirsk end, in the west, the new line would plug into the existing Great North of England Railway – which linked York and Darlington. At the Malton end, in the east, the railway would join the existing York to Scarborough line.

In the same year as the Thirsk and Malton railway was put forward, nearly five hundred other newly formed companies deposited their plans with the Board of Trade. Such was the pace of building that, in many cases, new lines sprang up to replace routes only a few years old; in 1844, for example, the York to London train took just under eleven hours. Tweaks to the route had shaved off two and a half hours of the journey by 1850 and then, only two years later, an even more direct route was made that could whisk a Yorkshire dweller into the capital in little more than five hours. Not all plans for new railway lines were approved; three separate

schemes were proposed for the Thirsk and Malton stretch, and only one could take the prize. The winning scheme was finally approved in 1846. It predicted that the cost of linking the two market towns would be a hefty £300,000 (about £18 million today) but, after a protracted series of delays, legal threats, and a scaling down in ambition to a more modest £100,000, work on the line finally began in 1851.

Construction went at a considerable lick – the whole line was laid in just two years – and on 19 May 1853, the Thirsk and Malton railway officially opened. Only nine days before the grand unveiling, the Board of Inspection had declared that the line wasn't actually safe; on his site visit, Captain Douglas Galton had not only expressed his concerns about the fact that three station platforms weren't even finished and that the track might not be suitable for heavy engines, but the timber railway bridge that now straddled the River Derwent at the Malton end was looking decidedly wobbly. 'I am of [the] opinion that the opening of this branch line', he wrote, 'from Thirsk to Malton would be attended with danger to the public.'[25] A little 'health and safety' never got in the way of blind entrepreneurial brio, however, and the line opened regardless.

The Derwent Navigation and the railways were now in direct competition. Any goods that sailed down the river represented a loss of revenue for the railway companies and so, determined to squash the competition, in 1854 the North

Eastern Railway Company (NER – a 'super-group' formed from the existing railway companies) – started negotiations to take the Derwent Navigation off the earl's hands. Fitzwilliam's agent drove a tough bargain – a year later he sold the Derwent Navigation for a handsome £40,000 and was awarded an NER directorship to boot. Under its new management, the Derwent Navigation was deliberately run into the ground – river tolls were raised, boat traffic declined, and maintenance ground to a halt. No other event captured the moment when railways sank the river trade better than an 1874 report bemoaning 'the navigation of this river is becoming so much impeded near Malton, by the silting up of the bed, that it is no uncommon occurrence to see the few vessels that now track to the town, stuck fast when near their voyage end. Yesterday, one stuck right in the centre of the stream right beneath the new railway bridge, and had to be lightened of its load before it could be moved.'[26] By 1913, commercial river traffic to Malton had ceased.

The Barn had a front row seat from which to view the unfolding drama. The new Thirsk and Malton railway line cut a swathe through the Barn's valley bottom and skimmed along the edge of the 200 acres that belonged to the farm. When the first carriages rattled through the basin, in 1853, the Barn's new farmhouse was yet to be occupied by the

Hickeses. Labourers and domestics still filled the rooms and, as they sat and ate a meal or worked away in the fields, they would have witnessed the moment when thousands of years of nature's gentle melody was shattered by the thunder of an approaching steam train. One can only imagine what these men and women, most of whom had never left Ryedale, would have made of the spectacle. For some, the railway must have represented an opening up of the world, a giddying chance to travel beyond familiar parish boundaries. In 1859, Samuel Smiles, writer and government reformer, extolled the virtues of the railway: 'The iron rail proved a magicians' road. The locomotive gave a new celerity to time. It virtually reduced England to a sixth of its size. It brought the country nearer to the town and the town to the country [...] It energized punctuality, discipline, and attention; and proved a moral teacher by the influence of example.'[27]

For others, it must have seemed as if the dank dreadfulness of mill-town pollution was creeping into their rural idyll. In 1844, William Wordsworth, in a campaign to stop a line opening in the heart of his beloved Lake District, despaired in a letter to the then President of the Board of Trade, William Gladstone:

Is then no nook of English ground secure
From rash assault? Schemes of retirement sown
In youth, and 'mid the busy world kept pure

As when their earliest flowers of hope were blown
Must perish; how can they this blight endure? [28]

Closer to home, one resident expressed his dismay about the coming of the railways in an anonymous letter to a Yorkshire newspaper:

'On the very line of this railway, I have built a comfortable house; it enjoys a pleasing view of the country. Now judge, my friend, of my mortification, whilst I am sitting comfortably at breakfast with my family, enjoying the purity of the summer air, in moment my dwelling, once consecrated to peace and retirement, is filled with dense smoke of foetid gas; my homely, though cleanly, table covered with dirt; and the features of my wife and family almost obscured by a polluted atmosphere. Nothing is heard but the clanking iron, the blasphemous song, or the appalling curses of the directors of these infernal machines.' [29]

While the workers in the field watched the new locomotive rush past the Barn, passengers on board the train would have experienced a journey like no other. For the first time, many parts of North Yorkshire's hidden countryside were open to view. Not everyone, it seems, liked what they saw. One journalist, who was documenting the maiden voyage on the

Thirsk to Malton line, described the journey starting from the Malton end. And, while he was complimentary about some of the villages he passed through, on reaching the little section of valley belonging to the Barn, his tone changed: 'Along on the right [...] Oswaldkirk Bank for the precipitous outline of the basin and on the left the woody heights of Gilling, crowned by the grim-looking Gilling Castle. Further on the right is seen the Roman Catholic College of St. Lawrence at Ampleforth, beyond which the scenery grows very wild, and the whole appearance of the country ungenerous.'[30]

By the time the Hickeses moved in, in 1855, five train services were rattling past the Barn every day – three passenger, a goods and a minerals train. Whether John objected to the smoke and clatter ruining his view, the practical and financial benefits would have quickly become apparent. The Thirsk and Malton railway soon became a regular carrier of coal, livestock, animal feed and timber. The freight trains also took vast quantities of limestone from nearby quarries, much of it bound for the ravenous blast furnaces further north, where it was used to remove impurities from iron ore. In 1871, eighteen years after the Thirsk and Malton line opened, a second section of track was added, branching off at right angles in the middle of the valley in front of the Barn. It headed northwards towards Helmsley and then beyond to another market town, Pickering. The Barn and its land were now framed on two sides by railway lines.

For John Hickes, now sixteen years into his tenancy, the possibility of new markets must have been exhilarating. He was spoilt for choice, with three new stations within spitting distance: Nunnington was a quick one-and-a-half-mile cart ride away; and Gilling and Hovingham stations just three miles distant in opposite directions. From all accounts, livestock travelled in vast numbers out of these local stations – in 1896, Hovingham station – just a small rural stop – handled 14,000 beasts in one year. The timing of the arrival of the railway and the construction of the large cow shelter, tacked on to the existing Barn, was not coincidental. John Hickes – never one to miss an opportunity – saw the potential of the railway to open up new markets and had taken a throw of the dice. As we'll see later, his gamble would save the farm.

The trains also welcomed passengers, rich and poor alike. When the carriages first started to run, there was a worry that not everyone would be able to afford to use them. In 1844, a Select Committee monitored the 'Effect of Railways on the Interests of the poorer Classes'. While railway fares were, initially, higher than the equivalent journey on a wooden-wheeled vehicle, investors were convinced that the time and hassle saved by rail travel more than compensated for the increase in cost. When the vice-chairman of Thirsk Union, one of the local workhouses, was asked for his assessment on the Great North of England Railway, he was clear: 'The railway had unquestionably extended the means of communication to the poor as well as the rich. The third class carriages of the Great North of England Railway are attached to four trains, each daily (for six working days), and the charge is about one shilling for nine miles, thus affording to the poor a cheap and regular conveyance.' His enthusiasm wasn't entirely unqualified, however. When it came to single people travelling, the train could just about compete. Take the family along, and the costs soon added up. 'The charge by waggon was about a penny a mile: but if a woman had two, three or four children, they were generally charged as one. The waggon, therefore, to a person so circumstanced was cheaper than the railway; for one person only the latter (especially if time be any value), is decidedly the cheapest conveyance.'

But he concluded on an optimistic note: 'I may mention after the last harvest I noticed many of the Irish reapers returning by the railway, and during last Martinmas, when the servants were at home with their parents for a few days, a considerable number passed on the railway, and many visited York.'[31] It's interesting that the workhouse official mentioned the Irish reapers. While they were undoubtedly some of the North Yorkshire train companies' best seasonal customers, it seems old prejudices died hard. Irish immigrants had a long history of travelling to Britain to escape poverty, and many of them ended up in farm work or helping to build the canals and, later, the railways. Many faced racial and anti-Catholic religious discrimination, despite their key role in Victorian Britain's growing economy. Irish reapers were known locally as 'July barbers'; they were expert scythe-men and asked little in terms of accommodation, often making do with a cold attic or hayloft. Yet train companies didn't want the Irish mixing with their usual customers. A letter circulated in 1860 insisted they be segregated from regular passengers. 'Care must be taken that these men when travelling by third class trains are not allowed to travel beside ordinary passengers, but that they travel in the third class carriages specially attached for their accommodation.'[32]

The Thirsk and Malton line also transformed the experience of getting to the seaside, a journey of about 30 miles from the Barn. Get to Malton station (and a few years later, Pickering station) and you could connect, by rail, to the popular coastal towns of Bridlington, Filey, Whitby and, crucially, Scarborough. Long before the arrival of the railway, Scarborough had started to attract tourists. In 1626, a local woman, Mrs Farrer, had discovered a natural mineral spring bubbling out of the bottom of South Cliff and the town soon gathered a reputation as the place to enjoy the curative effects of 'taking the waters'. By the end of the eighteenth century, Scarborough had expanded its list of enticements for the rich and famous from foul-tasting mineral water to sea bathing, sailing, afternoon gambling and horse racing along the beach. Despite being 240 miles from London, Scarborough drew in a surprisingly affluent crowd from all over the country. In one year alone in the 1730s, over a thousand visitors poured into the small North Yorkshire coastal town, including no fewer than two dukes, one marquess, seven earls, three lords, nineteen baronets and six knights.[33] But for most people during that time, Scarborough might as well have been on the moon rather than just over the moors. Before the advent of the railway, getting there was no mean undertaking. Scarborough had no navigable river or canal, so if you wanted to travel there from one of Britain's fashionable cities, you had only a few options: spend a few days hugging the coastline by boat; take the road to Lincoln and then a ferry over the Humber; or, after the 1750s, bounce your way slowly along in one of the regular stagecoaches on the newly turnpiked roads.

On 7 July 1845, the first steam engine pulled into Scarborough's shiny new station. It had departed from York just a few hours earlier and received a rapturous ovation from crowds gathered at every station along the way. However, the inhabitants of Scarborough welcomed the arrival of the steam engine not because they wanted more tourists but because they hoped it would provide a quick and cheap way of getting tons of locally caught fish and shellfish straight into the heart of West Yorkshire's industrial towns and cities. 'They would have been amazed, and perhaps horrified,' wrote one modern historian of the town, 'to learn that eventually the railway would transform their elitist resort into an excursionist mecca for millions of holidaymakers.'[34]

It's all too easy to assume that the arrival of the steam train revolutionised working people's travel expectations overnight. But for many people living and working in the countryside around the Barn, the notion of taking a train to the seaside for pleasure would have been a pipe dream. In the 1860s, a third-class ticket to Scarborough, for a farm labourer working for John Hickes, would have cost perhaps three or four shillings – a third of his family's total weekly income. Families living in the industrialised mill towns and cities of West Yorkshire, with their higher manufacturing wages, would have been better placed to buy a ticket to the beach than their country cousins. And even then, most families could only afford a day trip rather than an overnight stay. Yorkshire's rural labourers and live-in servants simply didn't have that many days off during the year. In the late eighteenth and much of the nineteenth century, anyone working in the Barn or the farmhouse would have enjoyed only Christmas Day, Good Friday and hiring fair days off.[35] While the 1871 Bank Holidays Act legally set in stone people's entitlement to an extra four days off – Easter Monday, Whit Monday, the first Monday in August and Boxing Day – these were still unpaid and often created more economic hardship than excitement. It wasn't until 1938 and the Holidays with Pay Act that workers from all walks of life were entitled to one week's paid leave a year. Any excited potential holidaymakers would have had to temper their excitement, though. Only a few years earlier, most of the Barn's local village stations had been closed to passengers as a cost-saving measure.

Even in the early twentieth century Scarborough was still dominated, as a holiday resort, by the middle classes. Where you sat on the beach front said something about your background. While the South Cliff was reserved for the great and good of northern money, the lower middle class made a beeline for the North Bay. Neither group would have entertained the idea of frequenting the fishing quarter, the preserve of the 'genuine proletarians'.[36] Holidaying at Scarborough, far from being a chance for all and sundry to frolic on the sand, ended up mirroring all the inequalities of daily life. British novelist V. S. Pritchett, writing in the 1930s, observed wryly: 'the "improper" classes can have the run of the magnificent modern North Bay or – if they are very improper – of the foreshore and the harbour, without being bored by the South Cliff and the Spa. The hills so divide Scarborough, in fact, that it has been able to tout for the masses without losing caste.'[37]

For most people who lived and worked on the land around the Barn, the arrival of the railway had little effect on how they got about from day to day. While farmers like John Hickes had access to horses and wheeled transport, his employees and their families still made most journeys on foot. One of the more curious clippings describing village life around the Barn is tucked away in an 1834 newspaper. With the title 'Pedestrianism', the article reads: 'We understand that Robert Skipper, the pedestrian champion of England, on Wednesday commenced, at Malton, the Herculean task of walking 64 miles per day, for three successive days. His route is by way of Hovingham, Stonegrave, and Helmsley, twice and back each day. He relies for the remuneration of his labour on the generosity of the public.'[38] It's a sport now lost in time, but in the first half of the nineteenth century, 'pedestrianism' enjoyed enormous popularity. It was one of the few mass-spectator sports, alongside boxing and horse racing, that everyone could watch and, most enjoyably, bet on.

The idea was simple, but the rules were deeply prescriptive. 'By Pedestrianism is understood, in racing parlance, the contest between two or more men, or between man and time,' the *Manual of British Rural Sports* grandly announced. The body should be 'inclined forwards and the heel touches the ground before the toes'. Using this technique, practised quick walkers could cover a bracing six miles in an hour and, in the case of 'very extraordinary pedestrians', an even brisker seven miles. Those who weren't quite sure how to pace in a straight line were advised solemnly 'to keep the knees supple and not too straight, and to make use of the arm as a balance-spring, or even as a kind of fulcrum; but in this respect walkers vary a great deal, some, like Mountjoy, using great action of the arms, and others keeping them as still as if they were glued to their bodies'.[39]

The whole affair sounds ridiculous until you appreciate the distances covered and the sums of money involved. One of the pioneers, Captain Robert Barclay Allardice, known as 'the celebrated pedestrian', power-walked 1,000 miles in 1,000 hours in 1809. When he finally hobbled to victory, Captain Barclay bagged 1,000 guineas in wager money (about £50,000 today) and earned those who had bet on his success £5 million in modern terms. Other pedestrians relied on donations from the public as they wandered past – rather like a busker – or the chance of a cash prize as they stepped over the winning line. Rather like the hullabaloo of a Tour de Yorkshire, the pomp and spectacle that surrounded a speed-walk provided plenty of free and much-needed distraction for bystanders. And, in a world where 90 per cent of the population didn't own any form of transport, including a horse, 'All a contender needed was the ability and will to walk, and working people did that all the time'.[40] Spectators could appreciate the struggles and strains of an arduous walk; there were no barriers to entry, no expensive clothes or equipment needed, just the sheer willpower to put one foot in front of the other. The improbably named Robert Skipper, the pedestrian walking back and forth past the Barn, would have drawn huge crowds, from the lowliest farm servant to the lord of the manor. Pedestrians were national celebrities. A few years earlier, Skipper had taken on Captain Barclay's record at Newmarket and smashed it; he had performed 'the extraordinary and unparalleled feat of walking 1,000 miles in 1,000 successive half-hours, on the same ground Captain Barclay walked 1,000 miles in 1,000 successive bouts'.[41]

The arrival of the railways opened up new opportunities for rural regions to engage in national trade, especially mining and quarrying. The Howardian Hills around the Barn proved to be a valuable source of limestone for industry, but other remote areas of Britain's countryside also enjoyed similar shots in the arm from the development of railways; places such as the slate quarries of North Wales, rural Northampton's iron ore industry and the lead mines of Shropshire. For John Hickes, at the Barn, the bustling local train stations provided access to markets that a labourer-made-good could previously only have dreamed of. The exchange went two ways, of course; thanks to the railway, John could also benefit from cheap animal feed, ground bone and human waste or 'night soil' shunted in from distant cities.

The decision to expand the Barn to focus on cows, at a time when many of the bigger farms were concentrating on large-scale arable farming, proved to be a smart move on John Hickes's part. The late 1870s witnessed a catastrophic, and almost terminal, plummet in grain prices during a period that became known as the Great Depression. At the end of the 1840s, Parliament had repealed the Corn Laws, effectively getting rid of any import tariffs on foreign grain. The British market wasn't initially flooded with a cheap influx of wheat and barley – the American Civil War had kept one of our major competitors otherwise occupied. But when peace returned in the mid-1860s, there was no stopping the flood; a combination of the opening up of the vast American prairies for farming, thanks in no small part to the railway, and the advent of speedy steamships meant that foreign grain could now be shipped halfway across the world and still outcompete our home-grown crops.

Prices crashed. In 1870, a quarter of wheat (approximately 13 kg) sold for around 55 shillings. Twenty-five years later the price had been slashed in half, to just 28 shillings. Moreover, the amount of foreign grain being imported over the last half of the nineteenth century more than doubled from 30 million hundredweight in 1870 to almost 70 million by 1900.[42] The invention and spread of the railways, which had accidentally helped decimate the arable farming sector, ironically saved small, mixed farmers like John Hickes and, after him, his son George. Perishable goods – strawberries, potatoes, peas, fish, fresh milk and butter – and live animals such as cattle and chickens, for which time is of the essence, found eager markets in rapidly expanding towns and cities. Far from being a universally felt depression, it was often the farms that had thrown themselves into high input, large-scale farming earlier in the century that felt the crash most acutely. High farming lay in ruins.

Goods also came back up the railway line into rural communities. Rita Jackson, a young child in the 1920s, remembers living at Nunnington station with her father, the railway porter. For her, the network brought not only employment and a home for her family but a taste of life beyond the parish walls.

'We were self-sufficient: there was a field to go with the station and a very big yard. We had a big garden for vegetables and fruit, and Dad loved gardening. We had everything and Mum was always busy: ducks, geese, hens; goats for the milk and for making butter [...] If Mum wanted some different chickens, she used to ring up Spinks in Easingwold in the afternoon and at night-time the chickens were on the train [...] The big houses at Nunnington and Laysthorpe used Nunnington station and, if they were having visitors and they wanted fish, they would ring York up and it was put on the train in the evening and the chauffeur would come down and collect it.'[43]

The Hickeses, similarly, grew much of their own produce and, in particular, tended a large and fruitful orchard. Apple, plum, bullace* and pear trees had been planted next to the farmhouse during its construction in the 1840s, a remarkable act of foresight on the part of the then rector. In fact, the villages and hamlets surrounding the Barn are awash with the remnants of these historic orchards, fruit trees that once formed a critical part of the North Yorkshire rural economy. Before the coming of the railway, everyone from cottagers to farmers relied on fruit-growing and -picking as a seasonal boost. Men, women and children would collect whichever fruit was in season – either from local farms, their own gardens or from the hedgerows – and take it to the local market to sell. Fruiterers, who acted as middlemen, would scoop up the local produce and sell it on to grocers, jam and condiment makers, brewers and other fruit-based businesses.

---

* Bullaces are an old variety of damson-like plum. They're acidic but wonderful when cooked, making them perfect for fruit preserves and fruit wine.

When the railway arrived, perishable fruit could travel even further afield - much of Ryedale's fruit ended up at Rowntree's and Terry's, both York-based confectioners, where it was turned into fruit pastilles, jellies and a myriad other treats for the Victorian sweet tooth. After the Second World War, local growers couldn't compete with cheaper foreign imports of fruit pulp and many of the region's orchards grew gnarly and unloved. By a stroke of luck, the Barn's orchard survived being grubbed up - probably because it was too close to the farmhouse to turn into a field, and on an awkward slope. Every year, trees that are now fast approaching two centuries in age produce local varieties of fruit that are no longer grown commercially - including the Green Balsam (or 'Farmer's Wife's Apple', because of its general usefulness) and Hunthouse cookers, an apple that North Yorkshire's very own James Cook took with him on his adventures to keep scurvy at bay.

This nationwide shift away from arable into other types of farming - livestock, perishable fruit and vegetables, and dairy - changed the face of the countryside forever. The amount of land dedicated to growing grain halved between the 1870s and 1900. At the same time, the amount of land kept for grazing livestock increased, only by a fifth, but enough to make a difference to the number of rural employees needed on any one farm. Grain production – especially before the days of mechanisation – was labour-intensive. Farms now had only three viable options, all of which needed fewer workers: livestock and dairy, market gardening or highly mechanised arable. The number of people working in the countryside had peaked. Between 1870 and the end of the century, despite the fact that the population of Britain as a whole nearly doubled, the number of rural labourers halved.

5

SOME H'AE LUCK, AN' SOME STICK I' T' MUCK

SOME H'AE LUCK, AN' SOME STICK I' T' MUCK
Some have all the luck and some stick in the muck

The first time I knew we had a well was when I fell into it. I had been attempting to repaint the side of the log store, next to the farmhouse, and suddenly felt my leg disappear from under me. Back in the 1950s, someone had hastily filled in the well with soil and debris and covered it over with timber. Over half a century, grass had grown over the top and the contents had settled. And, like any good trapping pit, all it needed was the weight of an unwary trespasser and the surface gave way.

Old, abandoned wells can be lethal but this experience was fairly benign – the hole was only a few metres deep and, luckily, only one leg slipped in. What the accident revealed, however, was much more interesting – the forgotten skills of a well-sinker. Anyone who has attempted to build anything from brick will know just how challenging it is to create elegant, mathematical curves with a series of rectangular blocks. And when you consider the pressure of being underground,

knee-deep in water and digging in an impossibly claustrophobic space, the well-sinker's feat seems almost Herculean.

Water is heavy. And yet every bucket needed by the farmer, the labourers or the servants would have been hand-pumped from the well and carried across the yard. One working horse could drink five buckets a day. A dairy cow even more. Add to that the needs of a thirsty family of eight, the farm's live-in workers and the day labourers, and the cast-iron handle must have barely stopped pumping from dawn until dusk.

In 1845, a particularly upsetting story appeared in an East Riding newspaper, the *Hull Packet*. In tiny print, the feature jostled for attention between a scoop about the brutalising of a cabin boy on the high seas and a Mr Cockles' sage advice on how to cure nervous indigestion. It led with the teaser 'Two Men Buried Alive for Some Days' and told the sorry tale of two Dundee well-sinkers, men whose job it was to build and repair water wells. The two men were 60 feet underground when the shuttering that was designed to hold the sides of the well collapsed, filling the hole with tons of earth and rubble. Amazingly, both men survived the initial burial. Villagers dashed to the well-sinkers' assistance, frantically trying to scoop away the rubble but to no avail; and so a plan was hatched to quickly sink another well alongside the first, and tunnel through from one to the other. Meanwhile, the trapped men were using up their limited supplies of oxygen and, no doubt, trying not to panic. The villagers managed to feed a gas pipe down to the men and carefully poured not only wine, port, soup and tea down it, but also words of encouragement to keep up their spirits in a situation that was looking increasingly hopeless.

After five days, miraculously, the rescuers managed to reach one of the men and bring him up to the surface. For the other, the agonising wait continued, his only method of communication the gas pipe and a small bell, which he tinkled occasionally for 'consolation, information and refreshment'. On the morning of the sixth day, however, 'The bell had ceased to be heard' and all hope was lost. 'Death has its terrors even when met in the brightest of human abodes,' concluded the reporter solemnly. Spare a thought for the well-sinker, he continued, 'in his dismal earthy prison, where days were passed with apprehension of an instant and most horrible death, without a countenance where he might read hope, and without a hand that could reach assistance'.[1]

The story, for all its wretched drama, was not a particularly unusual one. Well-sinking is an all-but-forgotten occupation. But for hundreds of years, few farms and villages could have managed without the well-sinker's services. The job was a respected but dangerous one; newspapers throughout the late eighteenth and nineteenth centuries are filled with tales of well-sinkers' deaths and near misses. Digging for water also involved a huge amount of manpower, expense and ongoing maintenance. To understand, therefore, why anyone would bother to build a well in the first place, it's important to know what John Hickes's options would have been when he moved in, in 1855.

The Barn is built into the bottom of a hillside. This slope is called Spring Hill, a rise covered in multiple, naturally occurring springs. These have dribbled, non-stop, with fresh, clean drinking water for thousands of years and, no doubt, partly explain the position of the farm and its Barn and any other building that predated them. But springs can be temperamental – in winter, the slope gurgles underfoot with saturation but in summer, the springs can be reduced to barely a trickle. The North Yorkshire weather also provides plenty of rainwater but, like the springs, it can't be relied on with any consistency. Local farmers like Hickes, therefore, had to come up with ingenious solutions to collect and store water. From underground brick cisterns, like the one used to hide the body of the baby at East Newton, to man-made ponds, the resourceful farmer had to adapt the landscape to even out the year's water shortages. Artificial ponds were often built near stackyards, for example, not only as a source of water for livestock but also in case the harvested crops caught fire while they were waiting to be threshed. Other farmers could make the most of nearby rivers and streams, and the Barn had Holbeck at its southern boundary; but none of these options was very convenient for the farmhouse. As the Barn expanded, and John swelled his ranks in terms of both livestock and family, the need for a reliable and constant water supply became a priority.

The job of a well-sinker combined engineer and miner, bricklayer and, in many cases, diviner. Deciding where to sink a well would have involved a heady mix of local knowledge, reading the natural environment, guesswork, and not a little showmanship. Dowsing or 'water witching' involved walking along the surface holding a pair of rods, twigs or a pendulum, and waiting for a twitch that told him there was water below. The well-sinker at the Barn found his perfect site right next to the end of the washhouse, news that would have no doubt thrilled the domestic servant, whose job it was to fetch all the water for the family's washstands and baths, clothes washing, cooking, house cleaning and watering the kitchen garden.

The process of digging the well started with a metal or wooden hoop, like the rim of a cartwheel, about four feet across. The hoop acted as a template, dictating the size of the hole to be dug. It was a fine balancing act – too large a hoop and the well would take too long to dig, too small and the hole wouldn't be able to accommodate a man working inside it, digging out its contents with a small pick and shovel. The problem with digging any kind of hole was that, fairly soon, there was a real possibility that the sides would cave in. And so the well-sinker had a clever trick up his sleeve – once he'd dug down to the point where only his head was poking above the surface, the metal or wooden hoop would be placed at the bottom of the hole. The well-sinker would then start to build on top of the hoop, laying brick after brick around the perimeter of the hole, to create the lining of the well. It was important that the bricks weren't mortared together – the well worked by allowing water to seep through the bricks and collect in the chamber. Once the well-sinker had bricked the sides up to ground level he could then continue to dig downwards, slowly scraping out the earth underneath the hoop and allowing the column of bricks to gently lower, all the while preventing the sides of the well from collapsing in. Buckets of soil were pulleyed up to the surface by an assistant, who then lowered bricks down in return.

The well-sinker would keep going in this way, moving the hoop down and adding new bricks to the sides of the well, until the required depth was reached. If the well was going to be very deep, extra shuttering might be used to shore up the walls until the well-sinker had finished his task. The top few rows of bricks would be mortared, to stop contaminated surface water seeping its way into the well water, and then the well would be capped in some way to stop animals and people accidentally falling in – a small wall around the perimeter or a wooden cover. The well-sinker would then fit a hand pump or windlass so that even the youngest, and slightest, of domestic servants or farm labourers could crank or pump a handle and bring gallons of water to the surface.

It's extraordinary just how deep down these wells go. Twenty feet was considered an easy dig, but many reached 50, 60, 80 feet or more until they hit the water table. The deepest hand-dug well on record was 390 metres (1,280 feet) and took four years to complete, at a Victorian workhouse in Woodingdean, near Brighton. Working at those kinds of depths, in suffocating darkness, must have required a considerable amount of courage, especially when well-sinkers were only too aware of the many dangers of their profession. There were plenty of things that could go wrong in the process of digging a well: along with the very real possibility of being buried alive, men and young boys were routinely asphyxiated by underground gases – two of the most deadly were hydrogen sulphide, known as 'stinkdamp' because it smelt of rotten eggs, and methane, which was also highly explosive. Such was the potency of these noxious fumes that a well-sinker at the bottom of a shaft would die

277

within minutes; many a news story told of rescue attempts where the original victim perished but so too did the brave soul who attempted to save them.

Carbon dioxide, or carbonic acid as it was known, was also an ever-present danger. Newspapers compared the toxic gas to water for its ability to 'drown' men within minutes. As one newspaper reporter of the day lamented: 'Many wellsinkers, a class of men who ought to know better, appear to be utterly ignorant of the fact that wells frequently contain an invisible water, which will as certainly drown those who plunge over head into it, even, for a very few minutes, as the visible and ordinary water ever can do,—much more certainly, indeed, inasmuch as the invisible carbonic acid is more insidious, and neither excites those convulsive efforts which prevent choking by the receptions of water into the lungs, nor buoys up the drowning body till the vital air is reached.'[2] If you were working at the bottom of a well, there was also the very real danger of objects falling from above. Whether it was a bucket of bricks from a snapped rope or an unwary farm animal accidentally tumbling in, the safety of the well-sinker below ground was only as good as his kit and the capabilities of his young assistant.

If, like John Hickes and his family, you had access to your own well, you were in an enviable position. Most rural villagers had to rely on a number of different sources of water, depending on what was close at hand and what the water was going to be used for. In her semi-autobiographical *Lark Rise to Candleford*, written at the end of the nineteenth century, Flora Thompson remembered:

'Against the wall of every well-kept cottage stood a tarred or green-painted water butt to catch and store the rainwater from the roof. This saved many journeys to the well with buckets, as it could be used for cleaning and washing clothes and for watering small, precious things in the garden. It was also valued for toilet purposes and the women would hoard the last drops for themselves and their children to wash in. Rain-water was supposed to be good for the complexion, and, though they had no money to spend upon beautifying themselves, they were not too far gone in poverty to neglect such means as they had to that end.'[3]

A communal well was often the only source of drinking water and fetching it was a woman's responsibility. For women living in Stonegrave during the nineteenth century, the options for getting drinking water were both limited and, most of the time, dicey. The two main sources of water were a handful of ancient communal wells dotted around the village or, if those dried up, the River Rye at Nunnington, a mile-long trudge across the fields. It's easy to assume that countryside settlements enjoyed free and flowing access to drinking water, and that this was one of the many bonuses of bucolic life. And yet, for many rural dwellers, water was no more drinkable than it was in the towns and cities. Unless a person lived at a substantial distance from a settlement, there was a good chance that any overland watercourse would be contaminated with either human or animal waste from upstream. For hundreds of years, Helmsley residents merrily tipped all their effluent into the River Rye, polluting the supply for anyone living downstream, including families drawing water at Nunnington.

In the mid-nineteenth century, however, great scientific strides were starting to be made in the understanding of waterborne diseases. North Yorkshire's very own John Snow had been instrumental in fighting cholera when he deftly illustrated a link between the disease and contaminated drinking water. Snow had been born in 1813 and raised in York by a poor labouring family. His childhood home was in one of the most deprived areas of the city, rubbing up against the foetid River Ouse, which also frequently flooded. As a child, Snow had experienced the foul effects of polluted water first-hand; every time the river broke its banks, it would wash filthy, stinking effluent into homes and businesses. While physicians of the day blamed 'miasma' or 'bad air' for cholera, Snow proposed a radical new idea – that it was something in the water making people ill. His theory – which he first put forward in 1849 – focused on a microbial origin for cholera, an idea that was initially pooh-poohed but started to gain traction as the field of medical microbiology developed over the next few years.

Typhoid was another waterborne killer. For generations, doctors had treated the disease with wearisome and often lethal rounds of laudanum and bloodletting. Again, it was a disease thought to be linked to miasma. No part of society was immune to its effects and Queen Victoria's husband, Prince Albert, would famously succumb to the disease. Around the same time that Snow was advancing his theory, a similarly sharp-eyed doctor, William Budd, from Bristol, made the link between an outbreak of typhoid in Clifton and the use of a nearby well by those afflicted. Frustratingly, the scientific community remained wedded to the miasma theory for another three decades. Only with the work of now household-name scientists such as Robert Koch and Louis Pasteur, in the 1880s, was 'germ theory' taken seriously. Armed with a new, scientific sense of purpose, many Victorian towns and cities made access to clean water and sewage systems a priority, while rural areas such as North Yorkshire often lagged behind. A Commons Select Committee in 1879 investigated the water supplies at the nearby market town of Thirsk. The report found that the small market town had 160 pumps but only one for public use; women were made to walk 'great distances across the town carrying heavy pails searching for water' and were occasionally seen fighting 'over a little pail of softer water'.[4] People were even reduced to slipping out at night to use the pumps, and to stealing or begging water from their neighbours.

It's tempting to blame logistics for poor rural water supplies but, as many great Victorian infrastructure programmes such as railways had shown, industrialists could achieve miracles when they put their minds to it. Demand from industry always acted as a greater lever than the few scattered voices of rural villages. It's telling that, even as late as the 1890s, typhoid was still rampant in and around the towns and villages near the Barn; Northallerton, a small market town about 20 miles away, had the worst typhoid mortality rates in the entire country at that time. By 1895 the then rector of Stonegrave, Reverend Edward Augustus Bracken Pitman, felt compelled to complain to the Local Government Board about the 'impure and deficient water supply' in the neighbourhood. 'Several cases of typhoid fever had occurred, and the cases were attributable to the drinking of the water of the River Rye.'[5] Reverend Pitman, a man whose patience was at the end of its tether, added firmly that the council should take up the matter at once and 'that there be no shuffling'. Pitman had been moved to press matters after a local medical officer, Dr Reid, expressed his concern that typhoid was tearing its way through Stonegrave and the nearby villages of Leysthorpe and East Newton, putting the Barn right in the eye of the storm. The doctor believed the source of the outbreak to be the 'impurities of the Rye, and the indifference with which the people in the villages drink it'. He added, with barely disguised fury, that it was an appalling thing 'to make up butter and cook food with liquid filth' and that the council should be aware that 'the infected area was a huge scandal'.[6] To add insult to injury, the only place designed to deal with the victims of local outbreaks – Helmlsey Workhouse – was woefully unsuited to the task and had been condemned only a few years before by the government inspector.

One of the more curious aspects of the case was Dr Reid's bafflement at why local people would choose to drink from the river in the first place. As a champion of health, he might have done well to ask local residents whether their decision to drink from the river was truly one of indifference or something more fundamental, especially as it involved trekking across fields to collect water rather than nipping down to the local pump. Indeed, if he'd bothered to check, he would have discovered that villagers had their own doubts about the freshness of the drinking water and had been going to the River Rye out of necessity. The mass strychnine poisoning, which had contaminated one of the public wells in Stonegrave, was also within living memory. Only a few weeks later, the villagers' suspicions were confirmed when a district surveyor took samples from the five different water sources

– four private wells and one public one – in Stonegrave, and found only two were fit for human consumption and that even these were liable to contamination. 'The water taken from the village pump', concluded the surveyor, 'was the worst of all.'[7]

Stonegrave wasn't alone in its frustration. Rural communities were often overlooked when it came to water supplies and sewage disposal. One of the main issues was the disparity in funding – local authorities in sparsely populated areas couldn't square the two opposing forces of limited finances and the high costs of provision to remote districts. Planning for water resources was done in a highly localised way, a mishmash of government money and private enterprise, with little coordination at any regional or national level. There was also an ideological battle going on between public and private ownership – trying to reconcile the interests of shareholders in private water companies, local officials, landlords, landowners, health campaigners and villagers proved near impossible. Remarkably, some businesses even actively resisted proposals to build new water schemes; even as late as the Second World War, a third of all rural households countrywide still had no piped water. For villagers, quite apart from the fact that the lack of decent water carried with it the potential danger of illness, lugging cumbersome pails of water long distances over muddy, badly made roads put a further strain on many women's already considerable daily burden of drudgery. The physical toll on women's health was extraordinary, with regular complaints of miscarriages, hernias and broken limbs after slipping over. And when a mother couldn't fetch the water, the onerous task often fell to her children; it's interesting to note that, when free schooling arrived, water-carrying duties were regularly cited as the reason for a child being late, or, worse, not at school at all.[8]

With all these different challenges and perils close at hand, it's no wonder, in hindsight, that John Hickes decided to employ a well-sinker. Once built, the well next to the farmhouse provided gallons of clean, clear water not only for John, Jane and their six children but also all the live-in servants and labourers that came through the farm, many of whom would have had loved ones in local villages affected by the constant threat of contaminated water.[*] John took the extra precaution of buying a charcoal water filter for the family's personal use – a trend started when Queen Victoria asked Royal Doulton to come up with a way to purify the royal household's supplies after Albert's sudden death from typhoid in 1861. The stoneware vessel, like a huge vase, filtered the family's drinking water through powdered charcoal, a purifying substance known since Roman times.

---

[*] In 1932, Malton had the dubious honour of experiencing England's last major outbreak of typhoid. The infection began in September, when a young harvester succumbed to fever, but in no time had overwhelmed 270 of the town's inhabitants, killing twenty-three locals and visitors in just a few weeks. Among the dead was a young mother of three from Stonegrave.

By 1918 the farm had been connected to the District Council's new mains water supply. Despite their remote location, the Barn and the farmhouse were plumbed into fresh water before many of their more conveniently located village neighbours. The First World War had wrought havoc on Britain's food supplies – not only was the nation's produce being sent abroad to feed soldiers serving on the front line but vessels carrying cheap imports of food, which had been squeezing the life out of British farming for decades, were being sunk by German U-boats. Britain was in real danger of being starved into submission. The nation needed its farmers to rise to the challenge and maximise their output; on the day war broke out, Britain was importing 80 per cent of all its wheat and relied heavily on foreign fuel and fertilisers. Since the 1870s, the British government had believed that importing cheap food supplies, especially grain, would reduce the nation's food bill, but the policy had left the country dangerously vulnerable. The only solution was a concerted national campaign to turn as much land as possible over to arable – no mean feat when the farming community was struggling to keep their young lads and their horses from being conscripted. Almost a third of all farmhands were sent to war, many of them recruited at the traditional hiring fairs. Once places of merriment and opportunity, the hirings became hoovers for cannon fodder:

'Those young men who had no intention of joining up were exposed to the attentions of army recruiters [...] and workers became reluctant to attend.'[9] Not only did this hasten the demise of the hiring fair as a key event in the farming year but it also made more difficult the task of recruiting the few men who were left behind. Of the rural families who supplied labour to the Barn and the surrounding local farms, forty-eight sent one of their men, fifteen sent two, and one family alone sent six. Seventy-eight went in total and sixteen died, almost double the national average. At the beginning of the war, John Hickes's son, George, was by now in his fifties and too old for duty. He also, thankfully, had no sons of his own to send.

The mighty task of boosting arable production, without many farmhands, was made even more challenging by the pressure on farmers to keep livestock numbers high to protect meat and dairy supplies. The connection of the Barn, with its thirsty cattle and crops, to mains water would have been vital to the war effort after decades of being left to draw its own supply. Even at the end of the Second World War, however, many rural dwellers still found themselves without the most basic of sanitary arrangements. When help did come, it was from an unlikely ally. Behind its genteel, marmalade-making façade, the National Federation of Women's Institutes had been campaigning to give rural women a voice. In 1943, the organisation sent out a survey to more than 3,500 regional branches to find out more about how the countryside was keeping itself clean. They were horrified by what they discovered. One author concluded that the W.I. survey revealed 'a truly appalling state of affairs [...] which in many cases showed sanitary conditions little better than those prevailing in the Middle Ages'.[10] Of the twenty-six different counties surveyed, at least half were still dependent on outside privies or 'bucket lavatories', many of which were shared with other families. Lack of any kind of coordinated sewage collection meant that, most of the time, rural families simply threw their effluent into streams, ditches or onto their own gardens. Two-thirds of the villages had access to a mains supply of water, but this was often no more than a communal standpipe, which tended to freeze over the winter months. Even as late as 1951, nearly half of the villages around the Barn didn't have an inside toilet and a fifth still had no mains water.

Until the first indoor toilet was plumbed in the 1920s, anyone who stayed or worked at the farmhouse and the Barn would have had to improvise when it

came to sanitary arrangements. Every bedroom in the house would have had a chamber pot, the emptying of which would have been the domestic servant's responsibility. In the 1870s, when the farmhouse was at its fullest with John, Jane, five of their six children, a governess and two live-in farm servants, this onerous and unpleasant task fell to their domestic servant, Ann Barker. Every morning, Ann would have had to carefully take the contents of her own pot, the farmer's, the farmer's wife's and their five boisterous children, and slop it outdoors. The live-in farm lads would have emptied their own. With eleven people racing about the house, accidents must have been commonplace, especially when a young servant had so many other chores to squeeze in. Accounts of domestic service are rare but Hannah Cullwick, working at the same time as Ann Barker, documented a typical sixteen-and-a-half-hour working day down in the then leafy Middlesex village of Kilburn, now a suburb of London:

'Opened the shutters and lighted the kitchen fire – shook my sooty things in the dusthole and emptied the soot there, swept and dusted the rooms and the hall, laid the cloth and got breakfast up – cleaned two pairs of boots – made the beds and emptied the slops, cleared and washed the breakfast things up – cleaned the plate – cleaned the knives and got dinner up – cleared away, cleaned the kitchen up – unpacked a hamper – took two chickens to Mrs Brewer's and brought a message back – made a tart and picked and gutted two ducks and roasted them

– cleaned the steps and flags on my knees, blackleaded the scraper in the front of the house – cleaned the street flags too on my knees – had tea – cleared away – washed up in the scullery – cleaned the pantry on my knees and scoured the tables – scrubbed the flags round the house and cleaned the window sills – got tea at 9 for the master and Mrs Warwick in my dirt but Anne (a fellow-servant) carried it up – cleaned the privy and passage and scullery floor on my knees – washed the door and cleaned the sink down – put the supper ready for Anne to take up, for I was too dirty and tired to go upstairs.'[11]

The Hickeses' servant would have had a number of options for where to fling the contents of the chamber pots – if John had a manure heap on the go, she might have just thrown it on that, depending on whether it was close enough to the farmhouse. Upending the contents of the chamber pots into a privy might have been another possibility, depending on how substantial the hole was. Some privies were no more than a shallow pit in the ground, covered with a temporary structure that could be moved once a new hole was dug; others were almost well-like in their depth and designed to be emptied, by hand, at regular intervals. The system actually worked well when it wasn't overused. The privy pit functioned effectively if it was treated rather like a compost heap, alive with healthy decomposition. If the hole wasn't filled up too quickly – which is what was happening in overcrowded urban areas – the liquid contents could slowly seep into the ground, leaving the dry matter to rot down. Adding some kind of fibrous, dry material to the pit – whether it was sawdust, soil, straw or dry leaves – helped keep the contents aerated and, hopefully, not too potent. Evidence of the Barn's privy is long gone, a hole no doubt filled in nearly a hundred years ago, but it's easy to make an educated guess where it might have been. Privies and pigsties were often placed next to each other on farms – the idea being that the old bedding from the sties could be added to the privy pit to help keep it 'sweet'. Once the privy was full, the farmer could empty it and spread it on his fields. Or, if he was feeling flush, pay someone else to do it.

Next to the Barn, in a corner close to the cart shed, the soil is thick with broken pottery and glass. This is the midden. Every time a new hole is dug in the ground – for a rose bush or a rescued bramble – the earth reveals a lucky dip of late-Victorian refuse. This time capsule of trash provides a sneaky glimpse into the habits and hopes of the Hickeses and their live-in servants. It also tells us about the radical shift that occurred in the late-Victorian period, when farmed food went from local necessity to a national commodity.

At the start of the nineteenth century, the overwhelming

majority of food that British people ate was grown or raised locally. This was because most of the population still lived in the countryside. When the farmhouse was first built in 1840, the labourers who lived here, followed by the Hickes family in 1855, would have generated very little waste. Food scraps went to a local pig or chickens. Anything that could be burned would go onto the fire and the ash would be reused for the privy bucket or tossed on the kitchen garden. Textiles were worn out and reused ad infinitum – clothes would be handed down, remodelled, cut down for children's clothes, then made into dusters. Even then their work wasn't finished; old rags could find their way into paper-making factories, be dug into hop growers' fields to improve the quality of beer or be transformed into rag rugs to warm up a chilly floor.

Very few items bought from a grocer's or butcher's shop came ready-packaged. Solid food was wrapped in brown paper or newspaper and drink poured into the customer's own jug or bottle to take home. The larder in the farmhouse would have contained an army of vessels designed for mixing, storing and bottling ingredients. As Tom Licence, an expert on Victorian waste, has noted: 'pastes, polishes, pomades, sauces, beverages, and a great host of other substances were confected at home'.[12] Glass, bottles and baskets would be reused dozens if not hundreds of times, and only be thrown away when they were damaged beyond repair. This kind of gentle consumerism and thrift left very little trace. As the century wore on, however, it became quickly apparent that urban populations – who had no space to grow their own – would have to rely on food brought in from the surrounding countryside. As we've already seen, the arrival of the railways transformed John Hickes's expectations of where his crops or animals might end up. To keep food from spoiling in transit, manufacturers had to come up with increasingly inventive ways to preserve food – from canning fruit to condensing milk. Often marketed as 'luxury' or 'healthful', prepared foods also began to catch the eye of rural householders, especially aspirational families such as the Hickeses. Other household staples began to come ready-made too – ointments and unctions, polishes and potions, many of which were marketed as 'labour-saving', a quality few busy farmers' wives, such as Jane, could afford to ignore.

Patterns of food and household preparation slowly began to change. Middle-class households started to throw away redundant, useable vessels in favour of shelves full of neatly packaged goods. What was on the outside of a packet became as important as its contents. Provenance changed from knowing the farmer to knowing the brand. Packaging was a direct and immediate way to connect with customers: 'Names and claims could be embossed on the bottles, transfer-printed upon stoneware vessels, or emblazoned on colourful labels. An increasingly literate public could read them too;

 or, at least, they might recognise the trademark.'[13] What people did with their packaging also changed. As the nineteenth century wore on, reuse was no longer automatic; for the first time in history, packaging was deliberately designed to be thrown away – manufacturers didn't want to see their jars, bottles and tins storing anything but their own products. Worries about food safety and hygiene, which often stemmed from very public adulteration scandals, also encouraged Victorian households to put their trust in known, hermetically sealed branded containers.

The Hickeses quickly became adept at throwing stuff away. The midden has yielded numerous treasures, many of which perfectly demonstrate the family's slide into consumerism. Where once the housekeeper or Jane might have made jams and sauces from the orchard's fruit, bottles and stoneware jars with familiar names such as Dundee marmalade, Yorkshire relish, Hartley's jam and Garton's HP sauce took their place. Remnants of cosmetics reveal the family's – especially Jane's and her three grown-up daughters' – preoccupation with Victorian ideas about beauty. Ceramic lids of Gosnell's cherry toothpaste, cold cream and Holloways Cure All promise youth and beauty in a pot. Bucketfuls of clear and light-green bottles – many completely intact – held everything from the governess's ink to Camp Coffee & Chicory.

The objects that were jettisoned also directly reflected the wealth disparities of nineteenth-century Britain. Bottle hunters, who now happily rifle through the contents of late-Victorian middens, find stark differences in the composition of rubbish from poor and well-to-do households. Middle-class families like the Hickeses not only consumed more than their less well-off neighbours, they also consumed differently. Those who had the money could afford to splash out on ready-made branded products, or luxury packaged items. Poorer households tended to consume much less, and fewer ready-made goods, but they were also much less likely to throw the packaging away when they were finished with it. Bottles might be returned to the grocer's to collect a small deposit or be cleaned and refilled. What couldn't be reused also had value – with any luck you could sell your rubbish to one of the hundreds of scavengers who wandered the streets buying up bottles, bones, rags, paper and other waste.

Changes in farming, food production and consumption created a whole new class of jobs, human 'recyclers' who eked out an existence by sifting through the rubbish of others. Most Victorian households – both rural and urban – produced a large amount of 'dust', ashes from an open fire. This dust, which often constituted 90 per cent of what was thrown away, had an intrinsic value – ash was central to the brickmaking industry and a useful soil fertiliser. Anyone who could be bothered to collect ash on a large scale could sell it on. Households would also hold back certain pieces of rubbish, knowing they could either give it or sell it to one of the many rag-and-bone men* who floated past regularly. Making a living from the flotsam of others' lives meant that rag-and-bone men were often viewed with an uneasy mix of necessity and suspicion; the precarious existence of a scavenger often left them in a liminal world somewhere between beggar and buyer. For some, the occupation was to be pitied and reviled in the same breath; writing in *The Times* in 1840, one commentator seethes about a 'disgusting nuisance which has grown up of late years [...] Within a few years there have been introduced among us a class of people, whose persons, like their occupation, are the most filthy and degraded imaginable.'[14]

Once the refuse had been collected, it was sorted and sold on. Scraps of cloth went to paper-making businesses. Old bones were turned into toothbrushes, combs or teething rings, while the rest were boiled and crushed for fertiliser. Broken glass made emery cloth and sandpaper, while animal carcasses and parts were gobbled up by glue- and soap-making

---

* There are some fantastic regional variations in the name, such as bone-grubber, bone-picker, rag-gatherer, bag board and totter.

factories. Even dead cats could be sold to furriers. London was so efficient at extracting value from rubbish that other growing cities, including those in the north, shipped theirs to the capital, where it would be auctioned off to the highest bidder. The Yorkshire cliché turned out to be true – 'where there's muck there's brass' – the value of the rubbish pile, in effect, paid for its collection.

By the end of the nineteenth century, the system started to falter. The first problem was a slump in the value of ash – prices for 'dust' were falling, partly because brickmaking technology and materials were changing, but also because farmers such as George Hickes were finding different ways to fertilise their fields. Owing to changes in how food and other household products were packaged, households were generating more waste than ever before. Dust collecting and scavenging could no longer keep pace. The Public Health Act of 1875 also made it illegal to establish an 'offensive trade', such as rag-and-bone collecting, without written consent from the local authority. Rag-and-bone men often got round this clause by either collecting waste for free or giving out balloons, goldfish, baby chicks and other trinkets as 'gifts' to children in return for salvaged items, but it became increasingly difficult to make a living from selling other people's rubbish.

At the turn of the twentieth century, the mass production of glass bottles and other packaging meant it was often cheaper and easier for companies to create new products from virgin materials than recycle old ones. The only way of disposing of the country's rubbish, therefore, was to bury it or set fire to it. By the late 1870s, cities had begun to burn their rubbish in incinerators or simply dump it unsorted. Because so much of the waste was either glass or ceramic vessels, much of it ended up under new roads or was used to reclaim agricultural land from the sea. Other piles went to infill quarries or helped to shore up railway lines. The fact that the midden at the Barn contains so many bottles and ceramics from after the 1870s reflects a dilemma the Hickes family must have faced. John, Jane and their large family were fully embracing the late-Victorian consumer revolution but struggling to find a rural business or rag-and-bone man willing to take away for free the empty jars, tins and containers it spawned in such profusion. Organised collection of waste was not a general feature of late-nineteenth-century country life. In most rural regions, rubbish collection was down to the efforts of the local Women's Institute group or particularly proactive and forward-thinking landowners. Faced with a haphazard and unpredictable system, and with no available facility for waste disposal in the immediate vicinity, the only solution for the Hickes family was to get their domestic servant to walk to the end of the cart shed and tip bucketfuls of bottles and broken crockery onto an ever-growing heap.

Even as late as the 1930s, campaigners were expressing dismay at the amount of rubbish being dumped in the countryside. Ugly piles of household garbage and fly-tipped waste were a long way from traditional images of pastoral England. A survey sent out to 4,000 Women's Institutes across England and Wales revealed just how desperate the situation had become. Only half of the areas surveyed had any kind of organised refuse collection – either by a voluntary group such as the WI or the local council. Nearly 40 per cent reported that people relied on 'individual disposal' – which in practice meant rubbish being thrown into woodland or over someone else's hedge, dropped into a hole to fill it up, dumped in a ditch or surreptitiously abandoned on the commons.[15] In 1937, North Yorkshire's gentle and housewifely Anti-Litter League were left so apoplectic by people constantly dumping rubbish on Newby Moor that they proposed to build a wicker man from the refuse and, very publicly, set it alight. Not only was the campaign greeted with approval from the council and police, it had been inspired by a similar group who had angrily burned a litter-lout effigy just a few years before.[16]

For the Hickes family, life at the Barn had been good. From their arrival in 1855, thanks to a combination of hard work, canny business decisions, and not a little luck, the family had risen from labourers to prosperous middle-class tenant farmers. John and his wife, Jane, had managed to raise six healthy children, three boys and three girls, all of whom – unusually – made it well into adulthood and went on to have good careers or marry well. Success in farming also gave them access to a whole new way of life – from their large new-build farmhouse, with its live-in servants, to the latest in packaged goods, private education for their children and their own wheeled transport. When John Hickes died in October 1890, at the age of seventy-eight, his eldest son, George, took charge of the Barn and the farmhouse. Promising to take care of his now-widowed mother, George ran the farm with the same care and acumen as his father, growing the cattle side of the business and making the most of the Barn's proximity to the railway.

Farming had experienced monumental changes during the Hickeses' time at the Barn. Many of the ways farming changed over the nineteenth century – from land use to mechanisation – affected labourers and farm servants acutely, but when the Great Depression and the collapse of grain prices came in the last few decades of the century, the fortunes of those who owned the land changed too. The Great Depression that began in the 1870s had the effect of slashing land values, rentals and confidence in farming as a guaranteed money-maker. For most of the nineteenth century, the majority of British millionaires were landowners and had made their money from the profits created by agriculture. Between 1880 and the beginning of the First World War, that figure dropped to just one-third and carried on falling in subsequent years.[17] Many landowners had borrowed heavily to finance 'high farming' improvements around their estates, or had concentrated on arable, and couldn't survive the downturn. While wheat prices briefly rallied during the First World War, thanks to government guarantees, by the 1930s prices were back down to the doldrums of the 1890s. Many landowners decided, or were forced, to give up – between 1910 and 1921, around 6 million acres of land changed hands; historians have called it the largest turnover of land since the Dissolution of the Monasteries.[18] Many estate fields and farms were sold to their sitting tenant farmers.

For its entire life, the Barn and its land had belonged to the Church. It was glebe land – tithes and then rental income from those who farmed the land contributed towards the upkeep of Stonegrave's rector. In response to the Great Depression and falling rents, the Glebe Lands Act was passed in 1888, which allowed clergy to sell the lands associated with their parish and reinvest the money elsewhere, often in government stock. On 23 November 1917, Reverend Pitman, rector of Stonegrave and the same man who had fought so passionately for clean water supplies, put the Barn, the land and the farmhouse up for sale. The sale particulars, for the auction at the local pub, boasted that 'the land is of good quality, in a capital state of cultivation, the farm having been in the hands of the family of the present tenant for over sixty years'. Tucked away almost imperceptibly in the glowing description of the Barn's 'excellent sporting rights' and potential 'building sites' was the extra detail that the tenants 'are under notice to quit on the 6th April 1918'. George Hickes had been given his marching orders.

At the time of the sale, George had been running the farm single-handed for more than twenty years. Now in his late fifties, unmarried, with only a grown-up niece and a housekeeper for company, the news that the farm was going to be sold must have been devastating. At the time of the sale, the farm was still making money and employing at least two full-time farmworkers, a responsibility George would have felt keenly. In reality, however, despite the family's careful and profitable running of the farm for over six decades, they had never managed to save up quite enough money to buy the land, the Barn and property outright. As the hammer fell, over lunchtime pints in the Black Swan, Helmsley, George knew he had less than six months to clear out from the only home and landscape he had ever known. John Charles Barker, a wealthy landowner from nearby Sproxton Hall, snapped up the farm for just over £4,000, no doubt sensing a bargain in the middle of a general economic fog. As for George, the prospect of life without the Barn turned out to be unthinkable. By February 1918 – just two months before he was due to leave the Barn – he was dead, at the age of sixty-two. The Hickeses' dedicated and fruitful custodianship of the farm in its wide and gentle valley had come to an abrupt end.

AFTERWORD

Yesterday, I took the dog for his usual afternoon walk. It was one of those days that you only get in late winter, when the weak sunshine tricks you into thinking you have plenty of daylight to play with. Before I knew it, I'd reached the edge of Hovingham, a lazy two-hour zigzag around field edges and scrappy woodland. I'd been wonderfully anaesthetised by the pinching air and solitude, and completely lost track of time.

Slightly anxious that the light was fading rapidly, I headed back a different way, along the abandoned railway line that once carried cattle, limestone and, briefly, holidaymakers across the valley bottom past the Barn. I could trace the route in my sleep, but it struck me that I'd never walked here in near darkness. The signs of twenty-first-century life had dissolved into the black and all I could make out was the narrow straight track, cutting through the woodland, and the warm, advent calendar windows of Stonegrave on the ridge in the distance.

It took another half hour to get within striking distance of the Barn. The railway line emptied me onto the lane, the same road that had witnessed the girl being thrown from the cart and the groom struggling to save her. Now in complete darkness, I had to take a sharp right, across the valley bottom, following a barely used footpath that refused to go in a straight line. I picked my way through a field, across gate after gate, over Holbeck stream, past a dark copse, and another, before the Barn, and home, finally came into view. The dog had spent most of the walk pulling on the lead and so, irritated, I'd let him off and he'd shot off into the darkness.

A few years ago I would have been frightened to walk in the dark, but instead I felt time gently unravel. After spending so long reading, thinking and writing about the people who had lived here before, I realised I was walking with 'ghosts' – not only the Hickes family, but also the workmen who laid the railway track, the waggoners with their horses, the children walking to their village school, the gleaning women, the labourers ambling home, sore from a day's work in the fields. Only by being alone could my thoughts conjure up their benign presence.

It also struck me that, in the grey distance, the outline of the Barn probably looked no different from how it had done a hundred years ago. And yet, at its heart, everything had changed. After the Second World War, farming took a different turn – one that almost preserved the Barn in aspic.

Despite the rallying of farmers like George Hickes in the First World War, it took the Second World War to really shock the country into realising it was too reliant on imported food – conflict with our foreign neighbours soon strangled the food supply chain and we were again hostages to fortune.

During the conflict, the country's farmers rose to the challenge of growing more food, quickly, and managed to nearly double their output of wheat, barley, oats and potatoes. When peacetime came, farmers were rewarded with the Agriculture Act of 1947, which set out to create a stable and efficient agricultural industry. Its aims were seemingly contradictory – to provide cheap food for the country but also to make sure farmers were generously rewarded for their efforts. The Act achieved this by guaranteeing prices for a wide range of farming products – sheep, cattle, milk, eggs, barley, wheat, oats, rye, potatoes, sugar beet and wool. The legislation also made it more difficult to evict tenant farmers, as George had been back in 1918, a security that gave many the courage to invest in their own farms and future.

The Barn and the farm carried on being rented out until the middle of the twentieth century. After George died, just days before his tenancy was finished, the farm was bought by successive men of means; first, as we already know, by John Charles Barker of Sproxton Hall and then, in 1941, by Major Gordon Bentley Foster, the owner of Leysthorpe Hall, a glamorous Arts and Crafts country seat that overlooks the valley and the Barn, just half a mile away. Neither of these owners lived or worked at the Barn, but carried on the tradition of renting out the farmhouse and land to a series of tenant farmers. The last of these families were the Wilsons, whose two young sons, in 1961, managed to raise enough capital to buy the Barn, the farmhouse and almost all its original 200 acres. Just eight years earlier, mains electricity had finally been installed at the farm, with cables and poles swagged across the fields like washing lines. New, larger prefabricated buildings, including a Dutch barn for hay, and grain silos were soon thrown up and the Barn, now dwarfed in comparison, became largely redundant.

The cart shed, with its two-wheeled transport long gone, became somewhere to keep cars and kit; the tractors that replaced the job of the horse were too big to fit in any of the cart shed's bays and instead found a home further down the farmyard. The threshing barn no longer suited the farmer's needs for animal feed and became yet another place to store machinery. The open fold yard, where once the cows had milled about, was roofed with iron trusses and asbestos sheets to create a huge covered barn. And by the 1980s, the family had turned its attention to pig farming, a profitable wave they surfed until the market nosedived in the noughties. Sensing which way the economic wind was blowing, the family sensibly sold off much of the land and diversified, setting up a successful children's farm theme park over on the North

Yorkshire coast. In 2007 the farm, the remaining few acres and the Barn were sold to us.

I sometimes get a sense of being watched. Not in an unkindly way, but rather a feeling that what we do here will be judged. The Barn has seen it all and now, with two non-farmers in charge, it must wonder what we have in store for it. For the moment, the answer is nothing. I love the Barn as it is. Practical. Unshowy. As a farm building should be. We grow our own food and keep livestock, but it's smallholding, not farming. Our lives, unlike the Hickeses', don't depend on the success of the next harvest or a fickle urban marketplace for our meat and produce, but every year we get to know the land just that little bit better - the patches of field that always flood, the frost pockets and the sunny corners. Each season, and often individual weeks, are marked in their own reassuring way; in spring, the blossom appears in a pleasing roll call: the blackthorn first; then the plum and cherry; the pear and the apple next; and finally the hawthorn. In a similar way, I always know summer is close by when our Soay sheep start naturally shedding their wool in great, straggly clumps, a genetic quirk that hasn't changed since the dawn of farming.

As my walk came to an end and I approached the Barn, my boots clarted up from a shortcut across the last field, I could see that the dog had beaten me to it. Someone had left the light on in the threshing barn and he was a silhouette, waiting patiently for his owner, as perhaps other farm dogs had done before. After patting his head, I flicked the switch and plunged us both back into the darkness, and together we headed back across the yard.

ENDNOTES

Prologue

1. Jackson, C., in the preface to Thornton, A., *The autobiography of Mrs. Alice Thornton, of East Newton* (Durham: Andrews & Co., 1875), p.ix.
2. *Leeds Mercury* (1 Aug. 1896).

Chapter 1 – Is t'a stoppin' on, lad?
(pp.13–75)

1. Norman, A. F., *The Romans in East Yorkshire*, East Yorkshire Local History Society (1960), www.eylhs.org.uk/dl/124/the-romans-in-east-yorkshire.
2. Read, H., *Between the Riccall and the Rye* (The Orage Press, 2011), p.96.
3. Siddique, H., 'Yorkshire is most Anglo-Saxon region in the UK, DNA analysis suggests', *Guardian* (28 Jul. 2016), www.theguardian.com/science/2016/jul/28/yorkshire-is-most-anglo-saxon-region-in-the-uk-dna-analysis-suggests.
4. Newman, P. (ed.), 'The Archaeology of Mining and Quarrying in England: A Research Framework for the Archaeology of the Extractive Industries in England', National Association of Mining History Organisations and Historic England (2016), p.36.
5. Hartley, M. and Ingilby, J., *Life and Tradition in the Moorlands of North-East Yorkshire* (Otley: Smith Settle Ltd, 1990), p.2.

6. Britton, J. and Hodgson, J., *The Beauties of England and Wales, or, Delineations, topographical, historical, and descriptive, of each county* (London: Vernor and Hood, 1812), p.136.

7. Woodforde, J., *Farm Buildings* (London: Routledge and Kegan Paul, 1983), pp. 16–17.

8. Holmes, R., *The Age of Wonder* (London: Harper Collins, 2009).

9. As quoted in ibid.

10. As quoted in ibid.

11. Woodforde, *Farm Buildings*, p.17.

12. As quoted in Hartley and Ingilby, *Life and Tradition*, p. 43.

13. Caunce, S., *Amongst Farm Horses* (Stroud: Alan Sutton Publishing, 1991), p.73.

14. As quoted in Hartley and Ingilby, *Life and Tradition*, p.17.

15. Verdon, N., *Rural Women Workers in 19th-Century England: Gender, Work and Wages* (Woodbridge: Boydell Press, 2002).

16. Kebbel, T. E., *The Agricultural Labourer: A Short Summary of His Position* (London, 1887), p. 174.

17. As quoted in Moses, G., 'Reshaping Rural Culture? The Church of England and Hiring Fairs in the East Riding of Yorkshire c. 1850–80', *Rural History* (2002) 13, 1, pp. 61–84.

18. Tuke, J., *General View of the Agriculture of the North Riding of Yorkshire* (London: McMillan, 1800).

19. Marshall, W., *The Rural Economy of the Midland Counties: Including the Management of Livestock, in Leicestershire and Its Environs; Together with Minutes on Agriculture and Planting, in the District of the Midland Station*, Volume 2 (London: Nicol, 1790), p. 22.

20. Mingay, G. E., *Rural Life in Victorian England* (Stroud: Sutton Publishing, 1998), p. 77.

21. Caunce, S., 'Making the Most of Memory: Farm Lads' Tales', BBC History, www.bbc.co.uk/history/trail/htd_history/oral/make_most_farm_lads_02.shtml.

22. Mingay, *Rural Life*, p. 73.

23. Kightly, C., *Country Voices: Life and Lore in Farm and Village* (London: Thames & Hudson, 1984).

24. Cole, G. D. H., *The Life of William Cobbett* (Westport: Greenwood Press, 1971), p. 16.

25. John Burnett (ed.), *Destiny Obscure: Autobiographies of Childhood, Education and Family from the 1820s to the 1920s* (London: Routledge, 1994).

26. *Bradford Observer* (25 Oct. 1875).

27. Cohen, M. N., *Lewis Carroll: A Biography* (London: Macmillan, 2015), p. 170.

28. *The Yorkshire Herald* (24 Jun. 1871), p. 9.

29. *The Trial at Large of John Bolton, Gent: Of Bulmer, Near Castle-Howard, for the Wilful Murder of Elizabeth Rainbow, His Apprentice Girl, on Sunday the 21st of August, 1774, Before the Hon. Sir Henry Gould, at the Lent Assizes, Holden at the Castle of York, on Monday the 27th of March, 1775. Taken Down in Shorthand in the Court, by W. Williamson* (York: N. Nickson, 1775).

30. Burnett, *Destiny Obscure*.

31. Burnette, J., 'Child day-labourers in agriculture: evidence from farm accounts, 1740–1850', *The Economic History Review*, Vol. 65, No. 3 (Aug. 2012), pp. 1077–99.

32. *The Yorkshire Herald* (11 Feb. 1875), p. 6.

33. As quoted in Boos, F., *Memoirs of Victorian Working-Class Women: The Hard Way Up* (Springer, 2017), p. 51.

34. As quoted in Boos, F. S., 'The Education Act of 1870: Before and After', BRANCH: Britain, Representation and Nineteenth-Century History. Dino Franco Felluga (ed). Extension of Romanticism and Victorianism, www.branchcollective. org/?ps_articles=florence-s-boos-the-education-act-of-1870-before-and-after.

35. Pfordresher, J., 'Charlotte Brontë's Teaching Career', *Lapham's Quarterly* (2017).

36. Tuke, *General View*.

37. *Extraordinary Life and Character of Mary Bateman, the*

Yorkshire Witch: Traced from the Earliest Thefts of Her Infancy, Etc Till Her Execution on the 20th of March, 1809 (London: Davies and Company, 1811).

38. Griffin, E., 'Diets, Hunger and Living Standards During the British Industrial Revolution', *Past & Present* (January 2018).

39. Griffin, E., 'Diets, Hunger and Living Standards During the British Industrial Revolution', *Past & Present*, 239(1) (May 2018), p. 71–111.

40. Tuke, *General View*.

41. Goodman, R., *How to be a Victorian* (London: Penguin, 2014).

42. As quoted in Slater, G., *The English Peasantry and the Enclosure of Common Fields* (Edinburgh: Archibald Constable & Co. Ltd, 1907).

43. Tuke, *General View*, p. 314.

44. Lloyd, A. J., 'Emigration, Immigration and Migration in Nineteenth-Century Britain', *British Library Newspapers* (Detroit: Gale, 2007).

45. Quoted in Read, *Between the Riccall and the Rye*, p. 95.

46. Dixon, J. T., 'Aspects of Yorkshire emigration to North America, 1760–1880', PhD thesis, University of Leeds (1981).

47. *Two Friends* ship passenger list: https://immigrantships. net/1700/twofriends740509.html.

48. Ibid.

49. *Leicester Chronicle* (26 Jul. 1834), p. 2.

50. As quoted in Sloan, B., 'An anxious discourse: English rural life and labour and the periodical press between the 1860s and the 1880s', University of Southampton (2013), http:// eprints.soton.ac.uk/id/eprint/356982.

51. As quoted in Butler, S., *Goodbye Old Friend: A Sad Farewell to the Working Horse* (Wellington: Halsgrove, 2012).

52. Hansard, UK Parliament, 'Systematic Colonization'. Volume 68: debated on Thursday 6 April 1843, https://hansard. parliament.uk/Commons/1843-04-06/debates/5cod9265-faf9-457e-b27e-4b9cab6903eb/SystematicColonization.

53. As quoted in Higginbotham, P., 'Pauper Emigration under

the New Poor law', *The Workhouse* (2020), http://www. workhouses.org.uk/emigration/.

Chapter 2 – We've gotten wer mell, hurrah hurrah! (pp.77–141)

1. As quoted in Hone, W., *The Year Book of Daily Recreation and Information: Concerning Remarkable Men and Manners, Times and Seasons, Solemnities and Merry-makings, Antiquities and Novelties on the Plan of the Every-day Book and Table Book*, Volume 2 (London: T. Tegg, 1838).

2. Brand, J., *Observations on Popular Antiquities: Including the Whole of Mr. Bourne's Antiquitates Vulgares, with Addenda to Every Chapter of that Work: as Also an Appendix Containing Such Articles on the Subject, as Have Been Omitted by that Author* (London: J. Johnson, 1777), p. 307.

3. Hartley, M. and Ingilby, J., *Life and Tradition in the Moorlands of North-East Yorkshire* (Otley: Smith Settle Ltd., 1990), p. 54.

4. Kightly, C., *The Perpetual Almanack of Folklore* (London: Thames & Hudson, 1987).

5. Opie, I. and Tatem, M., *Oxford Dictionary of Superstitions* (Oxford: Oxford University Press, 2005), p. 405.

6. Simpson, J. and Roud, S., *A Dictionary of English Folklore* (Oxford: Oxford University Press, 2000), p. 359.

7. Silter, J. (ed.), *The Cambridge Companion to Eighteenth-Century Poetry* (Cambridge: Cambridge University Press, 2001), p. 9.

8. Hardy, T., *Far from the Madding Crowd* (1874).

9. Kightly, C., *Country Voices: Life and Lore in Farm and Village* (London: Thames & Hudson, 1984), p. 123.

10. As quoted in Hartley and Ingilby, *Life and Tradition*.

11. Britten, J., *Old Country and Farming Words: Gleaned from Agricultural Books* (London: The English Dialect Society, 1880), p. 5.

12. Hartley and Ingilby, *Life and Tradition*.

13. Ibid.

14. King, P., 'Customary Rights and Women's Earnings: The Importance of Gleaning to the Rural Labouring Poor, 1750–1850', *The Economic History Review*, 44(3) (Aug. 1991), pp. 461–76. JSTOR, www.jstor.org/stable/2597539.

15. King, P., 'Legal Change, Customary Right, and Social Conflict in Late Eighteenth-Century England: The Origins of the Great Gleaning Case of 1788', *Law and History Review*, 10(1) (Spring 1992), pp. 1–31, doi:10.2307/743812.

16. Thompson, E. P., *Whigs and Hunters: The Origin of the Black Act* (London: Pantheon Books, 1975), p. 241.

17. King, P., 'Legal Change', pp. 29–30.

18. Whitlock, R., *Peasant's Heritage* (London: Herbert Jenkins Ltd, 1940), pp. 46–60.

19. *Essex Farmers' Journal* (16 Aug. 1933).

20. Kightly, *Country Voices*, pp. 19–20.

21. Harwood Long, W., 'The Development of Mechanization in English Farming', *The Agricultural History Review* 11(1) (1963), pp. 15–26.

22. As quoted in Hussey, S., '"The Last Survivor of an Ancient Race": The Changing Face of Essex Gleaning', *The Agricultural History Review*, 45(1) (1997_), pp. 61–72, www.jstor.org/stable/40275132.

23. *The Yorkshire Herald* and the *York Herald* (15 Sept. 1855).

24. Marshall, W., *The Rural Economy of Yorkshire*, Volume 2 (London: Cadell, 1788), p. 37.

25. Marshall, W., *On the landed property of England : an elementary and practical treatise : containing the purchase, the improvement, and the management of landed estates* (London: G. and W. Nichol, 1804), pp. 163–4.

26. Young, A., *Annals of Agriculture Vol. XX* (Bury St.Edmunds: J.Rackham, 1793), p. 248.

27. Bloy, Dr M., 'Rural Unrest in the 1830s: the "Swing" riots', www.historyhome.co.uk.

28. Quoted in Tuke, J., *Agricultural Surveys: Yorkshire, North-Riding* (Board of Agriculture, 1800), p. 137.

29. John Walker Ord, J. W., *The History and Antiquities of*

Cleveland: Comprising the Wapentake of East and West Langbargh, North Riding, County York (London: Simpkin and Marshall, 1846).

30. Bailey, J. and Culley, G., *General View of the Agriculture of the County of Northumberland: With Observations on the Means of Its Improvement; Drawn Up for the Consideration of the Board of Agriculture and Internal Improvement* (London: Mess. Robinson, and G. Nicol, 1797), p. 55.

31. Saunders, J., 'Mr Mechi on Agriculture', *The People's Journal - Annals of Progress*, Vols. 3 & 4 (London: Willoughby & Co., 1847), p. 45.

32. Jefferies, R., 'The Future of Farming', *Fraser's Magazine* (Dec. 1873).

33. Sinclair, Sir John, *The code of agriculture; including observations on gardens, orchards, woods and plantations; with an account of all recent improvements in the management of arable and grass land* (London: Sherwood, Gilbert & Piper, 1832), p. 141.

34. As quoted in Aitkin, A., *Illustrations of Arts and Manufactures: Being a Selection from a Series of Papers Read Before the Society for the Encouragement of Arts, Manufactures, and Commerce* (J. Van Voorst, 1841), p. 2

35. Hansard, 'The Andover Union', HC Deb 05 March 1846 vol. 84 cc625-76, https://api.parliament.uk/historic-hansard/commons/1846/mar/05/the-andover-union.

36. Merchant, C., *American Environmental History: An Introduction* (Columbia University Press, 2007), p. 20.

37. Hansard, 'The Andover Union'.

38. Semmel, S., 'Reading the Tangible Past: British Tourism, Collecting, and Memory after Waterloo', *Representations* 69 (2000), pp. 9–37.

39. Stannard Barrett, E., *The Talents Run Mad* (London, 1816).

40. Limbird, J., *The Mirror of Literature, Amusement, and Instruction*, Volume 1 (1823).

41. *Pittsburgh Dispatch* (29 Mar. 1889), p. 4.

42. Meager, L., *The Mystery of Husbandry: OR, Arable, Pasture, and*

Wood-land Improved: Containing the whole Art and Mystery of Agriculture or Husbandry, in Bettering and Improving all Degrees of Land, fertilizing the barrenest Soil, recovering it from Weeds, Bushes, Briars, Rushes, Flags, Overflowings of salt or unwholsom Waters, to bear good Corn, or become Meadow or Pasture (London: Onley, 1697), Chapter II, p. 8.

43. Johnson, M. L., 'The English House of Gibbs in Peru's Guano Trade in the Nineteenth Century', Clemson University (2017), p. 6, https://tigerprints.clemson.edu/all_theses/2791.

44. Wilson, Rev. J. M. (ed.), *The rural cyclopedia: or a general dictionary of agriculture, and of the arts, sciences, instruments, and practice, necessary to the farmer, stockfarmer, gardener, forester, landsteward, farrier, &c.*, Volume 3 (Edinburgh: Fullarton & Co., 1849), p. 556.

45. Ibid.

46. As quoted in Schnug, E. et al., 'Guano: The White Gold of the Seabirds', in Mikkola, H., *Seabirds*, www.intechopen.com/books/seabirds/guano-the-white-gold-of-the-seabirds.

47. As quoted in Johnson, 'The English House of Gibbs', p. 63.

48. Mayhew, H. as quoted in Eveleigh, D. J., *Privies and Water Closets* (Oxford: Shire Library, 2008), p. 19.

49. Johnson, D., *Lime Kilns: History and Heritage* (Stroud: Amberley Publishing, 2018).

50. *Sheffield and Rotherham Independent* (11 Aug. 1860), p. 6.

51. Radford, M. A. and Radford, E., *Encyclopaedia of Superstitions* (London: Rider and Company, 1947).

52. Croker, T. C., *Researches in the south of Ireland: illustrative of the scenery, architectural remains and the manners and superstitions of the peasantry, with an appendix containing a private narrative of the rebellion of 1798* (London: Murray, 1824), p. 80.

53. *The Yorkshire Herald* (12 Dec. 1835), p. 3.

54. Tuke, J., *General View of the Agriculture of the North Riding of Yorkshire* (London: McMillan, 1800), p. 149.

55. Mann, C. C., 'How the Potato Changed the World', *Smithsonian Magazine* (Nov. 2011).

56. Younger, J., *Autobiography of John Younger* (Kelso: J. & J. H. Rutherfurd, 1881), p. 128.

57. Hoggard, B., *Magical House Protection: The Archaeology of Counter-Witchcraft* (New York: Berghahn Books, 2019).

58. Sinclair, J., *Hints Respecting the Culture and the Use of Potatoes* (Board of Agriculture, 1795).

59. As quoted in Graham, B., 'Historical Notes: God and England made the Irish famine', *Independent* (3 Dec. 1998).

60. www.teazlesandteazlemen.co.uk/wp-content/uploads/2019/04/Chapter-1.pdf.

61. A Society of Gentlemen, *The complete Farmer: or, a general Dictionary of Husbandry* (1777).

62. McMillan, R. A. 'The Yorkshire Teazle-Growing Trade', *Yorkshire Archaeological Journal*, Vol. 6 (1984).

63. 'April 1652: An Act prohibiting the planting of Tobacco in England.', in *Acts and Ordinances of the Interregnum, 1642–1660*, ed. C. H. Firth and R. S. Rait (London, 1911), p. 580.

64. Tuke, *General View*, p. 163.

65. *North-Eastern Daily Gazette* (5 Apr. 1886), p. 4.

Chapter 3 – Ee couldn't stop a pig in a ginnel (pp.143–215)

1. Ridgway, J., *The Transactions of the Yorkshire Agricultural Society* (1838).

2. Tuke, J., *General View of the Agriculture of the North Riding of Yorkshire* (London: McMillan, 1800), p. 248.

3. Burke, J. F., *British husbandry: exhibiting the farming practice in various parts of the United Kingdom* (published under the superintendence of the Society for the Diffusion of Useful Knowledge, London: Robert Baldwin, 1847).

4. *The Builder* (1843), p. 193.

5. Giles, K. and Giles, M., 'The writing on the wall: the concealed communities of the East Yorkshire horselads', *International*

Journal of Historical Archaeology, 4(11) (2007).

6. *The Central New-York Farmer*, 3(1) (1844), p. 77.

7. Collins, E. J. T., 'The latter-day history of the draught ox in England, 1770–1964', *Agricultural History Review*, 58 (2) (2010), pp. 191–216.

8. Griffin, E., 'Diets, Hunger and Living Standards During the British Industrial Revolution', *Past & Present* (Jan. 2018), pp. 71–111.

9. Ibid.

10. Tuke, J., *General View*, p. 254.

11. Ibid., p. 149.

12. *Whitby Gazette* (25 Jan. 1963).

13. Comben, N., *The Durham Ox* (Nottingham: Adlard, 2007).

14. Parkinson, R., *Treatise on the Breeding and Management of Live Stock* (London: Cadell and Davies, 1810), p. 267.

15. Milne, A., 'Sentient Genetics: Breeding the Animal Breeder as Fundamental Other', *Journal for Eighteenth-Century Studies*, 33(4) (2010), https://onlinelibrary.wiley.com/doi/pdf/10.1111/j.1754-0208.2010.00324.x.

16. Hartley, M. and Ingilby, J., *Life and Tradition in the Moorlands of North-East Yorkshire* (Otley: Smith Settle Ltd, 1990), pp. 23–4.

17. Panton, J. E., *From Kitchen to Garret: Hints for Young Householders* (London: Ward & Downey, 1893), p. 222.

18. Atkins, P., 'Bovine tuberculosis: the human impact' in *A history of uncertainty: bovine tuberculosis in Britain, 1850 to the present* (Winchester University Press, 2016).

19. *The Yorkshire Herald* (4 Mar. 1899), p. 16.

20. *The Yorkshire Herald* (10 Jun. 1889), p. 7.

21. Darby, H. C., 'Domesday Woodland', *The Economic History Review*, 3(1) (1950), pp. 21–43, doi:10.2307/2589941.

22. Cobbett, W., *Cottage Economy, to which is added The Poor Man's Friend* (Good Press, 22 Nov 2019).

23. Kightly, C., *Country Voices: Life and Lore in Farm and Village* (London: Thames & Hudson, 1984), p. 75.

24. Ibid.

25. Malcolmson, R. W. et al., *The English Pig: A History* (London: Bloomsbury Publishing, 2003), p. 96.

26. Hardy, T., *Jude the Obscure* (Ware: Wordsworth Editions, 1995), p. 52.

27. Tuke, *General View*, p. 282.

28. Ibid.

29. Hartley Edwards, E., *The Horse Encyclopedia* (London: Dorling Kindersley, 2016), p. 43.

30. Aubrey, J., *Remaines of Gentilisme and Judaisme* (published for the Folk-Lore Society by W. Satchell, Peyton and Co., 1881).

31. Hartwell Horne, T., *The Complete Grazier, Or, Farmer's and Cattle-breeder's and Dealer's Assistant* (London: Baldwin & Cradock, 1830).

32. Tuke, *General View*, pp. 276–7.

33. *The Hull Packet* (8 Sept. 1871).

34. *Leeds Mercury* (26 Jul. 1887).

35. Cobbett, W., *Cottage Economy, to which is added The Poor Man's Friend* (Good Press, 22 Nov. 2019).

36. As quoted in Rosen, Dr B., 'Knackered', 4 November 2016, http://vichist.blogspot.com/2016/11/knackered.html.

37. *The Hull Packet* (14 Dec. 1883).

38. Ewart Evans, G., *The Horse in the Furrow* (London: Faber, 1960).

39. Kightly, *Country Voices*, pp. 46–7.

40. Hartley and Ingilby, *Life and Tradition*, p. 24.

41. Caunce, S., 'Twentieth-Century Farm Servants: The Horselads of the East Riding of Yorkshire', https://bahs.org.uk/AGHR/ARTICLES/39n2a5.pdf.

42. *The Yorkshire Herald* (8 Nov. 1890), p. 3.

43. Giles and Giles, 'The writing on the wall', *International Journal of Historical Archaeology* (2007).

44. Mallinson, A., 'When wagons rolled to the battlefields', *The Times* (10 Sept. 2011).

45. Butler, S., *Goodbye Old Friend: A Sad Farewell to the Working*

Horse (Halsgrove, 2012), p. 106.

46. *Yorkshire Herald* (5 Jul. 1900), p. 6.

47. *The Manchester Guardian* (5 Aug. 1907), p. 10.

48. *The Yorkshire Herald* (8 Sept. 1900), p. 3.

49. *The Yorkshire Herald* (28 Oct. 1899), p. 11.

50. Jopling, A. F. and Woodhead H., *50 Years of Progress: Jowett Cars 1901-1951* (London: Lund Humphries, 1951).

51. As quoted in Edwards, G. A. B., 'Land-Rover and its Agricultural Applications led to the Agrover and the Trantor tractor', www.trantortractors.com.

52. Kightly, *Country Voices*, p. 20.

53. *The Vermin-killer: being a compleat and necessary family-book ... also several excellent receipts for the cure of most disorders. And some useful directions for gardening and husbandry, etc* (London: W. Owen, 1755).

54. Anderson, D., 'Noyfull Fowles and Vermyn: Parish Payments For Killing Wildlife In Hampshire 1533-1863', *Proc. Hampshire Field Club Archaeol. Soc.* 60 (2005), pp. 209-228.

55. *Leeds Mercury* (20 May 1865).

56. Nagy, V., *Nineteenth-Century Female Poisoners* (Springer, 2015).

57. Shrubb, M., *Birds, Scythes and Combines: A History of Birds and Agricultural Change* (Cambridge University Press, 2003), p. 319.

58. Birkhead, T., 'Climmers and Collectors' in *The Most Perfect Thing* (London: Bloomsbury, 2016).

59. Quoted in ibid., p. 6.

60. As quoted in McCann, J., 'The Influence of Rodents on the Design and Construction of Farm Buildings in Britain', *Journal of the Historic Farm Buildings Group* 10 (1996). www.hfbg.org.uk/images/influence_of_rodents_on_design_and_construction_john_mccann.pdf.

61. Burke, *British husbandry*.

62. Burke, J. F., *Farming for ladies; or, A guide to the poultry-yard, the dairy and piggery*. By the author of 'British husbandry' (London: John Murray, 1844).

63. Table IV.I Average weight of animals sold at Smithfield (lbs), www.ncbi.nlm.nih.gov/pmc/articles/PMC2531035/pdf/medhistsuppl00026-0061.pdf.
64. Wykes, D. L., 'Robert Bakewell (1725–1795) of Dishley: farmer and livestock improver', *Agricultural History Review* 52(1) (2004).
65. Cleaver, E., quoted in Tuke, *General View*, p. 262.
66. *The Hull Packet* (10 Aug. 1838).

Chapter 4 – Yan mud as good stop at yam
(pp.217–267)

1. *The Yorkshire Herald* (2 Jul. 1870).
2. Marshall, W., *The Rural Economy of Yorkshire: Comprizing the Management of Landed Estates, and the Present Practice of Husbandry in the Agricultural Districts of that County*, Volume 1 (London: T. Cadell, 1788), p. 187.
3. MacMahon, K. A. *Roads and Turnpike Trusts in Eastern Yorkshire*, East Yorkshire Local History Society (1964).
4. Ibid.
5. Morison, J. C., *Gibbon* (New York: Arkell Weekly Company, 1895), p. 102.
6. Morison, J. C., 'Gibbon', Chapter 17 in Morley, J. (ed.), *English Men of Letters* (New York: Harper & Brothers, 1902).
7. Baring-Gould, S., *Old Country Life* (London: Methuen, 1892), p. 213.
8. As quoted in Perry, J., *The York-Oswaldkirk Turnpike Trust 1768–1881* (North Yorkshire County Record Office, 1977).
9. Bogart, D., 'The Turnpike Roads of England and Wales', p. 9., www.campop.geog.cam.ac.uk/research/projects/transport/onlineatlas/britishturnpiketrusts.pdf.
10. Baring-Gould, *Old Country Life*, p. 201.
11. *Journals of the House of Commons*, Volume 44 (House of Commons H.M. Stationery Office, 1788), p. 315.
12. Austin, Mrs (ed.), *A Memoir of the Reverend Sydney Smith*.

By His Daughter, Lady Holland, with a Selection from His Letters, Volume I (London: Longman, Brown, Green and Longmans, 1855).

13. https://en.wikipedia.org/wiki/Rebecca_Riots.

14. www.bbc.co.uk/blogs/wales/entries/5d65f917-5961-3e76-b5ac-ecoc8fb3cob6.

15. Tuke, J., *General View of the Agriculture of the North Riding of Yorkshire* (London: McMillan, 1800), p. 298.

16. Ibid., p. 303.

17. Ibid., p. 305.

18. *Derby Mercury* (8 Nov. 1754).

19. Jones, P., *Navigation on the Yorkshire Derwent* (Sidcup: Oakwood Press, 2000), p. 8.

20. Copsey, N., 'The Subscription Rooms, Yorkersgate, Malton', www.nigelcopsey.com/reports/malton/malton_the_subscription_rooms.pdf.

21. *York Herald* (4 Jul. 1807).

22. Jones, *Navigation on the River Derwent*, p. 47.

23. Howat, P., *The Railways of Ryedale* (Martin Bairstow, 2004), p. 3.

24. Fowkes, E. H., *Railway History and the Local Historian* (East Yorkshire Local History Society, 1963).

25. As quoted in Howat, *The Railways of Ryedale*, p. 5.

26. www.maltonhistory.info/Topics/Topics/River.html.

27. Smiles, S., *The Life of George Stephenson* (London: John Murray, 1857).

28. Letter from William Wordsworth to Prime Minister William Gladstone, 15 October 1844 (British Library), www.bl.uk/onlinegallery/onlineex/kinggeorge/p/027add000044361u00278000.html.

29. *Leeds Intelligencer* (13 Jan. 1825).

30. *Yorkshire Gazette* (19 May 1853).

31. As quoted in Fowkes, *Railway History*, p. 12.

32. Fowkes, *Railway History*, p. 18.

33. Hembry, P. M., *The English Spa, 1560–1815: A Social History* (Fairleigh Dickinson University Press, 1990), p. 211.

34. Binns, J., *The History of Scarborough: From Earliest Times to the Year 2000* (Pickering: Blackthorn Press, 2019).

35. Wilson Fox, A., 'Agricultural Wages in England and Wales during the Last Fifty Years', *Journal of the Royal Statistical Society*, 66(2) (1903), pp. 273–359, doi:10.2307/2339234, p. 287.

36. Walton, J. K., *The British Seaside: Holidays and Resorts in the Twentieth Century* (Manchester University Press, 2000), p. 53.

37. As quoted in ibid.

38. *The Newcastle Weekly Courant* (5 Jul. 1834).

39. Walsh, J. H., *Manual of British Rural Sports: Comprising Shooting, Hunting, Coursing, Fishing, Hawking, Racing, Boating, Pedestrianism, and the Various Rural Games and Amusements of Great Britain* (London: G. Routledge & Company, 1856), p. 442.

40. McRobbie, L. R., 'How Competitive Walking Captivated Georgian Britain', *Atlas Obscura* (29 June 2017), www.atlasobscura.com/articles/pedestrianism-george-wilson-walking.

41. *The Newcastle Weekly Courant* (5 Jul. 1834).

42. Perry, P. J. (ed.), *British Agriculture 1875-1914*, Debates in Economic History (London: Routledge, 2006), p. xiv.

43. Howat, *The Railways of Ryedale*, p. 29.

Chapter 5 – Some h'ae luck, an' some stick i' t' muck (pp.269–303)

1. *The Hull Packet* (26 Dec. 1845).

2. *North Wales Chronicle* (8 Oct. 1852), p. 8.

3. Thompson, F., *Lark Rise to Candleford - A Trilogy Incorporating The Three Novels Lark Rise, Over To Candleford, And Candleford Green* (Oxford: Oxford University Press, 1957), p. 7.

4. Ecclestone, B., *Pumps, Pipes and Purity: The turbulent social history of providing the public with enough safe water in the Thirsk district and North Yorkshire from 1875* (York: York Publishing Services, 2012), p. 1.

5. *The Yorkshire Herald* (19 Oct. 1895), p. 11.

6. Ibid.
7. *The Yorkshire Herald* (9 Dec. 1895).
8. Ecclestone, *Pumps, Pipes and Purity*, p. 3.
9. Verdon, N., *Working the Land: A History of the Farmworker in England from 1850 to the Present Day* (Springer, 2017), p. 132.
10. As quoted in Ecclestone, *Pumps, Pipes and Purity*, p. 222.
11. www.icons.org.uk/theicons/collection/mrs-beeton/features/victorian-servants-in-progress.
12. Licence, Tom, *What the Victorians Threw Away* (Cowley: Oxbow Books, 2015), p. 3.
13. Ibid., p. 12.
14. *The Times* (2 May 1843), p. 6.
15. Licence, *What the Victorians Threw Away*, pp. 15–16.
16. *Guardian* (12 Aug. 1937), p. 10.
17. Cannadine, D., *The Decline and Fall of the British Aristocracy* (Yale University Press, 1990), p. 91.
18. Rothery, M., 'The wealth of the English landed gentry, 1870–1935', *Agricultural History Review* 55(II), p. 256, www.bahs.org.uk/AGHR/ARTICLES/55_205Rothery.pdf.

ACKNOWLEDGEMENTS

There are a handful of people who you meet throughout your life who have a profound impact. My editor at Head of Zeus, Richard Milbank, is one of those few. His encouragement and insight have been life-changing, giving me the courage and freedom to challenge myself and, hopefully, become a better writer in the process. He also happens to be a hoot, which always helps. A million thanks.

ACKNOWLEDGEMENTS